SHANNON COUNTRY

To the memory of my parents,
who inspired my early wanderlust.

PAUL CLEMENTS

SHANNON COUNTRY

A RIVER JOURNEY THROUGH TIME

Paul Clements

THE LILLIPUT PRESS

'Rivers and the inhabitants of the watery elements were made for wise men to contemplate and fools to pass by without consideration.'

– Izaak Walton, *The Compleat Angler*

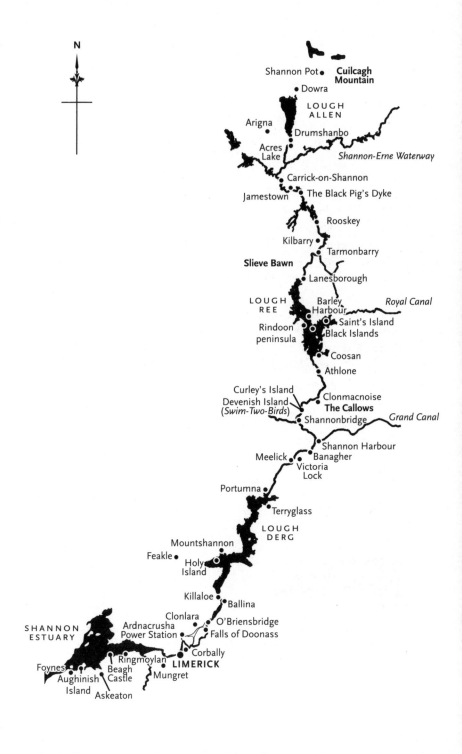

First published 2020 by
THE LILLIPUT PRESS
62–63 Arbour Hill
Dublin 7, Ireland
www.lilliputpress.ie

A CIP record for this publication is available from
The British Library.

10 9 8 7 6 5 4 3 2 1

ISBN 978 1 84351 783 2

The Lilliput Press gratefully acknowledges the financial support
of the Arts Council / An Chomhairle Ealaíon.

Set in 11pt on 14pt Monotype Bembo Pro by Niall McCormack.
Printed in Spain by GraphyCems.

CONTENTS

AUTHOR'S NOTE

THE JOURNEY recorded here was undertaken in various stages over a twelve-month period culminating in the summer of 2018. In a number of instances, the identities of several people described in the narrative have been disguised to respect their privacy and, in a world of much uncertainty, for the safety of the author.

PREFACE

JUST AS THE world was sliding into war at the end of the summer of 1939, the Irish travel writer Richard Hayward set off by car and caravan on a journey alongside the River Shannon with a photographer and movie cameraman. The trip produced an engaging book and film chronicling their adventures following the course of the river from the Shannon Pot to Ballybunion.

Where the River Shannon Flows, a handsome hardback with more than fifty illustrations, was the resulting book published in 1940, which expressed Hayward's love of both the river and of Ireland. It holds up a mirror to the 1930s and to a young country still trying to find its feet in the decade following partition. The accompanying film was shown as a travelogue at cinemas all over Ireland.

It was a journey into what were then little-known and unfrequented parts of the midlands. Writing with candour and in a bracingly honest, lyrical style, Hayward presents a snapshot of the social history of rural Ireland. He portrays families living on remote islands and secluded shores, writes about the country's neglect of its past, the lack of interest in protecting its built heritage, and considers its long-forgotten authors.

Richard Hayward (1892–1964) was one of Ireland's leading cultural figures from the middle decades of the twentieth century. Born in Southport, Lancashire, he grew up on the Antrim coast, later living in Belfast. A popular writer, he was also an Irish film star, stage actor, singer and radio broadcaster who spent his days promoting Ireland. He appeared in some of the earliest black-and-white films of the 1930s. *Irish Travelogue* was made in 1932 while his feature film, *The Luck of the Irish*, was released in 1935.

He also recorded 156 Irish folksongs and ballads with Decca and HMV, singing and playing with Delia Murphy, Anna Meakin, Sean Maguire and other artistes. He travelled around the country performing to packed houses at concerts and festivals, frequently playing and singing along to the harp.

From the 1930s up to the early 1960s, Hayward drove thousands of miles all over Ireland gathering material for eleven travel books. These were published as regional topographical accounts of each province; he also wrote separate books on the Corrib and Kerry. *Where the River Shannon Flows* was his second travel book and made him a celebrated champion of the area. A new edition of the book was published in 1950, while another, in 1989, commemorates the fiftieth anniversary of his journey.

Eighty years on from the distant days of the 1930s and with few tangible traces today of Richard Hayward, this meandering twenty-first-century journey, carried out intermittently over the course of a year from late spring 2017 to early summer 2018, looks at those who live and work along the river. Seen through the prism of the past, it reflects the deep vein and riptide pull on our imagination of the culture and landscape that is Shannon Country.

Paul Clements,
Belfast, July 2020

At the Shannon Pot

IT IS THE night of the full willow moon, and mystical figures move in ceremonial dress through the shadows beside a pool of water. They are here with a unified purpose, to harness the energy of lunar power and celebrate the water of the Shannon Pot through healing ritual, singing songs to the land and tapping into the tree energies of the area. The moon brings association of water and healing. The multinational group comprises seven women: two from Australia, one from Canada, an Italian, an Englishwoman, a northern Irelander and southern Irelander, plus Rover the dog with a noble German pedigree.

They are here for the practice of geomancy, the understanding of the invisible layers of the landscape. The group includes water witches, a shaman, sound-healers, and disciples of the natural magic found beside water. Their ritual is performed here because of the significance they attach to the Shannon and its importance as the source of the river, as well as its link to the goddess Sionna and the powerful mythological energy associated with her. In their diaphanous robes, gowns and votive long coats, they position themselves on the perimeter of the Pot, a steep-sided oval hole in pastureland. They are robed in mustard yellow, scarlet and gold. Necklaces cluster the throats of some, while others are garlanded with beads, brooches, pendant earrings; wrists are layered with bracelets. They are armed with bags of tricks and hazel sticks, staffs, willow wands and musical instruments. The willow is said to have been invested with the power of the moon and the traditional witches' broom is bound with a willow branch. The tree is also ascribed with femininity and dreaming, enchantment and deep emotions, wishing spells and protection.

Log na Sionna (or 'Lugnashinna'), the Shannon Pot, is ringed on one side by tall willow trees. The Pot is in a lush valley enclosed by densely forested mountains on all sides. From the west, the infant river falls through marshy countryside to Lough Allen from where it continues its journey through the centre of Ireland to the Atlantic. Because of the lack of recent rain, it is barely a metre-wide trickle. It is hard to imagine how this mere streamlet would later become a powerful river.

Alanna Moore, originally from Australia, is the mistress of ceremonies and welcomes everyone to the sacred spot. She hands over to Simone Ní Chinneide, a shaman practitioner who creates a theatre of calm. She talks the women through the four cardinal points, weaving in the guardians of each direction. These coincide with the four festivals in the cycle of the Celtic year: spring and autumn equinoxes and summer and winter solstices. Each of these periods has its own pantheon with specific elements and animals attached to it. I watch from the sidelines in fascinated estrangement. Standing barefoot at the Pot's edge, the women firstly look east, arms outstretched and palms open, embracing the energy of the moment. They face the hill of Tiltinbane on the western rim of the Cuilcagh mountain range where Cuilcagh Gap leads to the top of the flat mountain at 1949 metres. Its hillsides, scorched from wildfires, straddle the Cavan–Fermanagh boundary. They welcome the 'spirit of the east' where the sun rises and where solar gods such as Lugh, lord of light, are represented. The east is connected to the element of air, so, in 'water-worship speech', they call in the guardian of that element, perhaps a golden eagle, or an appropriate bird of their choosing.

A vigorous shaking of the rattle is the clarion call for the group to turn to face the south, dominated by the promontory of

Playbank mountain, which Cavan shares with Leitrim. With its sphinx-like appearance, it is also known as Big Dog mountain. Many kilometres beyond, as far as the eye can see, lie Bencroy and Slieve Anierin. Here the element is fire and the Great Red Fire Dragon is invoked. Fire, Simone says, is connected to a purifying aspect of healing; there is a synergy in using water and fire together. There is also a topicality to this since wildfires have been spreading out of control around the hills and heating the atmosphere. The participants move carefully around the Pot – a careless step in the wrong direction could result in an unscheduled bath or shamanic cleanse. They look to the west, said to be associated with water, gazing across lakes, streams, bogland, dark forested hillsides and heathland, to the horseshoe-shaped Boleybrack mountain, another part of the Cavan–Leitrim uplands where black patches are visible. Plumes of smoke rise high, blotting out the sinking sun. 'May you live unperturbed,' Simone whispers of the salmon of knowledge and its wealth of wisdom. In mythology, Sionna is said to have drowned after feeding on the salmon of knowledge, which resulted in her immortality and her name living on in the river in which she perished.

Their clockwise tour culminates with mechanical precision by turning to the north and the element of earth, representing a powerful animal, which could be a horse, stag or bear. There is an animistic belief that trees, rivers and animals have a soul. Views stretch beyond the Cavan Burren prehistoric park, across fields and the twin Macnean loughs into the heart of the Fermanagh lakelands. Enlivened by the opening of the circle, the women speak aloud their thoughts, well and truly in the zone. They want the earth to know of their appreciation. Alanna produces a small jar of rainwater that she had previously 'blessed' at home for the purpose by imparting beneficial thoughts and energies of harmony and well-being into it. She sings her river song, 'Waterways', pouring the rainwater into the Pot in divine manifestation so that the river will spread harmony, joy and peace:

Beautiful falling rain
Soak into soil again
I am your loving friend
Remember to come again.

Beautiful sparkling springs
Your bubbling laughter sings
Flow into rivers meandering
And take you my heart within.

For Eileen O'Toole, the space around the Pot is 'a bounty of magnificent energy'. She steps forward, rings a bell, and from a crystal bowl the noise is apparently transmitted to the Pot, where bubbles appear. Holding two body-tuning forks, she strikes them on a hockey puck to produce notes of C and G, creating what is known as a perfect fifth. After putting them to her own ears for a few seconds, she hovers the forks over the ears of each of the women. This helps, she says, synchronize their brains, balancing the left and right cerebral hemispheres.

A couple of tunes follow: 'An Indian in a White Man's Camp' and a Dakotan Indian song. The thuds of drums reverberate around the countryside, attracting curious sheep from a neighbouring field. Drawn by the noise, an older couple arrive to look around the Pot, stumbling unexpectedly on the ceremony. But the visceral excitement of the event does not interest them. 'It's a lot of gibberish' is the man's verdict, and they disappear as quickly as they had come.

Gibberish or not, there is a surreal side to these ancient rituals. For the next part of the performance, everyone in the septet makes a personal contribution. A stillness prevails as the willow energy around the Pot releases tensions and emotions. One woman speaks in unsteady tones of her grief, which is linked through the association of the willow's weeping stance: others tell of pain, while some break into song, recite poetry or recount a short story. As they speak, each lights a candle, placing it in a colourful ceramic bowl of water drawn from the Pot. They then light candles for groups of people in need of support: the firefighters; the homeless; the poor; the vulnerable. Gradually, the bowl fills with floating candles.

During a break, several women wash their feet in the Pot. I scoop the cold water ceremonially in my hands, then remove boots and socks, dipping my feet into the narrow newborn river, now just a trickle of water because of a shortage of rain in recent weeks. Aquatic insects perform whirls. Hundreds of tiny, colourful pebbles are embedded in the pure, clear water and I wriggle my toes through them. Several languid frogs doze on a sandy ledge. Flowerheads thrum with bumblebees, making the most of the blossoms. Showing off their brighter blue, water forget-me-nots and germander speedwell thrive by the banks.

Signboards state that the Pot is originally believed to be the ultimate source of the Shannon, but it is now thought that the water in it comes from several different places, flowing underground before emerging here from an unseen hole. Water-tracing experiments have shown that several of the streams that sink on Cuilcagh mountain flow underground to join the Pot. The farthest of these is the stream that sinks into the Pigeon Pots, over ten kilometres away in Fermanagh. Alanna, the author of books on geomancy, teaches dowsing and divination. I ask her about the recent 'battle of the sources' thinking, which states that the river's *fons et origo* is next door in Fermanagh.

'For us, this spot is the traditional starting point of the source of the Shannon. It is historically significant and a powerful place because the water is often upwelling very strongly although it may look calm today. Spending time here stimulates our energies as there is a high magnetic field, which stirs up the magnetic field in our head, helping to facilitate the visionary experience.'

Alanna has a long interest in geomancy, which started when she lived in London. She became fascinated with the medieval practice of dowsing, using rods to detect water, and for her, it is the greatest healing element. Over the years, she has found the Shannon flat, calming and peaceful and describes it as being wonderful for contemplation. 'There are no rapids on it and it is not flashy. It is a place to recreate yourself as the water gives a reflective quality and we can all tune into the magic,' she says.

Alanna is familiar with Richard Hayward and loves his writing. 'My husband Peter bought me a second-hand copy of his Shannon book and it intrigued him to go to places Hayward had been. I'm particularly interested in Crom Dubh, who is associated with Lughnasa Sunday. He writes about that because Leitrim was one of the last Gaelic strongholds of all those ancient gods and goddesses and those traditions were kept up.'

Eighty years ago, when Hayward came here with his caravanserai, few people visited the Shannon Pot or west Cavan. He described the countryside as 'fertile and green and comfortable', but noted that many writers habitually referred to the district as 'rather grim and forbidding'. These days the Pot is labelled a 'heritage property', coming under the umbrella of the grandiosely entitled UNESCO Global Marble Arch Caves Geopark. This designation has led to a proper tarred path from a car park and play area where interpretative panels explain the geology and history, packaged and sanitized for tourists. The first section of Hayward's Shannon book is filled with many stories of the mythical fairy folk, the Tuatha Dé Danann and other legends. He veers off frequently to explain the connections of pagan gods to mountains and festival days, and their place in mythology. He also questions where the starting point of the river is to be found:

> This limestone cauldron which we call Lug-na-Sionna is not in fact the source of the Shannon at all, but merely a basin beside a fault in the limestone through which the waters of many rivulets, gathering higher up on the side of Cuilcagh, issue in a copious stream. And this stream, child of many little mountain burns and brooks, cannot properly be looked upon as the actual head-water of the Shannon, but rather as a feeder of that head-water, which, strictly speaking is the Owenmore ... But a story is a story, and Lug-na-Sionna must remain Lug-na-Sionna.

Hayward walked a mile south-east towards Cuilcagh where he threw some grass into a lake, retraced his steps and back at the Pot found the grass rising to the surface of the water. He went on to point out that in his view all the lakes and streams in this area full of caverns, holes and subterranean rivers were connected with another.

As the evening shadows lengthen, the creatures of the night begin to stir. Alanna calls on everyone to regroup, forming a heptagon. The women, cradling two bodhráns, launch into a mix of chanting and song. The noise increases in volume and speed, ending in an adrenaline rush at a breakneck pace with an ear-splitting din echoing around the hillsides, emulating a Hare Krishna cult in full flow. The night air rings with song. Their exuberance is infectious. Animals are roused from their slumber. The group is joined by a small animal orchestra, a veritable Cavan bestiary creating a biophony rippling around the fields, bouncing off the hills, supercharging the air.

The prize for reaching the highest octave goes to Rover, whose great-great-great-grandfather was an Alsatian. Now a hybrid of sheepdog and spaniel, he is a hound of some nobility and sonar strength. His high-frequency howls drown out all other sounds. Elsewhere, a fish jumps in the water, distracting the chanters, while a frog scarpers to a peaceful corner. Cattle pause and look up from their nibbling. Two lambs wander into the zone, entering the highly-charged sanctity, bleating in unison until a farmer coaxes them back, scratching his head as he mounts his tractor beside a glitzy steel bridge that looks incongruous in the landscape. Troops of midges dance in the sunlight. A cuckoo sounds an alarming two-second salvo while lark song dries up. A snipe performing its percussive tick-tock drumming ritual somewhere indefinable rises in sudden flight and with a sharp call skitters away in panicky zigzags. Cabbage white and orange tip butterflies, which had been flitting through the performance, are spiral high, all aflutter. Dragonflies lose the run of themselves, whirring and twisting over the water.

So intensely focused am I on the proceedings, trying to record a video on my smartphone, that I forget to look behind me. In a misplaced footing, I snag on a tussock. My fall from grace into the Pot is sudden but no less impressive as I slide unstoppably down a bank. Fortunately, a sandy spit preserves me from the ignominy of a cold bath. But falling into the Pot itself brings an ingredient of laughter and fun. The two bodhránistas drop their instruments, collapsing into helpless merriment. Alanna breaks off from her bell-ringing, running across to help pull me up the grassy bank back on to terra firma. Luckily, I am wearing a thick skin, and although momentarily embarrassed, I shake myself down with nothing bruised except my ego.

Events reach a climax with the closing of the circle. One woman delivers a valediction that stands as advice for my trip: 'May your waters remain unpolluted all the time through the counties the whole way down your journey between here and the sea, and may you keep out of the water ...' Rover also bids me a watery farewell, leaping up, licking sand from my boots. Before leaving, Alanna told me that Sionna had appeared to her at the Pot in a mermaid form, stationed in a regal pose. 'She was a gracious presence,' she says, 'nourishing all around her and was delighted to reconnect with humankind and receive heartfelt wishes. You might take that as a blessing on your own River Shannon journey.'

In the world of writing about travel, there is often a journey that begins before the journey itself. I have broken myself into the Shannon's embrace, balanced my chakras and survived a fall. The thought-provoking ceremony sets me up for my trip. For these women, the river is the embodiment of grace and beauty. There is a certain sadness at the parting of our ways. I lag behind for a few moments of serenity as a shadowy melancholy prevails, and listen to the underlying sound of the landscape, but it is so quiet you could almost hear a tear drop from a weeping willow.

PART I

Upper Shannon

'He's gone: but you can see
his tracks still, in the snow of the world.'

Norman MacCaig,
'Praise of a man', *Collected Poems*

The Village that Vanished

MY VISIT TO the Shannon Pot marks the start of a journey in Richard Hayward's footsteps, following the course of a river that I have known about since schooldays but never properly explored. At primary school, the master, J.J. Hamill, hung up a coloured, torn oilcloth map showing two countries: the large John Bull island of Blighty, and the smaller island of Ireland adjacent to the west, shaped like a saucer. He pointed out some topographical features such as mountains, lakes and rivers. The largest lake was Lough Neagh, while the longest river in the British Isles – as the archipelago was then known – was the River Shannon. He delighted in telling us these simple facts, which have always stayed with me. In the tangled geographical history of the twenty-first century, the British Isles terminology has become contentious and is not much used.

But what I most remember from those long-ago schooldays is that all rivers are stories, connecting places and people, carrying history and lore. The Blackwater in County Tyrone was our local river that ran across an overgrown garden at the bottom of our house and alongside playing fields beside the school. Inevitably, many footballs ended up in the river from which as children we used to fish for pike which, like the balls, often got away. It was a watery backdrop to a childhood imagination. For a young boy, a river is a storybook and I was familiar with fictional ones, especially the Mississippi celebrated in Mark Twain's *The Adventures of Huckleberry Finn*, and the River Sark in Frank Richards' Billy Bunter books about life at Greyfriars school. Another childhood memory is listening to the hymnal cadences of the shipping forecast on radio and hearing North Utsire, South Utsire, moving on to Shannon, Rockall and Malin. It was an incantatory broadcast, although the Shannon reference relates to the estuary and the seafaring area of the south-west of Ireland, rather than the topography of the eponymous river.

When Hayward set out in mid-August 1939 with his fellow adventurers, their objective was to gather material as they followed the banks of the river from its source to the Atlantic seaboard. The journey of 214 miles, encompassing eleven counties, would take three weeks. Accompanying Hayward were Germain Burger (known as 'Jimmy'), who filmed a travelogue, while a photographer, Louis Morrison, provided atmospheric black-and-white photographs. They were joined at times and along the way by three other people. Their journey began on 16 August 1939 in an Austin car towing a Chesterfield caravan with what Hayward summed up as having a threefold purpose: 'To make a travel picture of the River Shannon from its source to its mouth; to write a book of similar scope; and to enjoy ourselves.' Three men in a car towing a caravan with their cameras, gear and supplies were a novelty at the time and sometimes locals trailed along behind them for a stretch. It was just twenty-one years since the end of the First World War, and on the eve again of momentous world events, Hayward presents a startling pastoral contrast in the preface about their departure: 'A warm sun in the sky, a genuine thrill of expectancy and joy in our hearts, and many and many a song in our mouths as we sped past the sweet fields of Ireland.'

Frequently in my own wanderings around the 'sweet fields' I crissed and crossed the river on many east–west journeys, never staying long enough to find out much about it. It was a place that seemed to keep itself to itself. I had often noticed, when crossing to the west side, the widescreen skies billowing with beefy cloud

Signpost at Dowra Bridge, marking the border between Cavan and Leitrim and the first town on the River Shannon.

formations. Not only does the river divide Ireland and represent many boundaries and a frontier, it also brushes against ten counties. After it leaves the Shannon Pot, it follows a haphazard course, slipping in and out of view until it reaches the first settlement, Dowra. An unprepossessing place and an inter-county village, Dowra is divided by the Shannon, with one half in the extreme north-west of Co. Cavan and the other in Co. Leitrim, or more correctly two-thirds in Cavan and the other third in Leitrim.

The Shannon joins forces three miles downstream from the Pot with the Owenmore, which Hayward mentions, and by the time it reaches Dowra with the Owennayla River, it is a fully formed adult artery spanned by an attractive three-arch bridge built with stones from Carrick-on-Shannon jail and from the village itself. The first houses date from 1860 when the police barracks was erected. The town is hemmed in by mountains, bleak moorland, windswept valleys and Lough Allen – the river's first major lake – while four roads converge on it. Dowra is in the ancient kingdom of Glan, whose rulers were the McGoverns, a common family name which still rules the roost in the area. Like other parts of south Ulster, certain names predominate. Neighbouring Fermanagh has the Maguires while next door in Monaghan the McKennas reign supreme, although O'Reilly is the renowned clan name of Cavan and the wider Breifne area. Hayward wrote that to ask for a Mr McGovern or a Mr Maguire would be 'nothing but a waste of time', something that was anathema to such a busy man. Apart from fishing and walking or paddling along the newly founded Shannon Blueway, there is little to detain visitors to Dowra: its attractions are low key, if not invisible. But as an example of a typical country village, it can claim a place for its throughotherness. Those reliant on public transport who wish to reach the area by bus can do so only on a Saturday when Bus Éireann operates a service to Drumkeeran, Dromahair and Sligo.

The moribund main street is a deserted straggle where cars are parked at odd angles. Half the buildings are abandoned or locked up, the shoddy legacy of the Celtic Tiger creating an ugly appearance on approach roads. One slated building beside the bridge was to have become a restaurant and has stood in a weather-beaten, unplastered state of half-completion since the get-rich-quick years. Buggie's Bar, which advertises *Ceol agus Craic* on boarded-up windows, has achieved local eyesore status and has not served any music or craic for many a year. The local mindset seems to be to abandon things as they fall. Clearly the place has had its ups and downs, although more downs than ups by the look of it. Very little, in fact, has changed since Hayward's time. He found it a decayed place and wrote that only with a stretch of the imagination might it be called a town. However, he described the people as gracious and friendly and took local advice from Mr Loughlin, the publican, about a camp site.

Because it is a crossroads town, a crop of cast-iron fingerposts and signboards lead to many different directions, including the newly formed Ancient East route that stretches from Cork up to Louth, and to the Cavan Way. I prowl around the streets. Scarcely a soul is about. The one redeeming feature of the built heritage is the renovated courthouse, which opens only on Wednesday and seems to be of more use to the swift population who are enjoying its eaves and chimney stacks. Originally built in 1932, it has been restored through an EU funding project, Harnessing Nature Resources, and is now used for what is termed a 'community creative arts space'. Tourism and enterprise initiatives across this border area are a huge bonus to many places yet little of that money has found its way to improving the appearance of Dowra, where a feeling of dereliction pervades. Dour Dowra has no church, Chinese restaurant or takeaway and is largely a caffeine wilderness. There is a sad emptiness about it.

For the past few days there has been a crisis in the uplands caused by out-of-control wildfires on mountains and uplands. April to early May is deemed here as 'fire season'. It has been a devastating week with conflagrations on a huge scale and firefighters at full stretch. Damage estimated to run into tens of thousands of euro has been caused to private and state-owned forests, which have wiped out animal habitats around Dowra, Killeshandra, Ballyconnell and Belturbet through fires deliberately started. Mature trees, gorse land and some newer plantations of Sitka spruce have been destroyed while the sunny weather and high winds exacerbated the problem, scorching forestry land for many kilometres. The popular boardwalk trail known as the 'Stairway to Heaven', leading to the summit of Cuilcagh mountain, is closed because of the fires. Along a country road, several fire-tenders whizz past me with sirens blaring. In the distance plumes of black smoke coil into the sky, spreading across plantations, reminiscent of a swirling mist. Dowra fire service has been working overtime to control the outbreaks and has been stretched to exhaustion. Machinery owners have been called in to help drive the fires back by dampening them with shovels.

The Cavan Way, which runs through Dowra and which I plan to walk a stretch of the next day, appears to have escaped serious damage. But a 500 m section of the nearby Sligo Way – a 34 km walk from Dromahair in Leitrim to Coolaney in Sligo – destroyed 4000 acres around Killery mountain. Dramatic front-page photographs and a flurry of newspaper headlines bear out the seriousness of the damage: 'Burn Out: Swathes of local habitat destroyed'; 'Out of control fires rage for days as dry weather continues'; 'Danger warnings from forest fires'. In Cavan's weekly newspaper, *The Anglo-Celt* (serving the community since 1846 and known to some as the Cavan man's bible), one resident is quoted as having seen hundreds of acres of shrubland go up in flames on Ben mountain bordering Leitrim. Hayward mentions the newspaper in one of his travel books:

> As a kind of commentary on the racial dichotomy of the County Cavan, it is significant that the only newspaper printed in the county is the weekly *Anglo-Celt*. The only bad thing I know about that paper is the execrable local pronunciation of the word *Celt* with a soft C. It does violence to my ear every time a Cavan man uses such an un-Irish sound.

Outside Loughlin's general merchants beside Dowra bridge, a man nods a good morning in the superheated air. 'We're not used to this hot weather,' he says. Oliver McGrail is sitting on a bench out of the sun's rays. He looks out to the hills, which are smouldering in places with a scorched-earth appearance.

'I was reading in the paper about what the law is regarding the fires,' he says. 'The general belief is that some of them are started on purpose by vandals, but others are an accident where people try to burn something and the whole thing gets out of control. The police have laid out the law about the burning of highly flammable dead vegetation such as gorse, rushes, sedges, heathers and hill grasses. They're ferocious blazes and when the moorland is bone dry like that they escalate very quickly.'

Oliver, a retired businessman who ran a hardware store, recalls that when he was growing up in Dowra in the 1950s, there were ten pubs: now there are two, but mostly just one.

'Dowra has lost an enormous amount by way of businesses and much more. When people go, everything goes and that's the problem. It is disheartening but the local people can't do any more.

Anything to bring in visitors will cost a big amount of money. I sometimes go out to where I was born and reared with a family of eight and the house is closed. When I go out to the home place and come back, I don't feel well and am worse than when I went out, so I don't go very often because it brings back all the good memories that have gone for ever. The world moves on and all the changes are connected to the decline of the population.'

Oliver cups his right hand to his ear as two tractors and a transporter trundle over the narrow bridge. I ask him about Jim Loughlin, whom Hayward met.

'The only thing I remember about Mr Loughlin is that he was in bed for nine or ten years that I was alive, and he died when I was eleven. His pub was next to where Loughlin's shop now is. He was a great organizer and loved getting things done and if there was a fair day he would be so nervous that he wouldn't be able to serve drink himself. He was clever and would have helped Hayward and told him where to go, a very intelligent man who knew people and knew the history of the area.

'The Shannon means nothing to people today because there isn't any tourism here although there is further downriver. People are friendly and helpful, very neighbourly and for the like of me that never left, the measurement would be better concluded by somebody who left and returned. My son is working in London and he is home five or six times a year and just loves coming here. In my childhood it was common to have fights, the same as playing cards, but there was no real seriousness to it, it was a bit of craic. Today they use knives or guns, but it would have been fists in those days.'

By next morning the fires have mostly been quelled. With binoculars I scan the black and charcoal high ground in the far distance. To get close to the Shannon's heartbeat, the section of the Cavan Way that I plan to tackle is part of a looped walk north of Dowra to Cashelbane where it meets the river. Near this point, according to my map, it appears with an eccentric kink before dropping into Dowra. The thin corridor of land in this part of west Cavan is made up of a bewildering network of un-signposted lanes, byways and boreens, although they cherish their townland nomenclature with signage every few miles: Gubaveeny, Corraquigley, Stranamart, while the map contains intriguing place names such as Dawn of Hope and Barr of Farrow. A road sign signifies Cathal Buí Country, a singer, balladeer and poet from the seventeenth century, described as an early version of Christy Moore. The early morning world glistens in spring sunshine. Pied wagtails curtsy on the rocks while magpies fidget in intensely green fields. I have arranged to walk with Bee Smith, an American who has lived in the area for fifteen years and is a freelance Geopark tour guide. We make our way along sunlit roadside hedges high with holly and berry and filled with a forest of ferns to the Old Coach Road, also known as the Smuggler's Road. The May blossom of the hawthorn tree creates a localized botanical snowfall in masses along the hedges. Radiant with wildflowers, it is a topographically pleasing area, but as Bee explains, Dowra has a dark side to its history.

'Initially the place was called Tober, which means 'well' in Irish, and up until 1862 it was the locus of population for this area when there was what is called "the great flood",' she says. 'Prior to that it had always been a thriving village with several shops and many taverns, a smithy, and fifty or more households who all attended mass at Doobally, half a mile from here. The landslides washed the whole place away and it is now known as the village that vanished. They held dances here and Cathal Buí visited the area. The local priest said he would excommunicate any household or tavern that entertained Cathal Buí as he was regarded as naughty because he was a rake-poet and a singer around rambling houses, which meant he was popular with people but not with the clergy.

'But one night at the presbytery an old woman, a real bent-over hag, knocked on his door and asked for bread and tea, and shelter for the night. The priest offered accommodation but said she would have to sleep with the maid. She said, "Thank-you, thank-you Father, you're very good and kind." Next morning at the breakfast table there was no maid to serve the breakfast and a note thanking him for his hospitality was signed Cathal Buí.'

We pause, admiring violet-tinged ditches and verges with the erect stems of bugle, bush vetch, milkwort, common dog violet and periwinkles. On the hedge banks a spring smorgasbord of flora and plants includes white globes of dandelion seed heads, while celandine and marsh marigold bloom in profusion alongside primroses and the cuckoo flower. The tapestry of colours includes carpets of sphagnum moss, early purple orchids and stitchwort, while stems of rosebay willowherb are not yet in flower. Luxuriant ferns add to the verdure. In the corners of fields, dense cylindrical silage sits wrapped in black plastic. The area is riddled with sweat houses, known as an early type of sauna, along with cairns and a megalithic tomb. Later we come to a large circular holy well, locally called Mary's well.

Bee explains: 'Hundreds of years ago there used to be faction battles at Lughnasa to mark the beginning of the harvest in August. At one point a fight broke out and blood was spilled in the holy well, which was regarded as a huge pollution. It was said at the time that the local priest cursed the well, which was a big deal because local tradition was that Our Lady had appeared there. This was told to me by my neighbour, who died at nearly 100. She said it was well before both her mother's and grandmother's time so we're going back long before Cathal Buí's time, perhaps even into the late medieval era when it was said that Our Lady had appeared here. Although there is no particular cure about the well, I suspect that it still has ancient fertility connotations because women who want children visit here. Still people came, but it fell into disrepair.

'Then the local landowner rebuilt it using a mason from Glangevlin. In 2012 he asked the priest to re-consecrate it and lift the curse. He was a Cavan man and went with it and I was present at the mass and a lot of the legend was told at the mass, which was held near Lughnasa. The curse would have happened and then came the flood, which was in the summer of 1862 – there were a lot of wet summers in the post-Famine period when they had what was called the "little Famine", which caused much hunger but not mass death. There would have been landslides and you can see how it slewed down and swept [the soil] away. The water is not in spate but is very powerful when it comes down and if you have a flash flood it thunders down here. At that stage all the businesses and households were wiped out – perhaps up to a population of nearly 500 living here – there was just a ford with stones where Dowra now is, which is why it's known as a Johnny-come-lately.'

Our walk leads through verdant countryside along traffic-free lanes. At the remains of a wooden bridge at Cashelbane the river has practically dried up because of the uncharacteristically warm weather. We lean over a white lattice-worked bridge where rocks and stones are visible on the riverbed, which looks as though it has been wrung dry. Large, multi-limbed oak trees come with ivy-wrapped tree trunks. Farther along the road uncurling, shiny patches of the prolific hart's tongue grow beside tall stands of the fancifully named fiddlehead fern with its distinctive looping, furled fronds. They are almost overwhelmed by horsetail, known as scouring rush, and grasses displaying a smaragdine haze of new growth. Bee points out mare's tail which, in folkloric tradition, was used for internal bleeding and stomach ulcers and for skin inflammation.

'A hybrid called Wilmott mare's tail is full of silica and can be brewed with garlic to make an organic spray that protects potato blight, so it had medicinal natural uses. Wilmott mare's tail was created here; it doesn't grow anywhere else and is hybridized in this unique environment, although I have never spotted it. It is undisturbed and is near a tributary and there is lots of it as it needs a damp environment, which is where Wilmott found it along a back river but did not say which townland – he might not have known the area's name.'

Since moving to live in the area, Bee has fallen in love with west Cavan and has developed a special fondness for the legends, folklore and mythology that surround it.

'This is a timeless place, a liminal place and a thin place. To me it is nature's entry to the Valley of the Kings, except that it is in Ireland and if you think about it, the Tuatha Dé Danann landed on Slieve Anierin, and Glangevlin is where the magical blacksmith of the Tuatha forged their laser swords. We don't get a cell signal – I had my first conversation inside our house a few days ago and the only reason is because it was windless and sunny since the Wi-Fi is affected by the weather.'

Bee says that Dowra was never properly developed for historical reasons, but she believes changes could be on the way to improve its image.

'People want tourism and it is bringing people in but it's very hard to sell Dowra. It was never energetically supposed to be a residential place. Other than the mart, it is quiet because historically Tober was where it all happened. It will be interesting to see what will happen now that the curse has been lifted and if things begin to thrive. Local people have tried to do their best to improve the place. The resource centre, the EU funding, the courthouse – but then something seems to happen to make things not happen. But without the funding things don't happen. People follow the money because they have to. There always seem to be problems or local difficulties when they try to plan something. My husband has been involved with the resource centre and there are schisms and disagreements and that is because there is something argumentative in the atmosphere. Don't forget, "the fighting men of Dowra" is an old phrase and will stand as long as the mart is there. People take a drink and there is bound to be a fight eventually. Some of the buildings are privately owned and have fallen into disrepair. There has been a fairly new development of houses at Shannon Ville but the petrol station in Blacklion got Nama'd and that is affecting things here.'

Aside from America, Bee has lived in several parts of the world including Britain and speaks about what it is like living as a blow-in to west Cavan.

'We came from Leeds in September 2001 and are very fond of this area. We had to rent a place and had two dogs and a cat living in the house with us. The Shannon was our back yard when we lived in Dowra and it was just heaven coming from a big English city. We loved the silence, so the river is important to us. I grew up in north-eastern Pennsylvania in an area known as the Marcellus and lived beside one of the longest rivers in the American north-west – the Susquehanna River, which is just a bit longer than the Shannon and which empties out in Maryland. I've always had a feeling for rivers and they seem to be part of my life – I want to live next to the sea but keep on getting stuck with rivers. I went to university in Washington DC where we have a couple of big rivers, the Potomac and the Anacostia, and then I lived in London where I met my husband. I loved the Thames of course, but more importantly the River Lea is where we lived near Walthamstow in east London – we did a lot of courting beside the river so it's a special place. You could say my whole life has revolved around rivers.'

THE CHARACTER OF Dowra changes on a Saturday with the influx of more than 150 farmers for the livestock mart, a long-established weekly highlight that brings much-needed business to the town. Cattle and sheep farming is the main occupation in this area and continues to provide employment, albeit in declining numbers. Through the decades, there have been many agricultural changes but one of the most profound is in the way in which the land itself is worked. Scythes, reapers and binders have been replaced by tractors and combine harvesters, and the hay is no longer forked into ricks. Hayward describes farmers in Cavan working in the fields, swinging long-handled scythes, and when he sees working donkeys, with creels, he remarks on how traditions such as thatching are still carried on:

> Over the rise of the hillside came several little mountainy donkeys, so deeply laden with rushes for thatching that it was almost impossible to see any donkey at all. I got out of the car and climbed over the ditch and found that the rushes were carried in rude creels slung on the sides of each little beast; and I was interested to observe that the creels, and what there was of harness, were made entirely of *sugan*, the Irish word for a rope which is made

by twisting hay or straw. The art of the rush-thatcher is still happily plied in this pleasant countryside, and I was glad to see that these gallant little donkeys, most faithful friends of the mountainy farmer, were in grand condition and obviously well cared for.

On this particular Saturday, cars and vans, trailers and cattle lorries, tractors and quads are parked on the approach roads to the mart. A yellow-coated steward directs traffic. The air resounds with the bellowing, snorting and grunting of animals mixed with the reverberations of an auctioneer's voice coming through speakers in the corrugated iron sheds. Parked alongside the Jeeps, Shoguns, Land Cruisers and pick-up trucks are a raft of gleaming tinted-screen vehicles with names such as Duster, Warrior, Discovery, Pajero, Defender and Invincible. In Hayward's time cars were prefixed with model names such as Austin, Morris or Vauxhall. On the lanes and roads during his driving days, they were given evocative names such as Hillman Minx, Singer Vogue, Riley Pathfinder, with Ford names of Zephyr, Zodiac, Prefect and Cortina.

The morning sales involve sheep while the afternoon is given over to cattle with dry cows, calf cows, sucklers, heifers and weanling bulls. To get a feel for how the agricultural landscape has changed since Hayward's time I contacted Terry McGovern, who runs the mart. In his office I study posters urging farmers to sign a petition: 'Save Our Sucklers'; 'Cattle not Conifers, Save Leitrim'. This energetic campaigning group wants to save the county's farmland, which they contend is being taken over by Sitka plantations, which in Leitrim alone amount to nearly 35 million trees. The farmers want to see more planting of their native hardwoods such as oak, beech, ash, hazel and larch. Terry points out the mart pens and the buyer's rings. It is hard to hold a conversation because of the volume of noise, so he shouts for me to have a look around, saying that if I call into the Melrose Inn after lunch he will arrange for some farmers with long memories to speak to me.

In one large pen, farmers lean over railings, looking closely as one by one the animals are prodded in with sticks. A woolly-hatted man beside me bids with his outstretched index finger for a well-fleshed Friesian but is outgunned. He talks about the importance of the animals getting home as soon as they have been bought as marts are stressful places for them and a potential source of disease transmission. Several metres back from the ring more than fifty farmers sit on wooden tiered bench seats, soaking up the atmosphere. A few speak on phones in this twenty-first century stock market. An electronic screen flashes up each beast's history as it passes into the buyer's ring, including place and date of birth, average weight, breed, previous owners, days in herd, test certificate, export details and a star rating ranging from one to five. On the weighbridge several cows slip and slide on the sawdust-covered floor. A few others play piggyback, receiving a smack like a naughty child.

Beef production is the most common type of farming in Ireland and the business at Dowra is concentrated on bulls and cows, with Charolais, highly muscled Limousin and stout Dexters to the fore. The ruddy-faced cattle auctioneer at the microphone is an expert at his job, although some of his phraseology is lost on me. He launches into a sing-song monotone incremental biding scale: 'Charley-bull again – nine hund-*erd* and sixty, forty, twenty … biddy, biddy, biddy … on the market … bull calf eight hund-*erd* and fifty, sixty, seventy, eighty … fibiddy, biddy, biddy …' He keeps a sharp eye on potential buyers through the syntax of his sign language: a flick of the wrist, head nod or hand gesture, his mallet falling to sign off a deal followed by a brief conversation with a woman at a computer.

As I walk down to the Melrose Inn, I glance over the bridge where the river races across rocks confettied with moss. Two grey wagtails, oblivious of the nearby echo chamber, bob up and down. At the road junction, a tailback of lorries, tractors, trucks and vans has formed. The owner of the bar introduces me to four farmers sitting around a table polishing off plates of roast beef and mixed grills. They tell me that they come from GLRC: Greater Leitrim, Roscommon and Cavan.

One farmer, a sturdily built man from west Cavan, talks about Dowra. 'It's only busy of a Saturday,' he says in a drawl. 'Dead the rest of the time but the town has a tragic past. This is the only place left to eat.'

I ask if any of them can remember their fathers or grandfathers speaking about life on the land two generations ago. Another Cavan farmer picks up the conversation.

'The biggest difference is that in the 1930s there was no mechanization ... it was all done by hand, whereas it's now industrialized. Farmers have an awful lot of money tied up in heavy machinery but they don't have many blisters on their hands. Years ago, even in the 1960s when I started, they didn't have half the machinery they have now, and nobody cared about health and safety. I bought my first Massey in 1965 for £500 and got many years' work out of it.'

A Leitrim farmer with a close-cut beard nods and adjusts his cap.

'In the 1930s hay meadows were cut in August but that work is done now in July. Most pastureland is rye grass compared with meadow grass and cutting silage instead of hay has had a big effect on insects, birds and animals. Even up to the 1930s, potatoes were all dug out of the ridges by a loy [an early Irish spade], which my father used. Nowadays they don't work in the fields at all and a contractor is hired to do the hay. The young ones don't want to do it and that's the height of it. If I had my time again, I don't think I would keep going at it.'

A farmer from Roscommon, finishing off his apple pie, says most of them are feeling the pinch and are just about breaking even.

'When I was growing up in the late 1950s and '60s there was no talk of education, it wasn't such a big thing as it is today. My parents didn't worry about me or my brothers studying to pass exams or doing well at school. You just went on to the farm and took it over from your parents. We grew our own vegetables, there was no such thing as going to the supermarket. The woman of the house baked the bread and the man provided for everyone. Now I have a son of nineteen and I would not encourage him to be a farmer – maybe a bit of part-time farming if he wants but he should learn a plumbing or electrical trade or go into public works and make a guaranteed living from that. He comes home at five o'clock and doesn't want to be working right into the evening.'

Nowadays large areas of the Leitrim countryside are under forestry, much of it non-native Sitka spruce plantations unwelcome to many farmers.

'The land itself is the same, there's still hedges and meadows with plenty of flowers, but the Sitka spruce are big, ugly, dark green blankets on the landscape,' says one man. 'They're also polluting the water quality because they use toxic chemicals, and aerial fertilization is being sprayed in the form of nitrogen and phosphate, which is draining into the rivers. On top of that, the rainfall has definitely got worse. It's increasingly uncertain and you can't rely on the forecast. The strategy is not right to cope with so many more cattle, the agricultural system is broken. We need some radical thinking and diversified farming with perhaps a return to tillage.'

This triggers another farmer who has listened attentively but said nothing. He places his red muscular hands on the table.

'Thing you gotta understan' is that there's an awful lot more red tape these days in being a full-time farmer, which is why there are so many part-time ones doing other work. The Common Agricultural Policy reforms and farming restrictions from Brussels, never mind all the E U directives on environmental matters, take up a lotta our time.' He blows out his cheeks and continues. 'I've also got strong views on the banks too but to be honest I'd be as well to keep them to myself.'

'In many ways the challenges are as great now as they were in earlier times,' says the Leitrim farmer. 'What has not changed are the problems over volatility of the prices and the weather, and of making ends meet. We've had disastrous years recently when the ground has been saturated for months on end with flooding along the Shannon and that has happened for a century or more, but it has been especially bad in recent years, causing several fodder crises. Traditionally farming was an industry that people went into because they wanted to work on the land with animals, but it is becoming increasingly hard now with cash flow a big problem, which is why so many small farmers have gone to the wall. The position here is that young farmers wishing to buy land cannot compete with forestry companies who are not making any contribution to the well-being of small rural communities. You're dealing with a government that wants to depopulate this area and the powers that be need to map out some sort of blueprint for the future.'

Coffee cups and saucers are produced and there is general talk about beef and lamb prices, farm inspections, planning applications lodged with the Department of Agriculture for afforestation, and the ageing workforce. The men are not so much fatalistic as practical and forthright about the next few years. One stocky farmer with a friendly face receives a call on his mobile phone that his two heifers are getting restless and he is needed at the mart. Before leaving, he sums up fluently the attitude of many in the industry.

'Farming is at a crossroads because the younger generation has a different mindset. There is no question that it's very hard to make a living from the land although we try to keep positive. 'Tis often claimed that farmers are always complaining but when all's said and done, we are still custodians of the land. It just seems to be changing now at such a fast speed that we have never seen before. But I'll tell you one thing, it's good to get a bit of whingeing off your chest – you feel the better of it.'

2

The Snake in the Lake

THE ROAD SOUTH along the east side of Lough Allen twists and spirals with glimpses of the lake coming and going, revealing its greater width at the northern end. Abandoned houses, victims of the recession, stand unfinished near Ballinagleragh while some are derelict, left to the forces of nature. Along other sections, modern bungalows are lined up overlooking the lake. Gorse embroiders high hedges, locked in a tussle with bindweed, and the road leads over several humpbacked bridges.

Lough Allen is bounded on the west side by Arigna mountain and on the east by Slieve Anierin narrowing to a thin tip at the southern end beside Drumshanbo. Its most distinguishing landscape features are the hills, something that gave Hayward particular pleasure on his travels. The mountains were an integral part of his writing and he paints a picture of an easy-going, carefree, climbing world with a friendship amongst the people he met. In Leitrim he was enchanted by Lough Allen – which he spells as 'Loch' – when he looked out at it from the door of the caravan at 6 am before enjoying a swim in the lake: 'I had been told that Loch Allen was not attractive, and that the brown hills which rise from its eastern and western shores are rather grim and monotonous, but with the scene of beauty before me I could not understand how anyone had ever got such an impression of this place.'

In those days a new strand had been artificially created following the lowering of the level of the lake with the introduction of the Shannon Electricity Scheme in 1929 at Ardnacrusha in Co. Clare. Hayward said this meant a great gain for the lake, which he describes as 'an uncommonly attractive sheet of water … and wholly compact of beauty': 'The water itself was glorious and had a soft and balmy quality which seemed to envelop my body in the manner of a warm velvet cloak. It was brown and peaty to look at, but lovely beyond belief as with soft fingers it smoothed away the last complaining remonstrances of slumber only just broken.'

Hayward often adopted a sunny tone but he was not so complimentary about the neglect of the canal that had been built by the Shannon Navigation Commissioners to connect the river with the Erne, and with the Leitrim–Belturbet canal, both of which he said now 'lie desolate and indescribably pathetic'.

Were he around today, he would be pleased that the canal reopened in 1996 at Acres Lake, a two-way lock where a visitor centre outlines the area's history. As I drive around the lough, the water melts in and out of view. The ebullient song of a meadow pipit cascades over the forests and hills while from a cluster of willow trees comes a combination of whistles, elongated soft trills, alarm calls and other grace notes. A flurry of forty scraggy-looking crows takes off in a raucous chorus heading for the tiny tree-covered island of Gubarasheen in the middle of the lake. One of the challenges I have set myself is to try to see a kingfisher, a bird that has eluded me in Ireland. It has a Shannon population but there have been few sightings of it along the riverbank and lakes. This is the point where the lough opens into a wide water sheet where it licks around boulders thickly clothed in moss. Infinitely grey and infinitely silent, the water is mirror calm. I shift my focus to the surrounding hills. Across the lake, in Roscommon, the blades of two dozen wind turbines turn slowly on Corry mountain. To the south, Kilronan mountain has another dozen.

At the southern end of the lake, the Lough Allen Centre classifies itself as an eco-tourism destination. Through its activities such as wilderness therapy, survival skills and adventure camps, it has built up a significant reputation, creating local employment. Sean Wynne, a teacher in the vocational school in Drumshanbo, is sorting out paperwork for a forthcoming group visit. He organizes activities through the community-run centre. His father worked in the coal mine and his family later bought the gatekeeper's house and the area became known as Wynne's Bay.

'It has been part of the fabric of my life,' he says as we survey the lake from outside the centre. 'Wynne's Bay was formerly known as Flynn's Bay and we have a small corner of it, which is where my father lived. The shoreline has been at the back of our house and we always made our own entertainment. We grew up with the lake, although it is not everybody's cup of tea. If you go into Drumshanbo – not even a mile away – and ask about the lake, you will find that most people know little about it. Just five or six families have only ever had anything to do with it. Equally, I often wonder how many people have been to the top of Slieve Anierin. If you were to ask local people about the lake and the mountains, they will tell you that they are too busy to make time to take part in activities. One of the most shocking things is that people don't appreciate what they have on their own doorstep.'

We walk along a stretch of the lakeside thick with alder and sally trees. Small wavelets lap into the edge. A solitary mallard glides through silvered water, performing a sudden U-turn. The lake is renowned for its natural history, with two rare orchids, Irish lady's tresses (which likes wet habitats) and the small white, both flowering in recent years. Its birdlife includes sightings of little egrets and an Arctic skua.

'The lake's triangular shape is related to the ice age,' Sean explains. 'The canal was built in 1810 from Lough Allen to the Shannon. There was coal mining and ironworks around the lake and there was a history of iron production going back into the mists of time. The canal was used until the arrival of the hydroelectric power station at Ardnacrusha. This meant that the lake was closed off from then until the mid-1990s when there was a campaign to reopen it and a lock gate was installed.'

Pre-Ardnacrusha days it was a fantastic salmon lake. 'Dead Man's Point, which is up near Ballinagleragh, has a strange history. People who had to be buried were put on a slab of rock with a flag and their body was brought out to the island for burial. It was the shortest possible distance as you see on the map between the island and the shore, so the remains were on the shore waiting for transfer. But if it was a windy day or bad weather, they had to wait around, and the area became known as Dead Man's Point.'

Lough Allen may not mean much to local people, but there is a reason for this. Sean attributes it to the fact that there are many legends associated with the lake – including a Lough Allen monster that is said to have several humps and an enormous head – which give it a darker side.

'The unfortunate reality is that there was a tragic accident on Good Friday 1831. A group of people from Corry at the north end of the shore went to Drumshanbo to collect their goods. They decided to head back late in the evening and instead of going by road they went on the lake and because of the wind strength, thirteen people drowned. That tragedy has led to fear right down through the generations. People are uneasy about it, which is strange because the number of accidents on this lake – compared to those on Lough Ree or Lough Derg – is minimal. If you were to carry out a survey of local people you would find there is an underlying fear of the lake, which I believe is still a legacy from that period.'

We gaze across the placid water with barely a ripple on its surface. But although it is a calm morning, the lake has a reputation for wind.

'Some say the name Lough Allen, or in Irish *Loch Aillionn*, is "the beautiful lake" but I think it stands for the "lake of the squalls" as the winds are funnelled through it and of course can change dramatically. Employment is seasonal and the important issue is disposable income. We are close to Fermanagh, so the sterling-euro difference can be significant.'

Flat-bottomed clouds cruise the sky and the sun is trying to make an appearance. The light evolves from a grey pallor to lemon shades, revealing the hills north of Corry. In the nineteenth century the lake was a popular place for regattas but the decades since have seen many changes.

'Regattas are recorded as having been held here in 1861, and the sailing would have been in large boats of sixteen ton or more. There was a viewing area and races took place from O'Connor's Island, marked on some maps as Inisfale, a nine-acre island but really more of a peninsula because the shoreline has silted up so you can walk out at low level.'

WITH THE DEVELOPMENT of walking, cycling and kayaking routes by Waterways Ireland, new commercial possibilities are opening up for local firms in an area traditionally bereft of visitors. The tourist board is capitalizing on what it calls the 'experiential' aspect of visiting Ireland by creating activities for visitors. Tourism authorities group visitors into different categories known as 'culturally curious', 'social energisers' and 'great escapers'. Encouraged by what Sean Wynne told me about the new boardwalk and Blueway, I have organized a ride along it with Eileen Gibbons, who runs a cycle hire company with her husband Seamus. While waiting for her to arrive, I browse the newly opened Acres Lake visitor information centre. Archival audio material from RTÉ makes up a considerable part of the display. I press buttons to hear clips of Turlough O Carolan, a blind early harper from the golden age of the late seventeenth century who travelled all over Ireland composing and performing his tunes. There is a strong tradition of flute- and fiddle-playing in Leitrim, particularly towards the south of the county, and one of the most influential musicians from the early recording era is John McKenna. Jimmy McKiernan on the fiddle plays a burst of 'Drowsy Maggie', while Brid Sweeney sings 'My Own Leitrim Home'. Banjo, harmonica, tin whistle, accordion and bodhrán are all to the fore as I push ever more buttons. The display states that the fortunes of music in Leitrim reached new heights of popularity in the 1980s and '90s and it now has an international following.

The Snake in the Lake, the local name for the Drumshanbo Blueway, walking and cycling path, County Leitrim.

Elsewhere the centre focuses on industrial heritage and the coal mining at Arigna, which closed in 1990. Amongst the framed wall pictures of flowers and birds is a delightful painting of a glamorous-looking electric blue kingfisher with a long beak, staring eye, small claws clamped to a branch and a flame orange underside. It is intensely vivid and reminds me that this is a bird I long to see close up – perhaps today will be my lucky Leitrim break. I mull over W.H. Davies' quotation from his poem, 'The Kingfisher': 'I also love a quiet place / That's green, away from all mankind; / A lonely pool, and let a tree / Sigh with her bosom over me.'

It is a bright morning when Eileen Gibbons pulls up with a van beside Acres Lake for our canal-side ride to Leitrim village. The large hump of Slieve Anierin is visible while a light wind ripples the lake where a barge and pleasure craft are berthed beside two anglers at a fishing stand. We cycle to the start of the curving boardwalk where we dismount and push our bikes along it to the southern end of the lake. Opened by Waterways Ireland in 2017, the purpose of the Blueways trail is to promote the lake, canal, river and its surroundings to a wider public. It is the first of its kind in Ireland and the idea is to encourage exercise or an adrenaline-fuelled day on the water.

According to Eileen, this stretch of the Blueway has re-energized the canal and river. 'The boardwalk has brought a new lease of life to Drumshanbo ... Because of the way it twists, it's known as "the snake in the lake" and walking along it gives you the impression that you're on a boat on the lake. It's floating and will move with rising water. Acres Lake is attached to the canal system and was created for the canal.'

Once over the boardwalk we join a tree-lined gravel path that runs alongside the Lough Allen canal. After a few kilometres along the traffic-free trail we come to the graceful old humpbacked Drumhauver bridge, smothered in ivy. Apart from gorse along one stretch, there is little in the way of floral colour. En route to Drumleague Lock, a jogger gives a new meaning to baby power by running with a pushchair, much to the delight of the swaddled infant. We swing right at the lock, crossing over the canal and head down another straight stretch to Battlebridge. Two cyclists flash past at speed. Dog-walkers are out in force while canal lovers and strollers take advantage of the mild morning, exchanging cheerful greetings. On either side, at Mackan and Bellanaboy, sheep bleat beside Sitka spruce planted in crowded, linear rows. Behind it a watery sun breaks through. As I stop to adjust the saddle of my bike, a horse nudges a foal and walks across the field towards the path, giving us a camera-friendly turn.

I consult the map to get my bearings. The qualification for the inclusion of place names concentrates on the 'Drum' prefix, coming from *Droim*, meaning ridge. A glance at the map reveals a veritable drum roll of nearby townland place names, including Drumderg, Drumgorman, Drumherrif, Drumkeelan, Drumbrisny, Drumboylan, Drumhierny and a score of others. Flitting from branch to branch, two great tits pause, settling only for a few seconds before scarpering when a magpie pulls up alongside. We hear the *seep* of meadow pipits and identify a blue tit that hops from the old timber lock gates on to the stone bridge and then the ground. I mention to Eileen the picture of the kingfisher hanging in the tourist office and wonder if she has ever seen the bird.

'I've seen them on the canal occasionally and they're very fast,' she recalls. 'They come out of the hedge and dart along on the water or glide on the surface before hopping back into the hedge. Sometimes you might see them doing another sprint down the canal with just a quick flash of blue. It's pot luck, although anywhere from the Drumhauver bridge to Battlebridge is a good spot.'

I had noticed on a crossroads sign in Drumshanbo that the emblem of the bird appears alongside place names. This, she says, is part of the Kingfisher Cycle Trail, started in the 1990s by the environmental charity Sustrans.

'That's an older route than the Blueway, which comes partly into Leitrim and the top loop of it runs through the Fermanagh lakes and then into Donegal in the shape of a figure of eight. The image of the bird appears on old brown fingerposts, but parts of the route are not well signposted. In Fermanagh they've embraced it with blue signposts, which stand out much better, and it's used quite a bit there.'

Electric biking is easy and stress-free. Occasionally the bike gives a jolt when I pedal to gather speed, but it is a comfortable spin.

'People love the electric bikes. It's like someone giving you a push on the back so you don't have to worry about hills and you can easily go wherever you want. We got a grant-aid from Leader for using them and decided that we would make sure that we had bikes for all different people's needs, so we have a good range for both children and adults.'

At Battlebridge Lock the route meets the Shannon and we travel uphill by footpath into Leitrim.

'Leitrim village and Battlebridge have always been a little bit touristy,' Eileen says. 'Leitrim is on the Shannon-Erne canal and even from the beginning of navigation on the River Shannon you could take a boat as far as the village, so it was always a turning point and important scenic hub.'

Eileen leaves me in Leitrim and I cycle down to the canal where a dozen barges are moored. At the harbour, black-headed gulls shriek and posture noisily while pied wagtails run around the waterfront, their long tails flapping. A plaque in a small park marks the 'Arms of O'Sullivan', an intriguing memorial to Donal O'Sullivan Beare who marched here on 14 January 1603 with his followers from west Cork. The plaque recalls a journey of 320 km from Glengarriff, which took fourteen days across harsh terrain. In total 1000 people – 400 soldiers and 600 other men, women and children – started with him. I am intrigued to read that a newly established route, the Beara–Breifne Walkway, has just been launched to highlight one of the most wretched journeys ever undertaken in Irish history and is being marketed as one of the central tourism spines of the region.

O'Sullivan was given the nickname Donal Cam, (meaning 'crooked'). He played a decisive part in the Battle of Kinsale of 1601 but lost his cattle, lands and other possessions. Munster had been subdued by the English and O'Sullivan could not remain in this remote part of the south-west so he attempted to make it north to Ulster where he could join forces with Hugh O'Neill. The odds were heavily stacked against him and those marching alongside him who included fighting men, cavalry and foot soldiers. The huge party was made up of porters, servants, grooms and horse boys who looked after the equipment. It was a dangerous south-north journey during a winter of poor weather where food was hard to find. They ate grain or raw beans, meal and barley where they could find it and stole ale. From the rocky hills of Beara they made their way through Kerry into the Golden Vale of Limerick and Tipperary, fending off their English attackers in many skirmishes. By this stage the dead, wounded and stragglers incapable of fighting had been left behind and their number reduced by one-third.

The next major obstacle the party faced was trying to cross the Shannon with their weapons, loads and animals. They halted at the banks of the river at a wide crossing point north of Lough Derg, at Redwood beyond Portumna. Since they had no boats, O'Sullivan killed some packhorses and a boat-maker who was with him made a currach using the skins of animals. Across

ARMS OF O'SULLIVAN
HERE ON JANUARY 14TH 1603,
BRIAN OG O'ROURKE WELCOMED
DONAL O'SULLIVAN BEARE
AND HIS FOLLOWERS
AFTER THEIR EPIC MARCH
FROM GLENGARRIFF IN 14 DAYS.
THOUGH ONE THOUSAND STARTED WITH HIM
ONLY 35 THEN REMAINED.
16 ARMED MEN, 18 NON-COMBATANTS
AND ONE WOMAN.
THE WIFE OF THE CHIEF'S UNCLE
DERMOT O'SULLIVAN.

Memorial to Donal O'Sullivan Beare, commemorating his epic march from Glengarriff to Leitrim village in 1603.

the border in Co. Galway further attacks at Aughrim involved hand-to-hand fighting with spears, pikes and swords. O'Sullivan kept up the pace with a firm commitment and belief in what he was doing. The final stages of their journey took the survivors through the Roscommon towns of Ballinlough, Frenchpark and Ballaghaderreen, sweeping in a hook shape around Lough Arrow and Lough Key and then from Knockvicar into Leitrim village where they arrived at the Castle of O'Rourke. By the time they reached it, the numbers had been seriously reduced and only thirty-five remained: sixteen armed men, eighteen non-combatants and a mysterious woman who some commentators identified as the wife of the chief's uncle.

I complete my own 'mini' epic twenty-kilometre journey cycling back through the Blueway birdsong. Although there are some minor roads along part of the route, it is largely unknown to most motorists. Like the O'Sullivan march, it is a trip through landscape and memory, encouraging contemplation and a contented state of mind. The historic aspect of this part of the river is never far away and I reflect on how every inhabited landscape is a palimpsest.

Later that night, back in Drumshanbo, a group of dancers take to the stage in the Lough Allen Hotel. The first to perform, a four-year-old girl with self-confidence, reveals an exceptional talent, shimmying along to a jig with precise and rhythmic youthful energy. She is joined by two older women step-dancing their way across the wooden floor, click-clacking their fast-moving hard shoes of fibreglass tips and heels. The dancers are choreographed to a group of twelve musicians in a loose circle, dominated by fiddlers and flute players. Blending reels, jigs and hornpipes, they signify the start of the *céilí mór* and the Lough Allen Dance Weekend.

A ginger-haired, ponytailed teenager sets the audience alight with high-stepping and is followed by a tall man, using all the space at his disposal, dancing with a graceful airborne style to a hornpipe amidst shrill whistles. A trio of young women performs a variety of modern Irish step-dancing and the evening launches into a raft of sean-nós, two-hand dances and set dances. During a break, Edwina Guckian, the event organizer and a teacher who has been dancing for twenty-six years, describes it as a unique concept in Ireland.

'There is a vibrant cross-generational dance tradition here,' she says, 'and it's getting bigger, so this is why I set up the weekend at Lough Allen, which is part of the Leitrim Dance Project. Along one side of us you have Arigna mountain and on the other side is Ballinagleragh and Slieve Anierin – and where you find good music, with flute players and fiddlers, you'll find dancers. If you take John McKenna on the far side of the lake, he played some of his tunes specifically for dances, including a great one called 'McPartland's Style', which is a hornpipe. McPartland was a champion step-dancer from here. Growing up as a child I used to see loads of men – and it was always men, never women – dancing, and they came across from Ballyfarnham and Arigna. A lot of them were miners in heavy boots and the dancing died out for a while but I recalled seeing them, which influenced me to help retrieve it.'

The sun has set over Lough Allen and darkness creeps in. Edwina speaks about what influence the lake has had on musicians and how it inspires dancing. 'Years ago, you would often hear musicians talk about people from one side of the lake playing tunes coming across from the other side so there was always that connection. The landscape of Leitrim and its lakes and rivers have a lot to do with this, as well as the way we speak, and there's no doubt that life around the lake makes it an ideal setting. It has clearly been inspiring for previous generations and we want to tap into that to ensure it continues.

'My great-grandfather was a dancer and my grandfather always spoke about how they would wear leather shoes, and to stop them from getting holes in them they would bring them to the tinkers and they would put tin on their shoes. Then they would put a donkey or a horseshoe on their boots and the last thing was hobnails. Around here the cottages all had flagstone floors and when the men were dancing with their hobnailed boots the nails would be warming up on the floor and they would knock sparks out of the floor, so it's a common phrase to say around here, "Oh he's a great fellow for knocking sparks," which means he's a great dancer.'

The musicians are restless and restart with 'The Doon Reel' and 'The Traveller's Reel', swiftly moving into 'The Foxhunter's Jig' and 'The Kilfenora Jig'. They coalesce well when a group of eight embarks on 'The Connemara Set', old-style step-dancing reminiscent of the type of crossroads social dancing that Hayward would have witnessed. Holding hands, they swing around, cross over and in skilful unison turn clockwise and counter-clockwise. The musicians accompany the dancers throughout their performance, a spirited marriage that includes two barn dances, 'Around the Fairy Fort' and 'The Chaffpool Post', also known as 'The Shannon Waves'.

The barman talks of the dancing before he is interrupted by three women ordering cocktails. One chooses the Lough Allen Cocktail, comprising Captain Morgan's rum, Malibu, Blue Curacao and orange and pineapple juice. When it arrives she immediately posts a photograph of it on social media. Standing beside me, a retired garda called Gerry nurses a brandy.

'Cuba Libre, a cocktail of Coca-Cola, rum and lime juice, is popular,' he says against a renewed background of stamping, kicking, quick-steps and side-steps. 'The drink here that has gone very big is Gunpowder gin, which is produced in Drumshanbo, but rum is my preference.'

Another brandy helps loosen Gerry's tongue and he confirms what I had already identified on the map. 'Apart from Arigna, this part of the Shannon does not have too many high places so 'tis a flat landscape, which leads to a flat imagination – that's why they call it the dead centre of Ireland. One of the things you'll find are a lot of townlands starting with "Drum". And because of that, some people feel this town would have a better ring to it if it was renamed Rumshanbo.'

3

'Little town of my heart'

A MAELSTROM OF motorcyclists slowly honks its way along Carrick-on-Shannon's main street with collectors rattling plastic buckets in the face of passers-by. Riding three and four abreast, more than seventy bikers wear luminous yellow and orange jackets advertising '32-County Honda Charity Challenge: Are we there yet?' The purpose of this scooter ride is to raise funds for a special ambulance, which operates a service for long-term sick children throughout Ireland.

'There's always something happening in Carrick,' says a woman pausing with her shopping bags to look at the spectacle clogging up the traffic. Minutes later, McLoughlin's glass recycling lorry crunches its way down the street, causing another long traffic jam around the corner into Bridge Street. Shoppers are queuing to use an ATM before crowding into the renovated Market Yard Centre for their organic garden produce. A woman curses at the ATM that refuses to give her any money. 'Awfully thick machines,' she shouts before stomping into the bank. Seated at the Market Yard entrance on a square of cardboard beside an old milestone, a baseball-capped Romanian plays a burst of 'Rondo Alla Turca' then waves at me with his fiddle bow. To one side of him are a dozen 25 kg sacks of Maris Pipers and an empty wine bottle. Occasionally he pauses, and with a toothless smile pleads for spare change to be thrown into his purple velvet-lined music case before launching into 'Que Sera, Sera'. At the Tattie Hoaker stall, the owner promotes shiitake mushrooms from Holland, Californian dates and a range of fruit that includes aubergines from Italy, pineapples from Ghana, clementines from South Africa, apples from New Zealand and peaches from France. Everything you could wish for is here, from artisan bread to farmhouse cheeses. Trestle tables at Reggie's Veggies are laden with strawberries from Spain, grapes from Peru, bananas from Honduras, as well as kiwis and oranges and apples, organic herbs and salads and other fruit grown on their farm. A tall man with dreadlocks and black leather biker gear picks through the produce from Dromahair selecting radish, cabbage and scallions. A Frenchman sells almond croissants, spelt bread, blue cheese, *fougasse*, jars of duck terrine and gherkins. He tells me that he comes from Amiens. 'You know Amiens Street in Dublin? Same thing.' Other stallholders sell organic meat, German sausages and fresh fish. Flower power is on display at Kealin Ireland's colourful Leitrim Flowers where the showy pink of cosmos, cousins of sunflowers, stand alongside many others. Kealin and her husband, originally from Dublin, moved to Carrick in 2008 when they set up business. She talks me through the array of flowers on sale.

'We have scented daffodils here, over there are beautiful tulips and anemones, then irises, lilac, sweet pea and sweet William, natural foliage such as pussy willow and birch, and small primula heather, all organically grown in Leitrim and chemical free. Over here is flowering currant, which has a unique smell and is related to blackcurrant or raspberry. Cosmos is a very ordinary flower, which can be grown easily from seed, but it is spectacularly pretty and comes in every shade from pale pink, white and cream right through to vermillion.

'We saw a gap in the market for product substitution so instead of importing expensive and exotic flowers from around the world we decided to grow our own. Carrick gets a very good through-put of visitors – in fact you could say it's a cosmopolitan town. It's thronged all year around, not unpleasantly, but busy and a place to hang around and have a coffee or a drink. It has a good agricultural base and we like it because it's not Dublin 4 but it's only two hours away so is very commutable.'

Kealin is also the local chairperson of BirdWatch Ireland. She recently had a good view of a kingfisher near Jamestown and advises me to go there. 'I saw a flash of blue and watched it feeding in the reeds, and of course you always remember seeing a kingfisher because of its beautiful iridescent colours. It's not that unusual and it's not an endangered species but you need to be patient, keep your eyes peeled and binoculars at the ready. We are surrounded by lakes, canals and rivers in Leitrim and while it is not the most unusual species, if you sit quietly for a while you may see one. Birding has been disturbed along the river a bit as they have been putting in the new Blueways so it could be a year or two before they are re-established. If you go to Jamestown you should also look out for the Doon, the remains of an old ditch still to be found there.'

Built in 1839, the Market Yard with its red window frames and old stone is an attractive place. Its main business for many decades was homespun linen and wool as well as market and farm produce. Formerly a market house and shambles, or meat market, it fell into disuse and was renovated after many years of neglect. It is one example of how the town is embracing an appreciation of its heritage, tapping into its past and preserving its finest architecture. A gust of creative innovation has seen new hotels (including a barge boatel), restaurants, bistros and gastropubs, their shelves groaning with craft beers, a bespoke coffee roastery and businesses nourishing local traditions. Old stone buildings have been imaginatively repurposed. The courthouse has become an arts and design centre, a neglected church has been converted into a tourism attraction, while the former Irish National Bank is now an elegant restaurant. Intriguing pieces of historic street furniture such as the town clock tower erected to Owen McCann in 1905 and one of the most enduring landmarks, have been repaired. The clock still presides at the junction of Bridge and Main Streets. In Hayward's time it stood on the road but in the 1970s it was moved back on to the pavement.

The town grew up around the river, which to this day plays an important role in Carrick's new-found confidence. The original Irish name for Carrick-on-Shannon, *Cora Droma Rúisc*, means 'the stony ford of the ridge in the marsh'. It is a place that became an important location for Hayward and meant much to him on his travels around Ireland. On his Shannon journey he camped beside the river, always aware, in his effusive style, of the history surrounding him:

> Carrick is one of the great ancient crossing-places of the Shannon, and while it is a small place it has always been important from this very circumstance of its situation. It is neat and clean, and one of the pleasantest little towns I have ever been in and is the centre of a district which cannot fail to delight the heart of any holiday-maker who has the good sense, or good fortune, to make it his headquarters.

Carrick was then a town with more bicycles and ponies and traps than cars but the fundamentals of the place are much as he would have known them. The purpose of my visit is to walk the same ground as he did, and see what traces of him are to be found. Indeed, resonances of old Carrick remain. The streetscape and the buildings look much the same and echoes of its history are all around. Shopfronts retain traditional facades although many have been restyled. Paddy Dillon's chemist shop that stood in Bridge Street in the 1930s is now a lash and brow bar. The Costello Memorial Chapel, the smallest church in Ireland, and reputedly the second smallest in the world, was built in 1879. Dwarfed by two pubs, it is still held in warm affection by the townspeople and has been renovated to prevent the fabric of the building deteriorating. Across the road, at the Post Office in St George's Terrace, Hayward had an encounter with J.J. Sheerin, who conducted his correspondence by telegram, which he called 'a darling contrivance'. Sheerin told him he recognized him from his appearances in the cinema and had heard him singing on

Radio Éireann. 'Jay Jay', as Hayward refers to him, was the author of a guidebook, *Picturesque Carrick-on-Shannon* (now a collector's item) and he presented a copy to him as a gift.

In the 1930s Carrick was full of huckster shops. Its population was 1200 and it boasted no fewer than thirty-one bars, three bakery shops and three grocery, hardware and timber stores. In those days, many small shops had a licence to sell liquor and this was frequently retained over the generations. It now has fifteen bars, some open only a few hours at weekends and many closed during the day. While the passage of eighty years has brought about considerable commercial transformation, the twenty-first-century town whose population has trebled to 3600 has its share of knick-knackery stores as well as discount and charity outlets. But its *raison d'être* now seems to be as a place where Italian-style shoe shops are juxtaposed with accessory boutiques. Hen and stag parties take over the town at weekends to such an extent that they have come with a new set of rules. These include restrictions on adult paraphernalia such as blow-up dolls and T-shirts with offensive or sexually suggestive language. Street-drinking, lewd behaviour, noise, violence, intimidation, residential disturbances, overcrowding, public safety and other issues are of serious concern to local people as Carrick develops its night-time economy.

While the essence of the town centre would be familiar to Hayward, the rural backwater that he knew, and with which he had a happy association, has all but disappeared. There is a strong whiff of affluence. The amount of new building – even since the demise of the years of plenty – would astound him; few small towns in Ireland can have benefited so much from the Celtic Tiger. There remains, though, a rural simplicity about the place. It takes a pride in its past but is not stuck in a time warp. Leitrim in the 1930s was a forgotten county where poverty was rife as it struggled to find an identity in the new state. 'We lean heavily on our history,' Joe Dolan tells me. He has been the manager of the Bush Hotel since taking it over in the early 1990s. With its white pebble-dashed walls and bright red door and window frames, the hotel occupies a long-block fronting on to the main street. Although Hayward was camping during his 1939 Shannon trip, he used the Bush as an organizing venue from where to get things done, frequently staying in the hotel in later years for his travel books of the 1940s and '50s.

As well as being an affable innkeeper, Joe is a consultant in the travel industry and has just completed a busy term as president of the Irish Hotels Federation.

'The hotel opened in the 1790s for weary travellers and tired horses on the scenic route of the Bianconi north-west coach road from Dublin to Sligo,' he says. 'So more than 220 years on we keep that old-world tradition and character alongside memorabilia from the past. During Hayward's time the hotel was run by the McDermotts, a long-established family. But by the late 1950s and early '60s, which was a depressed time, the hotel went into liquidation. Up until then it was a place for the elite and the gentry.'

Joe's grandparents ran the old County Hotel around the corner and he took over the running of the Bush in the summer of 1991. With help from the International Fund for Ireland to the tune of £60,000, he added twenty-eight bedrooms and a large function room and the hotel now has fifty-four rooms.

'It was very tough at that time as interest rates were 22 per cent and the place was falling down when we took possession. There were just eight lettable rooms. But in the 1920s and '30s it was completely self-sustaining with a very low carbon footprint. There was a piggery at the back with four acres of pasture and gardens where the car park now is. They had a farm and their own cows, so they supplied all their own milk, fruit and vegetables, as well as poultry, beef, lamb, pork and bacon. We've come full circle and are back to where we started. We were the first hotel in Ireland to win a European Union Ecolabel award for promoting high environmentally friendly awareness and practices. And in everything we do we minimize incoming waste potential, using local produce with as little waste as possible and renewable energy sources with low-energy light bulbs.'

The Bush offers a place where country people queue up for a traditional carvery lunch of roast beef, potatoes, carrots, peas and an ocean of gravy. Three men at a table are tackling rhubarb tart topped with two large dollops of cream as we walk past. The Bush still retains its old bedrooms and the layout of the long front two corridors has not changed since Hayward's visit. Joe takes me on a guided tour. He speaks proudly about the loyalty of his staff. 'We have a workforce of sixty-two today but when we started in 1991, we had eleven staff and eight of them are still here. We have a high retention rate and low absenteeism.'

The downstairs walls are crammed with black-and-white photographs of Carrick from different eras and front pages of newspapers from the late nineteenth century. Framed sketches of Carrick by Raymond Piper, who illustrated Hayward's later travel books, hang in a long corridor. The hotel celebrates the area's literary, cultural and social history. Rooms are named after writers with Leitrim connections, including Susan Mitchell, Anthony Trollope, M.J. McManus and John McGahern. On the door of a packed conference room, a sign reads 'Macra na Feirme: Forage Systems Meeting'. Aerial photographs of the river show how it writhes in a perfectly formed python shape into Carrick, the hub of the area. We make our way upstairs. Joe throws open a door and shows me into a square room with high ceilings and a solid mahogany bed.

'We use our local history, culture and heritage for competitive marketing advantages. This room, which was called the Judge's Room, has just been renovated and we have renamed it the Michael Collins Room. Collins stayed here during his visit to Carrick in the summer of 1917 so to commemorate the 100th anniversary we recalled his stay.'

The walls are covered with memorabilia and photographs. Collins had come to the area to establish Sinn Féin clubs in local towns. The front page of *The Western People* refers to his killing in an ambush at Béal na Bláth during the Civil War in August 1922: 'General Collins Dead'. A framed letter on the wall contains notes from Special Branch, who monitored his movements around the country:

Collins went to the Bush Hotel where he remained for the night and on following day he left here at 11 am for Gowel Leitrim Sub. Dist where there is a Sinn Fein Club, returning to Carrick on Shannon same evening and addressed a meeting from 9 pm to 9.45 pm for the purpose of forming a Sinn Fein Club – the speech was very moderate. At 10pm he drove by car to Drumlion, Co. Roscommon to form a Sinn Fein Club. And returned to Carrick on Shannon at 11.30 pm leaving by night mail train for Dublin.

The period-piece bedroom furnishings include a Continental typewriter, china cups and crockery, and an antique telephone with a rotary dial. 'About the only thing that has changed is this Samsung Plasma TV screen, and we stopped lighting the fires a few years ago. People often wonder about the bed and whether it is the original one that Collins slept in. What I say is that we have changed the mattress since then and that's the story I'm sticking to.'

Hayward generally bemoaned the lack of decent meals in hotels on his travels but did enjoy dining at the Bush. After one particular meal, he goes on to explain what happened next: 'We talked and we sang and we caroused, and we had what we call in Ireland a regular wee hooley, and during the night we met so many people I can't remember a quarter of them.'

A VERITABLE ARMADA of musicians has arrived in Carrick for a festival of traditional music, described as a weekend of forty-eight musicians and fifteen pubs, and known as Sessions at the Shannon. On a par with a fleadh cheoil but without any of the organizational niceties, it is an informal gathering of musicians and their friends, taking place from early afternoon to late evening. Nicotine-infused pubs were a tremendous source of knowledge for Hayward, who described them as 'a natural clearing-house for information'. I decide that I will not be able to get around them all but will try visit some as part of a musical fact-finding tour.

Carrick is effectively divided into two sections through its pubs. Close together, at one end of main street, stand The Swan, The Tipsy Tailor, Paddy's, Percy Whelan's, Murtagh's and the Buffalo Boy Whiskey Bar. At the other end of town, in Bridge Street, The Oarsman, Cryan's Teach Ceoil, The Anchorage, The Barrelstore, and McHugh's all vie for craft beer and cocktail money.

At the early afternoon sessions in the Landmark Hotel the playing is dominated by what a man beside me calls 'cool young dudes'. He agrees that traditional vernacular music is in no way uncool amongst the millennials; in fact, it is enjoying a resurgence of interest all over the country. One by one, more wandering minstrels slip in, produce their instruments unostentatiously and demurely join the company gathered around small tables. Within thirty minutes the group has mushroomed to a monster ceilidh, an orchestration of twelve multi-instrumentalists now gathered in a musical firmament. Fiddle bows are shooting back and forth at speed as they storm in a sustained onslaught into nautical-themed tunes: 'The Ship is in Full Sail', 'Launching the Boat' and 'The Three Sea Captains' followed by 'The Graf Spee', 'The Boys of Blue Hill' and 'Off to California'. The playing is amplified by the banjo, box, mandolin, guitar, uilleann pipes, harmonica, bodhrán and spoons, and a bouzouki, an instrument that has been integrated into the Irish traditional music scene. From his seat on a stool, a tall man plucks slowly on his banjo, stepping up the pace into overdrive, all the time remaining erect and motionless as he immerses himself in the music. One musician holds the fiddle in the crook of his arm while a woman beside him picks up spoons, creating a castanet-like sound before switching to a bodhrán.

Creative juices are surging in The Swan where a smaller ensemble of four musicians on tin whistle and banjo improvise with gusto and delicate cross-fingering in several tunes with local connections. These include 'The Shannon Breeze', 'Crossing the Shannon', 'The Humours of Tuamgraney', a hornpipe from east Clare, and 'The Shores of Lough Bran', a song that Hayward recorded with HMV. Across the road, slip jigs, double jigs and slides are underway in Paddy's Bar. But when I ask them, the performers are not sure of any of the titles. With flamboyant ornamentation, they play what is referred to as a BTST (a buncha tunes strung together), seamlessly whirling from one to the next with penny whistles howling like banshees.

I head for a stroll by the Shannon where boats and barges are being scrubbed at the jetty along Quay Road. A woman hangs curtains in a cabin cruiser while another owner tinkers with the engine. A couple of boats nudge slowly out while a team of eight rowers, their muscles straining, are slicing upriver with a rhythmical dipping of oars and grunts. As I clomp along the boardwalk, I note the names of boats: *Sapphire*, *Lady Lucy*, *Molly D*, *The Lady Gabrielle*, *C'est La Vie*, *Laura*, *Mary Ann*, *Samara*, *Anabell*, and the humorously named *Ship Happens*. In the water, bright red-faced moorhens, with their distinctive yellow bill, pick and choose insects from the surface. From a distance, the gleaming yellow eyes of a small party of tufted duck watch the proceedings, releasing a series of low whistles followed by growling calls.

On his summer Shannon journey, Hayward started each day with an early morning swim. For breakfast, he and his travelling companions often ate the leftovers from dinner the night before. The thunderous noise from a juggernaut of lorries, vans, cars and buses on the main road linking Sligo to Dublin jolts me back to the twenty-first century. A continuous stream of traffic and commercial transport skirts its way around Carrick from Cortober on the Roscommon side, squeezing across the bridge built in 1845, rushing to cities, ports and ferries. A recent addition has been the erection of a new steel footbridge, which has eased the pressure on the old bridge.

The old architecture of the streets contrasts with the teeming activity at the main marina across the bridge where opulent cruising boats and gleaming pleasure craft are moored hugger-mugger with a backdrop of new apartment blocks. In the 1930s the cost of mooring a cabin cruiser, Hayward writes, was three-and-ninepence per month per boat, while a charge of two-and-threepence is made for the passage through each lock or swivel. Carrick is the Shannon-Erne Waterway's twenty-first

Sketch in Dunne's Bar, Carrick-on-Shannon, of 'The Tale Goes Round' by Raymond Piper. Richard Hayward is seated third from left.

century boat-hire capital and the town's tourist trump card in a place defined by water. With its modern automated locks, the waterway was reopened in 1994 and scores of boats ply between the Shannon's broad banks, playing an important role in boosting the coffers of local businesses. It has become a gateway location from which to explore the waterways.

Back in town, Dunne's Bar in the main street curiously is not included in the sessions event. This is one of the pubs that Hayward knew well: in those days it was known as Dunne's Swing Door Saloon Bar, held no more than twelve people and was renowned for its after-hours drinking. The bar is divided in two but stretches back to the beer garden where smokers congregate. Young men, mostly in rugby shirts, drink Guinness without taking their eyes off the screen. Others sit around small wooden tables. A cheer goes up when Ireland scores in their Six Nations Championship clash with Wales.

Hanging at an arch is a small framed sketch to which few if any drinkers cast a second glance. It was presented by Gregory Dunne to the owners of Dunne's new bar in 2002 and hangs as a reminder of the esteem in which Hayward was held in a place that had a strong emotional pull for him. The line drawing by Raymond Piper, entitled 'The Tale Goes Round', features a group of six well-dressed Carrick businessmen, some perched on high stools with glasses in hand, shooting the breeze. Seated in the centre, a relaxed and puckish Hayward – his face radiating pleasure – wears an open-neck shirt with a sports jacket. Hayward's easy-going personality struck a chord with local people. His friends in the drawing are Paddy Dillon, the chemist, Jack Cassidy, the dentist, Patrick Dunne, the editor of the *Leitrim Observer*, Paddy Hyland, the paper's manager, John Dunne, jeweller and former owner of Dunne's Bar, and Tommy Flynn, the former owner of P. Flynn and Company.

Ponytailed women in baseball caps and fleeces stand in gangs in front of the sketch, slugging from bottles of Bud. As I study the drawing, one of them says to me, 'That's all my family up there but I don't know their names.' The women are captured on smartphone video grinning broadly in front of the sketch. One wears a T-shirt saying: 'Drink Sensibly, Don't Spill It.' It is not hard to imagine the banter and the yarns, the stories and songs, the repartee, rejoinders and the razor-sharp wit from the assembled Carrickmen as the night's partying wore on into the small hours.

A few doors away, in the window of Trinity Rare Books, Hayward's hardbacks with their brightly coloured dust jackets are in the window. Inside they sit alongside John McGahern's works and out-of-print volumes by other Irish authors. In bookseller's parlance, Hayward's books show some slight rubbing to the edges with price-clipped dust jackets. Others have minor foxing on the outer edges of the papers and a few come with protective wrappers to keep the jackets clean. A second edition of *Where the River Shannon Flows* is on sale for €70, while *Border Foray* with its enigmatic cover sells for €65.

In the shop, run since 1999 by Canadian bookseller Nick Kaszuk, the memory of Hayward and his connection to this busy boating town lives on. Nick says *Where the River Shannon Flows* is a standard local classic that attracts people interested in boats as well as readers who collect Shannon literature.

'Hayward's books are always sought after,' he says. 'I search for them and find them in Australia, America and all over the UK. His books are listed on the Internet and they just seem to keep on selling.' Nick attributes this demand to Hayward's writing style and his popular technique combining research and meeting people.

'He was an informative traveller, a very good writer, and he always seems to form an attachment to the areas he visits. The way he describes places makes them come alive. For example, there are some areas that he mentions in Manorhamilton that I have driven through but have never stopped to explore. He seemed to do a lot of research and he writes accessible history. People sometimes write to me requesting any of Hayward's books, but it is his book on the Shannon that is so popular here. River lovers come from all over and they want to find out about the Shannon's history and its literature. It is one of my top ten standards and anyone who appreciates topography will like this book.'

Along Bridge Street a veritable river of music flows as freely as the beer in the pubs, mingling with the restaurant smells of chicken tikka masala, fried rice, pasta, and stale urine. The piercing, breathy timbre notes of a tin whistle come through the open windows of McHugh's, enticing me inside. A polka, 'The Sprig of Shillelagh', being played with dash and flair when a group of white-shirted, black-trousered men with a priestly mien, who could pass as a choir, come in behind me. It turns out they are on a stag night and are not here to sing. They order twelve sambucas, then in their very own Riverdance in the middle of the bar begin their version of the Carrick-on-Shannon highland fling.

On the other side of the street, jaunty reels, jigs and barn dances are flying with dexterity around the Anchorage Bar, capturing the spirit of the moment. Perennial favourites range from 'Last Night's Fun', 'The Sligo Maid' to 'The Boys of Ballysadare'. 'We call it a fusion of music, but some others refer to it as a con-fusion,' one musician says.

In the Regatta Bar of Cryan's Hotel, which links through a passageway to its sister venue, Cryan's Teach Ceoil, Patsy Hanly and Sean Ward are tuning up concert flute and fiddle while waiting for the crowd to drift in. Sean's reels had featured in the musical history exhibit that I had seen in Drumshanbo. I was told to look out for them by a local man who said they are from the 1970s.

When I mention this to Sean, he questions the period. 'I'd say more like the 1870s, to be truthful.' I recite a nutshell version of my quest, asking about tunes which Hayward sang or recorded. When I show them the cover of his sheet music book *Ireland Calling*, which features a picture of a bowler-hatted Hayward, a flicker of recognition appears on their faces. The book is a mix of tunes and songs that he played and sang at venues throughout Ireland as well as on Radio Éireann and on BBC Radio, in some cases with Delia Murphy. One of the duets that he recorded with another singer, Anna Meakin, was 'The Shannon Shore'. Patsy has come across Hayward and is familiar with Sean Maguire, the fiddle player with whom Hayward recorded an album, *Words and Music of Ireland*, in 1957. For his Shannon journey, Hayward chose a theme tune, 'Nora Lee', a song of his own, which he recorded and said, 'goes to a very sweet air'. He was known for promoting and cross-referencing his songs and books and told the reader that 'a small matter of commerce will bring it into your possession'.

For what might be called a 'Hayward tribute act', honouring his memory and connection to Carrick, Pasty plays a graceful version on his flute of the sweet notes of 'The Bonny Bunch of Roses'. This was a Hayward party piece, which he said was a Co. Tyrone ballad of Napoleon and his mother. Patsy talks about the festival which has been running for more than twenty years but is held only every three or four years.

'What happens in Carrick is that the musicians are put into sessions with other musicians whom they may or may not know. This, in my opinion, is good, as I have made friends with people who otherwise I would not have met. Tonight we're playing a lot of tunes which were recorded in America in the 1920s by one of the all-time great Irish fiddlers, Michael Coleman, who was born in Killavil. Paddy Killoran and James Morrison were also part of that era and their tunes are still widely played so when in unfamiliar company, we all have the same versions from these recordings.'

After the break the musicians launch into a long uninterrupted burst of reels including 'The Devil in Dublin', 'The Humours of Lissadell', 'The Queen of May', 'The Copperplate' and 'The Hare's Paw', segueing seamlessly into 'Strike the Gay Harp'. The tempo is slowed for the 'Killavil Jig', 'The Scotsman over the Border', and 'Tenpenny Bit', ending a surfeit of beguiling tunes and feast day of Shannon showmanship concentrated in just two streets.

I raise my glass and a farewell hand to the musicians. On my way back to the Bush Hotel, I mull over how many of these traditional tunes have stood the test of time. If, by some quirk of time-travel fate, Hayward was to walk down the long main street of the county town of Leitrim, I wonder what he would make of the place where his name endures in art, music, journalistic history and literature. He remains imprinted in the minds of Carrick people, albeit as a distant, far-flung memory. He may even be enjoying a merry ceilidh amongst the stars, celebrating the fact that this vibrant town has reinvented itself, although part of him may feel that that town is a bit self-satisfied. After two 'wild nights', Hayward renamed Carrick-on-Shannon 'Cirrhosis-of-the-Liver'. In 1945 he was made a freeman of the town for his services to the Inland Waterways Association of Ireland in recognition of his work promoting the Shannon in his writing and filmmaking. Hayward never forgot the camaraderie, which for him exemplified the commonplace soul of Ireland. His ghost has never left the place he called 'dear friendly Carrick, little town of my heart'.

4

Along the Worm's Ditch

SVELTE MOTORWAYS BURN their way across Ireland, east to west and south-west with only passing regard to local culture or topography, built for speed by European Union money in the first decade of the twenty-first century. Signs point the way to places on Ireland's Ancient East, an eccentric zigzag route inaugurated in 2016, which covers a huge area from Cork to Cavan and Monaghan, with no real unifying theme. These motorways throbbing through the landscape mean that people have lost their engagement with villages. Small towns come with bypasses and numerous roundabouts to rush visitors through what some call the Cinderella country of the midlands (a name from Middle English, *mydlonde*, first used to describe the midlands of England).

Fáilte Ireland has launched a new regional tourism branding scheme, 'Hidden Heartlands', a route running from Sligo to Limerick, taking in both banks of the Shannon. A multimedia advertising campaign slogan revolves around the concept 'Yours to Uncover' along with some corny headlines on stories such as 'Water Way to Spend a Day'. In tourist terms the midlands is acknowledged as 'a black hole', lying in the shade of the other brands, and has been neglected and treated unfairly. The Tourism Minister, Shane Ross, described the 'Hidden Heartlands' as a 'seductive' project, saying the Shannon was an area with many hidden treasures. Selling the midlands is a tough call – it lacks the drama of the wild Atlantic. The region receives coverage in the American *Fodor's Essential Ireland* guide, which states that the area is 'Perfect for the relaxed visitor who values the subtle over the spectacular, although it is also known for its super-narrow B roads.'

The 'super-narrow' roads of the surrounding area between Lough Allen and Lough Ree are filled with the heritage of an older Ireland. Instead of driving north–south, I stray a few miles east–west in either direction of the river for a diversionary tour in search of 'hidden treasures'. On the fringe of my territory, through Keshcarrigan and Fenagh, then across to Keadew, Cootehall and Knockvicar, the towns are, to use a current term, 'jam' – just about managing. There is a sense that the past was a better place than the present. Some of the saddest sights are the rusting one-pump petrol stations that have not dispensed for perhaps forty years, standing as a Shell or Esso skeleton. Emerald green wall-mounted post boxes, along with cast-iron road signs and occasional thatched houses complete the picture of an Ireland that would have been familiar to Hayward. Juxtaposed with all this is the face of the new Ireland: boarded-up shops, half-built estates, villages without a post office, garda or petrol station, or in some cases even a shop. Unoccupied trophy homes from the Celtic Tiger years stand idle while numerous houses have been abandoned at the breeze-block stage. There seems little danger of this area ever being veneered by tourism.

A few kilometres south-east of Carrick-on-Shannon, the river turns sharp left at Lough Corry, then pauses in its journey, sweeps back on itself north at Jamestown – the only time in its course the river flows north – before looping around and falling into Drumsna where it hurries with unaccustomed vigour. If Carrick represents the brash new face of the twenty-first-century river, then Jamestown evokes an older riverine aspect where water bubbles over a weir on the way in. The village's historic buildings are identified with plaques recording their posterity. The auxiliary workhouse was a mill store in 1730 and later used to help with the Carrick paupers. Nowadays it is boarded up, smothered with yellow lichen and cobwebs. The town was named after James I and chartered in 1622 when the wall was built for the protection of the settlers. The sole surviving archway, which formed the north gate, is the only remaining trace of the old walls. Commercial life in Jamestown is restricted to two bars, Mulvey's Arch and Kenoy's, both closed during the day, and the Cottage Restaurant, which opens in the evening.

Adhering to Kealin's instructions, I follow the road from Jamestown in search of the Doon, or even – binoculars ever ready – the chance of a kingfisher sighting. Five black-clad, French fishermen are preparing to set off in two boats. They come from the Champagne region and one of their party, Pierre, who speaks English, talks about the bird, which in France is called the *martin-pêcheur*. My sighting of kingfishers in France has included one just west of Nantes on the island of Noirmoutier, and on another occasion in the Loire Valley. The fishermen carry provisions down steps to load up the moored boats. A supply of baguettes, croissants and sugary glories such as madeleines, éclairs and macaroons will help while away the time during a long fishing weekend. Their well-stocked cool box contains bottles of Pouilly-Fumé, Sancerre and Pastis, while food hampers reveal truffles, hunks of Brie and square chunks of Maroilles, which comes from the milk of cows in the Nord *département*. Pierre tells me that in olden days it was called *merveilleux Maroilles*. Two swans sail across to the steps hoping for an offering, but the olfactory mingle of ripe cheese puts them off and they quickly disappear.

After crossing Jamestown bridge, a sign for Co. Roscommon is my signal to turn on to a single-track road. High hedges obscure views of the river until I come to Ardanaffrin bridge. A tiny quay and picnic area overlooks Jamestown Canal, an offshoot of the Shannon. I scan the countryside with my binoculars, freeze-framing a motionless, black donkey beside a hedge, a thick-set, swaggering hooded crow reconnoitring the land and a poster on a sycamore tree advertising Circus Corvinni in Kilmore. It is hard to pin down any physical remains of an embankment. I pick up a glimmer of something resembling a corner of a ditch near the river but because of the shape of the land and tree cover, it is largely concealed from view.

I study the map closely and it is clear that the Doon, marked by a broken red line, runs adjacent to the Shannon. Traces of a short, two-metre-wide twisty and gently rising path runs between either side of a low section of plain, empty ditch about six metres deep. Silver and grey lichen blushes the stones. From the bank, I gaze over tall reeds and high grasses to the listless water of the Shannon, the colour of strong tea with ripples and golden patches. Above the tops of trees carrion crows break the silence with their loud and continuous harsh *kaaw*.

Originally an elongated Iron Age walled fortification made of earth and stone, the Doon was also called the Black Pig's Dyke and was known under other names in different areas. It ran from Donegal, through Leitrim, Roscommon and Longford to Down. Definitive dates are unclear but some archaeologists believe it was built around 200 BC to protect the Seat of Connaught, 22 km south, from northern enemies. Another school of thought says that it was erected to defend Ulster against marauding Connaughtmen from the south. Whatever the reason, it was a formidable frontier consisting of half a million tons of soil and trees with formal palisades along its length stretching through the loop to Drumsna. Its purpose may also have been to act as a short entrenchment, dividing property or making large-scale cattle rustling more difficult since livestock larceny was prevalent. The river hereabouts at Cuiltyconway follows the course of what is recognizable of the Doon for up to a hundred metres over to the other side of Ardanaffrin.

I walk a stretch of the ditch until my progress is halted because of dense foliage. The field rises uphill to a yellow farmhouse where a man chopping firewood points out the route of what he says is known colloquially as 'the worm's ditch' because it was thought to be the cast of a giant worm. It appears intermittently in sections with large gaps, and he tells me another part of it is found at the other end of the Jamestown Canal. The defensive aspect of it, he believes, is against the north, in particular defending the fording points around the loop of the river. The gist of the Black Pig legend is that a cruel schoolmaster with magical powers was transformed into a large pig by one of his pupils and pursued across the countryside leaving in his wake large indentations in the ground – now the present discontinuous linear earthwork – before drowning in the river. Like most Irish legends there are variations on this story. It is easy to miss the Doon but once spotted it is hard to overlook and is worth seeking out. On my mini-tour I find no hidden treasures, my kingfisher-hunting comes to naught, but I have at least satisfied a geographical conundrum and paid homage to the remnants of the mysterious worm's ditch.

From Drumsna the river plunges through a series of small lakes while the road veers towards Dromod where I briefly re-join the N4 before turning off into Rooskey. There is a startling contrast with the roads of today and those of the 1930s, which were in a terrible condition. Hayward frequently complained about the state of the dusty boreens. He travelled roads close to the river, which were so poor that in some cases he could reach speeds of only ten miles per hour. One of the most memorable descriptions of his trip was his drive along the Rooskey to Tarmonbarry road in Roscommon:

> We had not travelled more than a mile of this little road before our car and our caravan, and everything within and without them, lay under a thick layer of white powder, which had such a degree of penetration that for a full three months after I had left this limestone country it would continue to creep out from the joints and crevices of my car every time it was hosed. In appearance we had all aged thirty years in five minutes, for the dust had made our hair and eyebrows quite white and as we stopped to inquire the way we were all enveloped in a great cloud which stretched behind us as far as we could see. Such dust I have never seen before, and such dust I hope never to see again. For myself, who detest dust as one of the chief plagues of man, it was sheer misery.

Rainbow over Rooskey Bridge, built in 1845, signifying where Roscommon and Leitrim counties meet.

Rooskey itself is divided into two halves. On one side of the river, which used to be known as Georgia, most premises, including the Shannon Key West Hotel, are either locked up or derelict. The hotel has been closed for seven years, its car park fenced off with chains and padlocks.

Across the bridge the nerve centre of the town is Tighe's supermarket, a historic building. According to a plaque on its pebble-dashed wall, the RIC barracks was based here until after the War of Independence in 1922. At the checkout till, a woman speaks about the town's decline. 'We useta have a great bacon factory here with plenty of jobs but that was in the days when Rooskey *was* Rooskey.' She points to the building opposite, a former restaurant and café. 'The boats would've pulled up there and it was a busy place but between that closing and the hotel shutting up shop, it's not the place that it was. They're trying to develop the canal, putting in a walkway and a canoe trail so maybe something will come from it.'

Three locals join the conversation, scoffing at the idea of hidden midlands treasures. A man with a newspaper, loaf and carton of milk says they badly need immediate investment. 'They'd want to spend about two million here – it's godforsaken. There should be a complete upgrade that would revamp this place. It has suffered badly in the last ten years and has been left behind. For a start, y'see, you take your life in your hands walking across that bridge. There should be a pedestrian bridge, the same way as they got one in Carrick-on-Shannon a few years ago, but after that y'see they musta run outta money. We get nothin' here, there's no pride in the place, no community spirit and I've never seen any of these so-called treasures. They don't give two damns about us and that's the height of it. Funerals are about the only things that happen here. Is it any wonder we've nicknamed it the hidden-up-your-arse lands?'

A woman chips in to say that life was equally tough in the 1970s and '80s. 'There wasn't any money around and there were very few jobs, so the good old days weren't all that good at all. You couldn't blame the young people for going abroad to find work. And it's the same again today, the heart's gone out of Rooskey, nothing has changed. There's a school full of children but nothing for them. The busiest people here are Rooskey Active Retirement who organize outings all over Ireland as they're keen to get outta town. The whole place is a victim of the Celtic Tiger blues.'

Another man, with a jutting granite chin, hisses about the hotel.

'It needs to be reopened, and pretty damn quick. Don'tcha know that when a hotel closes, a town dies. It's a perfectly good solid structure from the boom years and needs a coupla hundred thousand to bring it up to scratch. Do you know anybody interested?' He offers a parting shot. 'Watch yerself on that road, the tractors fly along it, and all the Dubs who've moved into new houses there don't heed the bends.'

From Rooskey, a brown fingerpost brands the L1415 turnoff to Tarmonbarry as the scenic East Roscommon Drive. Hedges and ditches are lined with large toadstools, plantain and ragwort, and purple thistles lit up with shoals of light. Since Hayward drove it, the road has been tarred and widened. Along its thirteen kilometres, prosperous houses and trim bungalows sit beside each other. Drivers of two New Holland tractors nod as we pass. Roofers are busy at a new house. The distinctive primrose-and-blue chequered Roscommon flags lie limp from trees and telegraph poles. Yellow road signs warn of dangerous bends while the words 'Slow' and 'Slower' are painted on the tarmac. As was the case eighty years ago, the road still runs parallel with the river although trees, high hedges and shrubbery means that it is flowing incognito. Hayward found it a dull, flat, monotonous road.

Along a verge, a 'flying saucer' has come to rest, one of the ubiquitous hubcaps that litter roadsides. I pull over by a farm gate to saturate myself in the mellifluous townland names that tumble from the map: Moneenbog, Cloonafill, Pipers Town, Cloonfad, Sharvally, Ballymagavie and Kilbarry. A safety notice in red lettering warns of the dangers of livestock. Six bullocks stare at me. Circular bags of shrink-wrapped silage stand in a field where jet-black crows jostle with each other. Far-carrying sounds break the silence. A chainsaw howls, a dog bays from a distant farmyard, and somewhere else a motorbike is kick-started into life. This is a route made for meandering.

Following a signpost for St Barry's holy well, I drive slowly on a minor road to Kilbarry church, passing a field with a scattering of sheep. An inquisitive Hayward came here to find out information about what he had been led to believe were the seven churches of Kilbarry; but despite his enquiries he was unable to trace anyone who knew about them. A woman told him there is only one church and that she had never heard of seven churches: 'And is it any wonder I didn't know what you would be at, for there's no seven churches in it, not even one itself, but nothing but a few old stones (God keep us all from harm!) to put you in mind of days gone by.'

Today the remains of two churches survive and the site preserves stones of a round tower. A square-headed doorway denotes the antiquity of the ruined church. A farmer from a nearby house comes over to talk about the site. There is, he says, a local legend that a night spent within its walls will cure the mentally ill. He is not aware of the seven churches label but sends me off in the direction of the holy well along a rough mucky track. Hedges

Statue of St Barry, near Tarmonbarry, who in the fifth century used a large boulder to cross the Shannon.

overflow with rustyback and maidenhair ferns, entangled with bramble and ivy, herb Robert, and masses of the soft green leaves of common nettles. A tall episcopal statue of St Barry robed, in a cream gown and with a terracotta staff, gazes into the distance, his mystery lacquered into history. He wears a lugubrious face with beard and crown. Fresh tubs of flowers have been placed around the base where a sign says the statue was erected in Jubilee Year 2000. The well is surrounded by a low circular wall and it is said that there is never a time when it runs dry. Steps lead down to it, cinctured with leaves and twigs. Someone has left a white votive candle with the words 'Bringing you the gift of hope'. Piles of stones have been deposited by worshippers performing the Stations of the Cross. Alongside are several small statues: one says Medjugorje, another is of St Anthony, and mother clutches child in a third. St Barry, a disciple of St Kevin of Glendalough, dates from the fifth century. When he was searching for a place for his settlement, he reputedly used a large boulder to cross the Shannon because he had no boat.

TARMONBARRY, WHEN I eventually reach it, is a loose straggle of houses with a population of 518. It consists of a supermarket, restaurant, pub and a historic hotel. Right on the Longford–Roscommon border, Keenan's styles itself as a boutique hotel. High above the river, electricity lines link both sides of the Shannon. I count over a hundred starlings on the lines, clothes-pegged in tight formation, a nightly cross-Shannon ritual. Amidst a confusion of warbling, clicking, squeaking and semi-musical whistling, they produce their own gigawatts. They keep a beady eye on the panorama of life on the bridge and on the metallically motionless Shannon. There is little river traffic until *Scruples II* pulls off from the quayside and heads downstream under the lifting bridge, causing a tailback of livestock lorries, tractors, vans and cars.

The starlings continue their restless activity. A few of the more aggressive ones engage in argy-bargy while others raise throat hackles. Suddenly, a single avian wanderer takes off, followed by twenty whirring in a small black cloud, then another handful rises in the same direction. *Sturnus vulgaris* are on the move, heading over to the thickly vegetated Longford shore, drawn in by the Leinster air where they are heckled by a dozen crows. The river as a physical and geographical barrier is unimportant to them. Wood pigeons emerge shouting loutishly while a cloud of midges circle around me. Two cyclists whoosh by on the towpath. I stroll past patches of red clover, bush vetch, dog violet, teasel and rough hawkbit. Beyond the weir and sluice gates, three white swans on evening gliding manoeuvres add a touch of luminescence, while two fishermen pack away their tackle. The evensong of birds fades into silence and I leave the roost and the river to the creeping creatures of the night.

At the bridge, a signboard states that the Shannon 'majestically cradles Tarmonbarry as it winds its way through the centre of Ireland'. In the gastro bar at Keenan's, Mickey Kelly is majestically cradling a whiskey and chaser on a corner stool. The octogenarian has lived in Tarmonbarry all his life and is familiar with the road to Rooskey, having driven lorries along it for Bord na Móna.

'It was hard work but there was no other employment around here,' he says. 'There might have been a small bit of rural electrification but Bord na Móna was a good company to work for. They built houses in Lanesborough and other towns and there were hundreds of men, women and children cuttin' turf. I knew all the roads well. I'd say at one time that road to Rooskey was probably the worst country road in Ireland. There were a few horses on it in the 1930s but that would have been the height of it. In the winter there would be muck on it and it was prone to a lot of potholes. The country was full of bicycles and there was no need for locks or helmets then.'

I ask Mickey about the man that Hayward met and he concludes that he may well have existed although he reckons no one would know now who he was. 'Y'see up there in Kilbarry they're very learned men, very intelligent people. I wouldn't be surprised about their fancy words because it was a place of scholarship. They were nice people and were all clever men.'

Mickey taps his empty glass to indicate he might be persuaded to accept a refill in exchange for more anecdotal lore. With ease, he unspools his memories of local transport life. 'In Tarmonbarry I remember seeing only two cars in the 1940s and there might have been about 100 people living in the village then. The first car was at an old schoolhouse, which is now a guesthouse. Thomas Reilly, who ran a grocery store, bought it and was an undertaker too. He also had a horse-hearse, which was two horses and a smashing-looking carriage. He owned one of the working horses and my father would have loaned him his horse and he would put a super harness on it. The man that was driving the horses sat up on top wearing a hard hat. In the time when Hayward was here there would have been horses and donkeys and carts on the roads.'

Mickey's passion is collecting car registration number plates and story after story pours from him. 'Tommy Reilly had a Ford V8 and the registration number was DI 2282. When he changed it, he bought a similar one again and that number was DI 2717.' The numbers were known as alphanumeric marks and were issued by the local authority. 'Ned Brehon had a car for his own use and his number was DI 2175. After that, another man, John Murray, built a house up the road and he started the hackney business and had a V8 and it was DI 2145. Each county had its own numbers. Longford next door was IX, Galway was IM, but DI stood for Roscommon whereas today DI is the number of the Lord Mayor of Dublin's official car.'

Mickey possesses a razor-sharp recall of the registration numbers. 'It's not that difficult as they were initially the only two cars in the village. But they were great cars and so too were the Minors that you could drive for ever. Everybody's father, or grandfather or neighbour, owned a Minor. The very first car I had was a baby Ford and its number was DI 1916 so I remember that one well as it's a collector's item. That would have been probably in the late 1940s. They were different days with different licensing laws. You couldn't open on a Sunday but if you were what they call "bona fide" you could have a drink. That meant if you lived three miles away from the pub you could have a drink in the evening, so some local people used to sneak in because you weren't supposed to have a drink if you lived nearer. 'Twasn't a bad place to live in those days but there was no wage packet coming in. People were trying to live on the price of a couple of cattle and the houses weren't great – there was no running water nor electricity.'

I mention to Mickey the feathery profusion of the Tarmonbarry starling serenade and it sparks a memory for him.

'I remember when the electricity came into Tarmonbarry in the 1950s. The ESB were working in the Killashee area just across the bridge and it was always the done thing that when the switch came on that there had to be a hall and the government minister came but there was no hall in Killashee, although there was one in Tarmonbarry. The ESB brought the electricity across the Shannon, and that's why you'll see the two poles across the river, which are very high up – they had to go up twice as high as normal to make sure they cleared the river, which is why they attract birds. The switch-on was in the Tower Ballroom. The minister at the time was Erskine Childers, a lovely man who switched on the lights

Mural of heron on gable wall of the Shannon Bar, Tarmonbarry.

and made a speech. He said the next most important thing is the telephone and how right he was.'

Mickey has lived all his life in the village and has early memories of the river. 'I remember in Tarmonbarry when there was just one boat and it was called the *Lavague*, owned by Dr Delaney who was a great man for the Shannon. 'Twas the biggest one on the river at the time. More boats started to come and there were rallies into the 1950s and '60s. Quite a few barges or canal boats transported Guinness and brought flour from Limerick to here. But the whole thing changed, the boating and especially the fishing. The river has not changed much – it's the same as ever, the boats sail up and down on a summer's day but it's very expensive to hire a boat these days. The anglers loved coming here and they would pre-bait, which the younger generation don't do. They stayed in rooms over the bar here but eventually that died away. It was a main attraction for people from England, they could fish in comfort. Some great characters used to come and we had an Irish night on a Monday night. Looking back, it was a completely different world that we lived in. Who knows where the time goes?'

5

In Casey's Kingdom

WALKING PURPOSEFULLY down the main street on his twice-daily mission, Dan Kavanagh cuts a familiar figure in Lanesborough. Without fail, every day for thirty years, Dan 'the duck man' has turned up at a pond beside the Shannon at 10 am and 5 pm to feed his beloved ducks. Collectively known as a paddling, they hungrily anticipate his arrival. The breeds include pintail, mallard, Appleyard, call ducks and the ungainly Muscovy ducks with their long bill. They are enclosed behind a fence in a circular pond with an island connected by a miniature bridge. Some breed in canvas-covered nesting boxes placed sporadically around the island and hidden by foliage. Dan carries a distinctive yellow bucket filled with barley and oats mixed with maize, and a sliced wheaten loaf. The ducks show their noisy appreciation, gathering around him. He shakes out the bucket of feed and walks slowly along the black felt surface on the edge of the pond. The waterfowl fall silent. A few stand on his toes.

'They're not very particular about their diet,' Dan says. 'They might eat five or six times a day if they could. People are always coming to give them stuff to eat, they're not fussy.' Waddling around in circles, the ducks quack, nibble, pinch and poke each other, comedians of the bird world. 'They go mad for the snails and enjoy worms too, as well as the grass. Some people will tell you bread is bad for them but we're feeding them bread for years and it's never had any effect on them. They wouldn't eat meat since that would not be good for them. If I wasn't coming, they'd be hungry and would have to fly out on to the Shannon foraging for duckweed, crustaceans, insects or frogs.'

The ducks are an inalienable part of the riverscape. A riot of colour, they come with red beaks, white and silvery-grey or bottle-green heads, narrowed black tapered tails, buff side whiskers, blue and green flanks with black-and-white polka-dot feathers. Dan talks about the history of the pond, which was built by the local council in the late 1980s.

'We started off in 1990 and believe it or not we just had two ducks and now we've over a hundred although some are out nesting on the river. The white call ducks are very small and are a bantam breed of domesticated duck that are kept mainly as pets. They love upending in the water and are very skilful. You can see that the call drake has a curl on its tail, which the females don't have, and the sun brings out a rich purple sheen on it. It's easy enough to spot the pintails too as they have long necks, small heads and a tail that tapers. They're dabbling ducks, as opposed to diving ducks, and there are about twenty of them here.'

A couple of house sparrows hop on to the ground searching for food, keeping their distance. Dan points to one defiant duck swimming on its own at the far side of the pond. It flew in a month earlier from the Caribbean.

'It's a West Indian whistling duck, which you don't see very often, so it came a long way to get here. They're brown birds with black-and-white speckles, they've an elongated neck, long legs and very big feet, so they're different to some of our own and like their own peace.'

Like waltzers in a local version of *Strictly Come Dancing*, some pintails spin around in the water while others have less sense of direction. Energy levels are high, especially after a nutritious morning. A woman with two young sons throws bread and mangled crusts into the food mix, leading to a renewed stampede of the Lanesborough duck buffet. Amongst the crowd is a group of small chicks, a particular interest for the children.

'It's amazing the people who come down to look at them and feed them,' Dan says. 'They're well known around here and the children love them too. The chicks are only after coming out and this is their first time on the water – they hatch in the island. Some of them are a cross between mallard and call ducks. One of the biggest problems is the big gulls, magpies and greybacks will go for them. A few of the ducks are volatile but most are more interested in eating than shouting and they are fairly relaxed and produce a calming effect on people.

'Most of them have an easy-going temperament and you'll find a fight breaking out now and again but they all love the water and are great swimmers. Quite a few of them will be hatching on the Shannon and later in the year they could number more than 200. The Muscovies, with their red faces and glossy black, come in a range of colours but they are wary. You'll know them because they have long claws but fairly weak quacks. They're a lazy 'oul duck and never stray too far.'

Muscovy is an old term for the region of Russia near Moscow, but despite their name these birds come from South and Central America. They are not native to Russia and arrived in Ireland more than a century ago.

'The ducks sleep on the island and get on well together but the main threat to them are foxes from Rathcline wood who attack them and the hens. The fox won't cross the water so they're fairly safe there as the bridge gate is closed so they can't get over it.'

Dan does the work on a voluntary basis out of sheer enjoyment and buys his own feedstuff. 'I love checking on them, looking at them and feeding them. You see people for a good 'oul chat so it's a social thing and meeting place. I get a kick outta coming down here and am interested in wildlife and in checking on the nest boxes. The little chicks will be ready to fly in about eight weeks' time and are quite a sight. When I arrive they come over to the alder trees to meet me because they know they're going to get grub ...'

Suddenly a fight breaks out, and Dan moves into referee mode, shooing and hissing. 'When you have too many drakes, they'll kill the ducks – there could be as many as fifty mallard drakes, which are too many. They kill the ducks when they get too plentiful but it's in their nature to fight over females.'

Dan has seen many other species of birds, including kingfishers, one of his favourites. 'Kingfishers are not too plentiful. I saw one some time ago down at the sand beds here and I saw one a few years ago. It was a close-up view – lovely bird and a memorable sight but very rare.'

He suggests I call with Seadna Ryan who is involved in improvement schemes around the river. Dan, the duck-charmer, picks up his empty bucket and heads home. Ducking under the branches of alder trees, he takes a final look back at his contented avifauna squatting on the grass and at the faint cackling of mallards waddling like overweight bouncers outside a nightclub.

BY LATE MORNING there is a dreamlike quality to the powdery light that produces shimmering surface flashes in the Shannon. One section has taken on the appearance of a silver lamé fabric caused by the elemental interplay of cloud and sun. The surrounding low hills may lack drama, but the towering choreography of the cloudscapes make up for it. I mull over what John Constable once said about the emotion to be found in clouds rather than in the grey signatures of rivers. The Lanesborough skyline is particularly good for cloud-spotting: Shannon cloud shadows rarely race, but slumber sedately, almost imperceptibly. These ones come in a mixed colour palette, some pure white, others with a gun-puff look, swirling off and dissipating into the sky. Far overhead, wispy cirrus clouds blow in long streaks. Within a few minutes, the sky grows more chaotic with a raggle-taggle of new cloud shapes materializing into what look like giant birds stretching out their wings.Halfway across the bridge, two plaques declare the meeting of two counties, Longford and Roscommon, acknowledging the county boundary, signifying the division of the provinces, Leinster

The county boundary is marked by the Shannon, which separates
Lanesborough from Ballyleague.

and Connaught, and reflecting the transit nature of the area. Flags
from different countries flutter in the wind following a recent
international coarse fishing contest. Like many of the Shannon
bridges, this one also links two separate river towns: Lanesborough
and Ballyleague. Signboards along the walkways promote
biodiversity, celebrating its flowers, trees and butterflies. The main
street of Lanesborough has a despondent look where trucks hurry
through to Connaught. Flower boxes overflow with geraniums
and the bridge's metal railings are gleaming from a recent power
wash. It is floodlit from both sides with underhanging lights and
old navigation buoys. Tiny whirlpools of water form and reform
and a couple of Polish fishermen try their luck.

Looking back more than eighty years, it is fascinating to think
that terms such as biodiversity, climate change and global warming
were not in the vocabulary in Hayward's time. Biodiversity first
originated in the 1960s as 'biological diversity' and was reduced
to biodiversity in the 1980s, while Bord na Móna was set up in
the 1940s. It was thought that it would mark the beginning of a

more affluent age and would lead into the emerging of the EU prosperity. At the end of the second decade of the twenty-first century fascinating changes are underway, which will transform the face of this landscape. Intensification of agriculture has led to a reduction in biodiversity throughout Ireland with Bord na Móna ceasing peatland harvesting. The machinery will fall silent and the company will have a new contract with nature. It is moving into new businesses such as recycling and generating electricity to replace the loss of harvesting and processing. This has been dubbed its 'brown to green' strategy. Ecological experts predict that a new wilderness will be created in the next fifty to a hundred years. One scheme being discussed is the possibility of turning the bogs into vast cannabis farms. Bord na Móna has been carrying out a study into whether the cultivation of marijuana for medical use could replace traditional turf-cutting.

No one can say with any certainty what may happen, but the ecologist, author and environmental historian John Feehan has written about how he believes the landscape will be depicted. He suggests that new wetland habitats will come about and extraordinary changes will take place in the landscape. He has predicted that it will be 'a lacustrine landscape in the future when Bord na Móna and the bogs are turned off – and a new wilderness will be created'.

Living in the here and now interests me more than the apocalyptic vision of the future and at the office beside St Mary's parish hall, Seadna Ryan agrees to show me around town. 'There are recent developments along the shorefront with signage and most of it is now a walkway leading into woodland. We are building a plaza and developing this area so we have great areas for walks.'

We look out on the bay and through a navigation buoy to what is known as The Cut leading into Lough Ree. International fishing competitions have been held to encourage tourism and try to emulate the business they enjoyed in the 1970s. This was the era in which Seadna grew up and of which he has fond memories.

'There were many children in the village as we were the first generation of the Bord na Móna and ESB workers, which were the main influences in the development of the town. In the mid-1970s the power station started to emit hot water into the Shannon and it has been developed now for coarse fishing, mainly for tench, roach and bream. During the 1970s and '80s a lot of coarse fishermen from England came here but angling declined and they started going to other markets.'

The population of Lanesborough is about 2000 while across the river, Ballyleague is around 1000. They have both developed a strong community ethic. 'It's a commuter town for bigger places such as Tullamore, Mullingar and Athlone, as well as the county towns of Longford and Roscommon, which are equidistant from Lanesborough. There was always a distinct difference between the two villages. They are two different parishes, counties and provinces, different electoral areas, people went to different schools and played in different football clubs. In recent years, through a variety of joint events and festivals, both sides are starting to blend into one.'

Seadna firmly believes that the spirit of the river is alive in Lanesborough and he sees the new Blueway as playing a factor in helping. 'In the past ten years we have developed a triathlon club and with the advent of the wetsuit more and more people are using the river. We have just put in a swimming ramp and Waterways Ireland are encouraging people to take part in kayaking and cycling. The local scout troop are salvaging a barge called *The Fox* that ploughed the Shannon during the 1930s and '40s. It is a heritage barge, which belonged to a family from Athy in Kildare and is being restored by the scouts as their headquarters. We have an area called the sand beds, which is a sheet of limestone that comes out from two quarries and runs into the shoreline and was overgrown. That naturally heats during the summer and we restored it and put a beach around it. There was another area that people flocked to called Elfeet Bay, a natural sandy bay that was very popular and I went there as a child.

'Back in the 1970s I remember a visiting speaker came to talk to a group of professional architects in the Prince of Wales Hotel in Athlone and he accused them of being behind the times. He justified it by saying that when he came into town for the first time, one of the only windows that was looking on to the river were the toilet windows in the Ritz Cinema. When we were kids there were factories along the riverside and the cinema and the castle. In our generation we have tended to turn towards the river, which the previous generation neglected. We didn't utilize the river from an economic point of view in the past but now with the festivals and events it might improve. The cruiser traffic, which was huge in the 1970s, has all but disappeared.'

We walk along the waterfront and through parkland where white smoke comes from the milled peat power station north of town. The two-storey building, which is fifty years old, is Lanesborough's tallest building and believed to be Longford's largest structure and a classic example of government-sponsored functional architecture. It has been part of the social history and a landmark in the area but is now closing its operations.

Hayward thought Lanesborough a neat little town and an important station of the Grand Canal Company. He was impressed with the solitary mass and sudden elevation of the Sliabh Bawn ridge of hills, which he said looked imposing because of the sudden rise of its Upper Silurian rocks from the level of the limestone plain. For him it was a reference point and with the single exception of this hill, he compared the country all around to the level lowlands of Holland. Its name is said to have been taken from 'white mountain' from patches of corn that appeared white at harvest time. He describes seeing it in early morning light: 'Our old friend Sliabh Bawn looked like part of a mirage in the miraculous light, and the air was laden with some invigorating essence which seemed to charge the body with energy and a marvellous sense of joy and well-being.'

Sliabh Bawn now represents an encroachment of the present on the past with the giant turbines operational on a new wind farm catching our attention. It is the same hill as Hayward saw but is engulfed with several additions: Coillte forests and marching phalanxes of towering, white wind blades turning slowly and spaced at north-south intervals over an area three kilometres wide and seven kilometres long. The wind farm,

Sliabh Bawn wind turbines and Coillte forests have changed the face of the mountain.

a joint €90m venture between Coillte and Bord na Móna, is located in Doughill forest on the mountain itself. Twenty-two turbines have been placed on the hillside, one of the biggest developments in the area. Turning over the dark green hills, the turbines bring an industrial edge to an area well used to it. Although only a few kilometres away, seen through binoculars, they look a towering presence, or what the writer Tim Robinson called 'jerkily gesticulating giants'. In the flat midlands, a little bit of elevation goes a long way.

Ireland's relationship with wind energy has deepened and there is no getting around the fact the turbines are a major development that have changed the face of the landscape for ever. Opposition came from some quarters with complaints of nimbyism and the impact they would have on the area, including noise from a south-westerly breeze, shadow-flicker, visual blight and health issues such as epilepsy. Others appreciate them as a sign of hope, of a new Ireland tuning into a cleaner way of living and doing their bit for the climate. Just one megawatt is enough to power about 650 homes. Those running it claim it will produce clean electricity for homes, farms, schools and businesses, and will have an export capacity of fifty-eight megawatts, which is enough energy to supply nearly 40,000 homes. It also includes a community benefit scheme to deliver improved local amenities and recreational facilities and support local projects. In 2009 every EU country committed itself to the steady reduction of their carbon and methane emissions. In an era of green energy and carbon reduction, there is a new coming-of-age environmental approach in the offing that will see an ever-increasing reliance on 'renewables'. Seadna describes Lanesborough as an energy town, which is set to become a post-industrial centre.

'We have the windfarm as you see, and another planned here when they retire the boglands, so they are a contrast to the older traditional type of power. And you wonder will there be geothermal energy, which is heat energy stored in the earth and is clean and sustainable. Perhaps the Shannon will have another chapter in its history and new uses. The ecology would have been influenced by the peat-milling so that will change. But the ecology of the river today is changing because of circumstances after we had an infestation of Asian clams on the fishing stretch. It is an invasive species that was found in the River Barrow and is now in the Shannon, so the authorities are monitoring this. There are plans to make the islands more accessible by putting in pontoons, which means people might appreciate the lake more.'

Lanesborough and Ballyleague have also been selected to become Ireland's first 'digital hub town' with money from the Roscommon Leader Partnership. The purpose of this is to encourage more people to embrace the Internet and bring new technological initiatives to the doorstep.

'It's only in recent years that we've begun to appreciate what Lanesborough has to offer as it's a smashing place to live that is looking to the future. Food is now one of the biggest elements, bringing people in and food towns such as Dromod and Carrick-on-Shannon are developing this so it's something we are building on.'

With appetite piqued, it is time to head to the Wooden Spoon café, a place to watch the river of life float by from an outside table. It is bin collection day and black wheelie bins have been left out. With its flashing orange lights, Mulleady's Renault bin lorry makes gradual progress along the street. I am amused at the motto emblazoned on it: 'All our time goes to waste.'

On my travels, I subscribe to the philosophy that until you have wasted time in a place, you cannot pretend to know it, or in other words: 'The time you enjoy wasting is not wasted time.' People often talk about the demands on their time through idiomatic expressions. They 'buy' time as if it were something you could purchase in a shop or online. They 'spend' time like money, they 'invest' time or 'put time aside', they 'find' time for 'quality time' and they 'save' time. But what they never do to is 'waste' their time, because time is money. In the 1970s Raymond Gardner went on a riparian journey along the Shannon and other Irish waterways, calling his book *Land of Time Enough*, meaning there is no hurry. In recent years I have spent a considerable amount of research time in France and discovered there are thirty places called Perte-de-temps ('waste of time'), most of them now deserted. A river provokes themes of time too. The Shannon defies time. Since the 1930s this is largely the same river and landscape that Hayward admired. As a chronicler of the river, he was one of the first in the twentieth century to write about it. Since then its essential nature is no different, representing a sense of timelessness, while the light on the water is the long light of time itself. And as Mickey Kelly, and my old Latin teacher, used to say, '*Tempus fugit.*'

I round off this part of my journey heading back to Tarmonbarry, crossing the bridge and turning off to the Grand Canal at Clondara. In the Richmond Inn, fifty people are sitting down to lunchtime plates full of beef, salmon or pies. It is an example of a community pub, which the owner says is well supported by locals and visitors. 'Busy all the time. We get all sorts in here – boat and business owners, anglers, builders and tradesmen, staff from supermarkets, tourists, and passers-by like yourself. We serve very good food at great value.' He takes my order and within a few minutes produces a half portion of roast beef, potatoes and veg. I remark on the blistering speed of the service to which he replies: 'You look like a busy man and we wouldn't want you to waste your time.'

ON SHANNONSIDE RADIO, the 11 to 1 show is concentrating on Irish country music and mawkish faux-American lovelorn ballads. For the best part of an hour, a sentimental soundtrack of homilies of life and death, happiness and loneliness, divorce, betrayal and regret provide the driving music – not necessarily to my taste, but as my car CD player has a broken heart, I do not have much option. The sonic journey helps focus – driving me, if not around the bend, then around many bends and a maze of winding traffic-free back roads, mysterious hidden corners and unexpected angles through south-west Longford on my way to Barley Harbour. The peninsula is a network of staggered crossroads, T-junctions and Y-junctions, bog-train level crossings, stone bridges and, at Derraghan, a ruler-flat one-kilometre stretch of road. Signs warn of the danger of flooding and cars skidding, while posters on a run of telegraph poles give vent to the emotive feelings of locals: 'No to wind farms here.' The landscape is peppered with bogs far outnumbering lakes. Short boreens end abruptly at the water's edge or turn into cul-de-sacs.

In the era of the soulless satnav, it is heartening to unfurl an Ordnance Survey map with its tactile reassurance of place names reflecting the fact that at one time the parish was heavily wooded. More than 1600 townlands throughout Ireland have been recorded with the 'Derry' suffix, and just a few centimetres of my map are sprinkled with a score of townlands, headlands, bogs and lakes including Derrycolumb, Derryshanogue, Derryglosh, Derrygowna, Derrymany, Derrindiff, Derrymacar, Derrycolm and many others, all from *doire*, meaning oakwood.

Longford has always felt one of those neglected counties – justifiably so. In 2017, for example, Fáilte Ireland awarded the county the grand sum of €2000 for tourism promotion. This came out of a national budget fund of nearly €4 million. A local county councillor, quoted in the *Longford Leader*, described it as an insult to every man, woman and child in the county, saying it represented 'nothing but contempt' for rural areas. In between radio birthday greetings to listeners and a sprinkling of songs from Declan Neary, 'Give Me One More Kiss', and Nathan Carter's 'Jealous of the Angels', the news bulletin reports on funding that has just been announced for rural development under a town and village renewal scheme. It is to be spent on enhancement projects such as improving footpaths and lighting, bus shelters, allotments, flowerpots, playgrounds, streetscaping and stimulating economic activity by using vacant sites. Newtowncashel, where I am heading, is being awarded a €20,000 windfall.

Along the road to Barley Harbour there is no dancing in the streets but a quotation on a wall from a local poet states: 'My native place of matchless grace, the hills above Newtowncashel.' As I follow the minor roads across this isolated corner of Longford, I notice some remarkable bog wood sculptures. These are made by Michael Casey and his son Kevin. Having heard about the imminent closure of the bogs, I want to find someone who works in them and arranged to meet Michael. He greets me outside his showroom at Barley Harbour on the eastern side of Lough Ree and tells me that he helped mastermind funding for Newtowncashel. Understandably, he is happy with the award that has just been announced in Granard that morning with a defiant declaration by a government minister: 'Rural Ireland is alive and well.'

'It's a major boost for Longford,' he says, 'but a real pity we didn't apply for €40,000 since other small places got that. We lost our post office, shop and garda station, so this will improve things and help revitalize the place. It's a good day for local communities.'

The village, with a population of just fifty, has worked hard to enhance its appearance. In the Tidy Towns awards ceremony in 2017, against fierce competition, it increased its overall figure on the previous year by three marks. With our hands wrapped around coffee mugs, and a pleasant aroma of wood and beeswax washing over us, we sit in a showroom filled with numerous examples of both Michael's and his son's sculptured artefacts. Most pieces are made from bog oak, a semi-fossilized wood that has been buried deep in the Longford bogs for thousands of years. Michael explains his work as both landscape architect and artist.

'The work for me developed from carpentry and travelling in America, Canada and England. I came back here in 1962 and started on my own with no training and it has grown from that. In the early years I worked with elm but that is gone from Europe, killed off with Dutch elm disease in the 1970s. Initially we created vases, Celtic crosses and small gifts. Then we got to the big sculptures that you see here. We discovered in the bogs this wonderful black wood. A farmer was pulling some of it out, but until that time I never knew what it was. I brought a bit of it home and tried to turn it on my lathe and it remained black. We made enquiries and found that this wood was buried in the bog 8000 years ago. For some climatic reason the bogs have grown up by one solid inch every hundred years, which gives you an idea of its age.'

Michael's work with oak, yew and pine involves weeks and months of painstaking cleaning, washing and drying, then time is spent sanding the wood. 'Don't forget it was down at least fifteen feet in the bog and full of moisture when we got it. After we have gone through all the processes of preparing it until it is ready for working, we then follow the shapes of the timber. The second type of wood that we work with is the yew tree found in graveyards. The wood on them is yellow, but in the bog it turns a rusty brown. We have some slices of big roots that are pleasing to work with. We get magnificent pieces from the bog and follow the shapes but for most of them we don't give them a title. The reason for this is because people will get tired of it so we let them put their own name on it.'

Michael's bog timber work has been likened by some art critics as having a 'Michelangelesque attitude'. This comes from the sense that the artist is removing the art from the hands of nature, lifting the form from the natural block and adding a unique human element. Like his historic near namesake, many of

Michael's bigger pieces furnish churches and sanctuaries, and he has created altars, tables, lecterns, baptismal fonts, ambos and seats. 'We had a priest who wanted a small tabernacle for his church and when he came and saw this nine-foot piece with the wings on it he fell for it, but he had to bring his bishop out to show it to him first to get approval. In 1996 we had a request for a chalice for Pope John Paul II for the beatification of an Irish saint, Edmund Rice, in Rome. I couldn't find anything for it for many months but then in the middle of a big root I saw the hand holding the bowl. It takes time to find the right piece.'

Michael shows me around his handiwork – a fantastical mix of colours, textures and balletic gracefulness. Sitting on shelves and nooks are mythological creatures, fish and birds such as curlew, swallow, snipe and the salmon of knowledge all chiselled, carved, shaped, sanded to perfection and frozen in wood. A siege of long-legged grey herons stands to attention in exquisite poise. From a corner shelf, a startlingly beautiful kingfisher stares back at me so intently I almost blush. Perched bold as brass with a can't-catch-me look, this one is lacking the cerulean glory. In bird folklore, they are said to be spirits of good luck, traditionally a symbol of peace and prosperity, and because of their elusive nature have been enfolded in mythology.

'The kingfisher is made out of bog yew,' Michael explains. 'We apply the same principles that we use to make the other birds and the yew gives the kingfisher a richness of tone, although we can't obviously reproduce the dazzling blueness. People love them because of the colouring of the yew and we get many requests for them. It's a small bird and this one is based on a picture of it on a brochure and is almost the actual size. I have a memory of seeing one many years ago on a canal, but they are shy birds.'

In the centre of the showroom stands an intriguing piece of artwork with contorted shapes. It is based on a story that was told to Michael by a local man years ago. 'Along the shores of Lough Ree, a low-lying swampy area is known as Lismagauley Meadows. Until recently it was believed that a race of people called the *lucht na fathi* (the swamp people) lived there. One autumn evening, when the mists came up, the days grew shorter and the imagination raced, those frog-like creatures came to life. Jimmy Feeney who died in 1970 and was then ninety, told me about them and described them as little men that he used to meet. He painted a picture of them and I have tried to recreate them in bogwood – but don't forget he was leaving the pub when he described them.'

Michael's work is much sought after. Over the years, a diverse range of commissions has come from hospitals, colleges, schools, libraries, county councils and private individuals such as Nelson Mandela, Yasser Arafat, Seamus Heaney, Ian Paisley and Noel Dempsey.

'I don't feel famous, but the pieces have travelled quite a bit. We cover the whole spectrum as bog oak knows no boundaries. There are an awful lot of pieces of wood that will never get that new life but it's exciting when you see the thing in it. Suddenly to see the image in a piece of root or to see the wings in something and visualize the head means that people can get very excited. It's that inspiration in the moment that brings it out. No one knows where that comes from – you either have it or you don't. A musician or a painter might have it but you have to come to it.'

Michael kindly offers to act as a cicerone to give me a feel for the topography of the area. A robin is singing outside his showroom as he serenades us off on our whistle-stop tour of backroads. We drive firstly down to the end of the peninsula and to the cut-stone Barley Harbour. There is no sign of any barley or fields of gold, but willow, ash and birch trees flourish along the lakeshore, which is designated a Special Area of Conservation.

Built in 1960, Barley Harbour provides safe mooring for boats along the lakeshore. Michael has the distinction of having named it. 'The proper official name is Collum. I don't know what that translates as, but in 1960 an old man told me they used to draw barley from here a century or so earlier. When I came, all the land was in bushes and rocks so I'm not sure where they got the barley from, but I liked the name Barley Harbour although it wasn't on any maps. I put it on my postal address and now it has become the official name for it and appears on signposts although on the census forms it is still Collum. This is the mid-point of Lough Ree and as we stand here at the harbour, the lake it is at its widest point. The island point is the Quaker island that Hayward mentions and is always known as Quaker, but the proper name is Inchcleraun. Quite a few of the islands were inhabited when I came here. It has been well documented since Viking times.'

The scale and size of the lake surprises me. For decades Michael has walked these shores, visiting many islands. He has come to know local people, discovering a love of trees and animals, all of which feeds his imaginative territory, informing his artwork.

'You will often see the heron down here. They're always solitary, standing on a rock and that might be a small influence, but it may also have other influences deeper down. I love the water, and love sitting on the rocks, so it is working on you. The pull of it is endless and we are always delighted to find a new piece of root or tree bark. The Shannon is not like an ordinary river and its history is still growing every year.'

The past is a preoccupation of Lough Ree but it is also a living presence. We survey the lake, our horizons bounded by water and trees on the far side. Michael points across to tree-covered areas.

'It hasn't changed that much since Hayward's time whereas Lough Derg has. There are some ancient woods on the Roscommon side. One is St John's Wood, which is over 7000 years old and is a local natural wood of self-seeding oak. It is one of the most ancient post-ice-age forests anywhere in Ireland. Mount Plunkett is an ancient hazel wood too and is part of a nature reserve with a biodiversity farm so they are looking to the future.'

Michael recalls a particularly fierce winter in 1962 when the lake froze over. 'We took medicine out to the two islands over three weeks – there were no helicopters or mobile phones to help people then. The ice eventually started to crack but it was a tough time for everyone involved. We were worried about a man called Paddy Welsh who lived on Inchcleraun. We got medicine and supplies out to him too but he wasn't in the least bit worried about food, he was more concerned about running out of tobacco.'

Along dirt tracks and hedges of white bindweed, we rattle over cattle grids. The road takes on a potholed dimension with room for barely one vehicle. Then we come to an arm linking the lake to the mainland via a long straight causeway taking us on to the triangular-shaped Saint's Island, *Oileán na Naomh*, which consists of one road running around its northern half to a dead end.

We look around the Augustinian church. Sir Henry Dillon of Drumrany founded the monastery for the Augustinian Canons before 1244, possibly on the site of another church. It was here that Augustin Magraidain wrote *The Annals of All Saints* two centuries later. This was a collection of Latin annals beginning in 1392 and continuing until 1407. When the church was built in the thirteenth century a decorative cloister was added and portions of this still survive. The east window of the church was inserted in the fifteenth century, after which the monastery declined although it may have continued to exist into the seventeenth century.

Even in the twenty-first century, families are still making use of the graveyard and each August a 'Cemetery Sunday' is held on the island. We walk through the graveyard filled with many large Celtic crosses. Michael points out some recently erected headstones saying the marble for them was brought in from China because it is so expensive in Ireland. Many people, especially poets, writers and artists, have drawn inspiration from the island. Ted Hughes came here in the 1980s and while fishing on the lake wrote a haunting four-page poem, 'Saint's Island', about the mayfly, the bait of trout fishermen and the dapping, which he called 'a lace of brackish crystals'. The poem was dedicated to the artist Barrie Cooke. Hughes referred to the 'grey crumble of Monastery', defining it as 'A day for small marvels / The Mayflies are leaving their Mother.' In his poem, 'The Kingfisher', which is very much the poets' bird, Hughes wrote that his colours might have 'Escaped from the jeweller's opium'.

The final stop of our tour is a visit to Dernagran bog, where Michael wants to show me examples of bog trees in their raw state. We pull over and park at an opening to allow a crawling Bord na Móna vehicle to pass. We step out into the bog where a turf smell pervades the damp air and walk along a grassy path to a four-metre-long tree bark that has been discarded to one side.

'This is a piece of bog oakwood that looks burnt but when you delve into the bark you see it's pure black, which has taken 6000 years. The geoscientists at Queen's University in Belfast carbon-dated it for us. Their research unit said that in the case of the bog yew, the date of growth of the wood is between 2000 and 2200 BC. For the bog oak, the date of growth is between 3300 and 3600 BC, while the bog pine's date of growth is between 3500 and 3900 BC.'

Michael runs his fingers across the wizened bog oak. It is wet and soft and will take up to four years to dry. 'After that we cut it into lengths and shape the pieces out of it. The root creates strange shapes. All you see now is bog dirt but when the power hoses wash it out, the whole thing comes to life. Then we hope to see some movement of what it is going to become. We don't cut the root because that would be a sin. The bark is functional but I prefer working with the shapes and inspirations that comes from the root. You can feel how tough it is, as you peel a few pieces of it. Can you imagine that bark was lying there for 6000 years? It would have had an 80 per cent moisture content and although the wind has affected it, it has weathered well but bits are coming off with the sun.'

Slowly, Michael rummages around his *materia prima*: large twisted roots and gnarled stumps of trees that suggest ideas to him. We look out on a tenebrous flatland, a brown desert stretching for up to five kilometres with straight drains. Trees delimit the horizon and the margins around us. The bogland carries the furrows of deep time and are rich reservoirs of biodiversity. In the past fifty years, much peatland in the midlands has become forestry but Ireland still holds more than 50 per cent of Europe's intact bogs. We wander across a section which melts underfoot, producing squelches and squirts of water over juicy peat, leaving our boot prints alongside lorry tyre tracks. The natural world of the bog is not in the least flamboyant-looking and could pass for a place devoid of interest. But is a mosaic of habitats. Parts of it are thrumming with water spiders, flies and beetles while the bog pools are full of uncharismatic mini fauna. In one corner, plastic has been placed over large chunks of wood to keep it dry. The bog is a place with a powerful imaginative pull. Michael gestures around an area of immense silence and peace in which he is most at home.

'You have to remember that before the bogs were forests, so thousands of years ago this was all covered with trees. It was so thick it was said that a monkey could swing from tree to tree between Dublin and Galway and only had to swim the Shannon. It developed after the ice age, and when that climatic change came the trees fell down and the bogs developed. When Hayward visited in the 1930s he would have seen heather here, and right up to the early 1950s you could still see rows of heather. Then Bord na Móna drained it so they have gone down and left it as cutaway and pulled all these trees out of the way. To them they're just a nuisance. These roots and sections of bark are fairly heavy, so we have machinery nowadays, but when I started, we cut it in the middle then came down with a tractor and pushed it up on to the trailer.'

A bolt of sunlight breaks through clouds, creating a strange alchemy in what some call 'the land of the squelch'. It produces a glittering chiaroscuro effect, sponging up the sunlight and sending our senses soaring. Michael pauses and surveys his kingdom, a lonely and windswept mosaic with big skies. A visionary artist in love with nature, he has succeeded in moulding the natural block from the dark sods, adding the unique human element, imbuing it all with a Celtic mysticism.

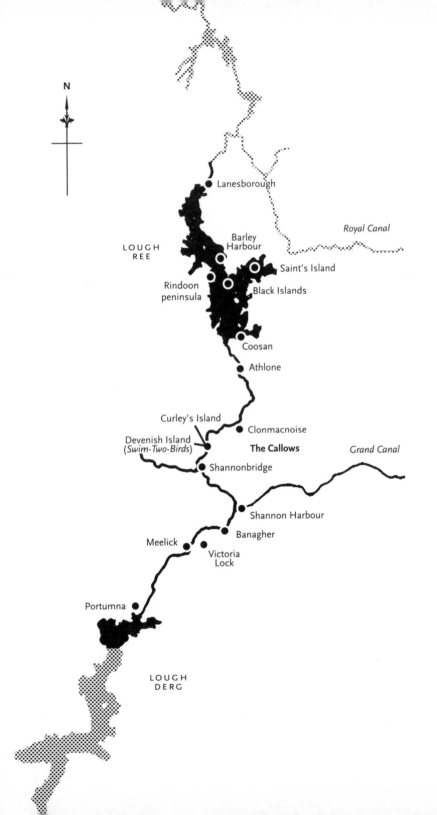

PART II

Middle Shannon

'The city dweller who passes through a country town and imagines it sleepy and apathetic is very far from the truth: it is watchful as the jungle.'

John Broderick,
The Pilgrimage

6

The Road to Rindoon

WHEN HAYWARD REACHED Lough Ree on his Shannon journey, he spent time on the Black Islands with the Hanley and O'Hara families who made their living by farming, and fishing for eels and trout. The islands were inhabited until the mid-1980s but since then have been derelict. One of the women Hayward met was Mary Hanley whose nephew Paddy Hanley has agreed to take me out in his boat to the island.

Needle-sharp sounds pulse through a curve of woodland along the edge of Lough Ree as I wait beside a large rock near the slipway at the tip of the Rindoon peninsula. The symphonic purity of birdsong chatter fills the air. One by one, robin, blackbird, wren, song thrush, great tit, greenfinch and willow warbler call out a series of clicks, sighs, stutters and plaintive whispers in three- and four-second bursts. Some are singing to attract a mate, others to repel one. It is a dry day with cloud cover, the sun half in, half out. There is no one else around. Out on the placid lake, the clear whistling of chevrons of wigeons sounds like a congregation of kettles. Curlew used to be plentiful on these islands but there are now only a few pairs remaining, most in the northern part of the lake. I scan the water's edge on my quest to see a kingfisher but they appear to be having an away day. A pair of mute swans, their long necks kinked like a U-bend, dive in perfect synchronicity.

They replicate their upending in harmony, each remaining in the water for fifteen seconds, then coming up for air before dunking and repeating their actions. Coots busy themselves fidgeting in another corner of the bay.

Paddy circles round Warren Point from the small harbour at St John's Bay. He cautiously pulls up alongside a slipway at a narrow channel, stretching out a hand for me to jump into his fibreglass open-lake boat. We nudge out of the secluded bay into the wide waters of Lough Ree where the waves are becoming lumpy. Scintillas of light play off the water and there is a steely sheen to it. In the far distance, the archipelago of the Black Islands comes into view. The boat lurches and shilly-shallies. The sense of movement so close to the water is exhilarating. Paddy revs up to 12 kph and the waves become stronger. I shift my weight on the seat, gripping it tightly. He shouts over the whine of the outboard motor.

'You'd get a few rogue waves on her and she can be violent betimes when she wants, so it can be difficult. You can get a northerly or southerly breeze and swells build up, which means she can be tempestuous. You do have to be careful, watch the weather and know your way around it. We'll be doing a little dancing here and there, but I'll slow down if it's too much for you.'

As Paddy reads the water and the landscape, his watchful eyes and measured talk is calming. Accompanied by his cameraman and photographer, Hayward came out to the island with a local boatman Jimmy Rigney. On their return journey they got into trouble as he ran out of petrol in poor conditions amidst 'ominous little waves' and they were forced to use the oars. I had a concern that history might repeat itself. Travelling in the footsteps can sometimes have too literal an approach. Hayward's film of the Shannon was illustrated with shots of fishermen hauling in trout nets, and eels being caught on set lines. As many generations had done beforehand, they would later row their boats into Athlone and land their boxes of eels for despatch by rail. Paddy talks about the fishing on the lake today.

'There are about twelve licences for brown trout on Lough Ree but there's very little salmon – you might stumble on the odd one. It would be like winning the lotto to get a good salmon. The last one I caught was twenty years ago, maybe about 12lbs. I don't do any fishing now, just some farming. I've a suckler herd of ten and farm twenty acres, which belonged to my mother.'

One of the aspects of island living that most surprised Hayward was when the semi-aquatic cows tired of the grass on one island, they simply waded over to another one:

> Into the water they go, and away to their new pastures with chins well up and their four legs propelling them along with the ease and speed of a Channel swimmer. I had always known that cows, in common with most animals, were more or less amphibious, but I had no idea that they could be brought up to enter the water of their own accord and swim the considerable distances between these seven islands with the ease of a spaniel.

Lough Ree is the nerve centre of the mid-Shannon. A sprawling lake with numerous islands and antiquities, it embraces 1500 years of historic settlement and stands at the junction of two provinces, three counties and four dioceses. Every island and rock has a story. Dotted along the edges with sheltered jetties are sporting lodges, grand summer residences and lakeside houses in private hands. As we move across, Paddy surveys the water, pointing out our destination; a covey of low-lying islands, which he knows better than the bow of his boat. He calls out their names: Nut Island, Sand Island, Long Island, Horse Island, Red Island, Girls' Island and our objective, King's Island, which was the only inhabited one. They are all sheltered and most are small. Every island in the group has a story attached to it. There are also two aits to the north called the Brearoge Islands. We slow down and he speaks with affection for the lake and islands.

'I love the water and always think I breathe differently when I'm out on it and of the peace, the scenery and nature. There isn't a big influx of traffic most of the time. There's not so many Germans coming nowadays but we still get a few and some Swiss.

They especially enjoy two things: the boating and the pubbing. One family that I know have been coming for thirty years. They like to have someone who knows the lake well and they are happier when I'm with them. They start from Shannonbridge with a ten-berth boat, which is a big responsibility to watch the weather and keep an eye on where you're going.'

After twenty minutes we arrive at a small rocky cove on King's Island and Paddy skilfully steers the boat in tight to the bank to allow me to step off. He has been coming back and forth to the island since his schooldays in the 1940s and lived with his aunt and uncle on it from the mid-1950s until he left it for good in 1985 when he resettled on the mainland. Along with a neighbour, Nancy Conroy, he was the last person to leave the islands. We walk up a tree-lined grassy path to the 'street' – a name that amused Hayward – where three single-storey whitewashed farm cottages stand in a row. In the 1930s they were thatched but now have asbestos roofs. Paddy lived in the middle house, which is surrounded by a low stone wall.

''Twas a normal enough life I suppose,' he says, 'a good life, but a hard life. You didn't know anything else and you didn't question anything but just got on with a bit of farming and fishing. There was no running water or electricity, they never had it on the island. My aunt and uncle were happy with their life although they hadn't a lot. That's how it was in Ireland back then.'

Hayward called the Hanleys 'princely' and said he was treated like a king because of the hospitality his party received: 'Mary Hanley made a grand meal of good strong tea, fresh boiled eggs, and bread, baked by herself, light as a feather, and fit for a king. Indeed, it's a cunning hand the same Mrs Hanley has for the baking, and her husband a luckier man maybe than he knows!'

Hospitality was traditional in the Ireland of the 1930s and strangers were made to feel welcome. Paddy endorses the view.

'My aunt Mary was friendly and easy to get on with even though she came in from the country near Longford town. She found it different but adapted quickly to life on the island. They had potatoes and other vegetables such as cabbage, carrots and

Paddy Hanley at his old cottage home on the Black Islands, Lough Ree.

onions and as Hayward mentioned they kept cows for milk and butter and had apples and plums. They were self-sufficient and burnt wood and turf fires. Fish was a big thing for them and they would have lived on eel and trout, which were popular in those days. Mary died in 1971 and was living here right up to the end of her life so it was a special place for her.'

The Black Islands are in County Longford so his aunt stayed within her native county. Paddy was just four when Hayward visited the islands. 'I remember hearing Mary talk about him. Everyone would have been known about him then and word would have gone around that he had come to the islands. I often heard them speaking about his book later in life.'

From the outside, the cottages look in sound condition. I am curious to see what the insides are like. Paddy turns the key on the front door of Nancy Conroy's, pushing it on its creaking damp-stiffened hinge as it springs open. Cobwebs brush my face. It consists of parlour, living area and bedroom. We look into well-proportioned, long-unvisited rooms where wallpaper is peeling. Curtains are still intact along with a fireplace and mantelpiece. The frame of a bedstead and spring, an old kitchen table, wooden chairs, cupboards and trunk are just as they were left, now with a layer of dust. The bedroom lino remains in place with rolls of netting wire on the floor. Faded yellowing newspapers lie on the windowsill. There is a dank smell of the unlived. I feel a shadow pass over me. Despite the lack of amenities, it must have been an idyllic place to live, although a constant struggle. The comfortable houses were in an unspoiled setting right beside the water. But it was a tough life, growing vegetables, looking after cattle, fishing and working the land. There is a melancholy feel to it all and an overwhelming sense of isolation alongside an echo of previous lives.

'The house has been vandalized and we had to move out some of the furniture,' Paddy says. 'They smashed windows and I had to put up iron bars and wire mesh on the windows for protection. The vandals were continually burning it and it was going on for years. They came out on a boat, probably from Athlone, took anything they could get their hands on and sometimes burnt furniture in the doorway. They could be on drink or drugs, you wouldn't know.'

We reflect on the fact that there is no longer any human life on the island to disturb the goats, nesting ducks or birds. King's Island, which is eight hectares, is a floristically diverse jungle of tall plants. We walk across verdant and spongy grass that has been left to run wild. In some places nettles and thistles have taken over with wild abandon, vying with a tangle of brambles. Paddy points out the silvery foliage of wormwood, a plant with a distinct aroma that was used for medicinal purposes and to flavour alcoholic drinks. We also find celandine, wild garlic, swathes of the delicate ferny leaves of sweet cicely with its aniseed scent, known for its therapeutic uses as an antiseptic. Multi-limbed trees surround the cottages. We duck and weave our way under overhanging branches of ash, alder, sycamore and blackthorn. Wildlife is disturbed by our presence. We hear rustles in the undergrowth but cannot see any animals. Behind a bright yellow splash of dandelions and cowslip lies an unsightly

The Hanley and O'Hara families pictured on the Black Islands in Hayward's Shannon book. Mary Hanley is on the far left, Hayward is third from left.

pile of empty beer bottles and cans. The long grass also contains discarded utensils such as a metal teapot and saucepan, some old milk bottles stand to one side of a house; vegetable patches and potato ridges are long overgrown.

As Hayward's party was preparing to leave after their visit, they sang their theme tune 'Nora Lee' to the Hanley and O'Hara families. He describes how the notes of their song mingled with cries of farewell, floating together over the placid waters of the lake. Paddy tells me that the islands are now for sale.

'The asking price for the whole lot is €750,000 so you never know who would be willing to take over. They're solid enough houses and as you have seen they're in good shape. But you wouldn't be allowed to do any developments because it's all protected heritage under law.'

We spent three hours exploring the lake, island and cottages. Paddy seems in no hurry to return. Time stretches out. Although the sun has disappeared, the wind has dropped and there is a wistful lostness about the day. I later discover that, in estate-agent-speak, the islands are described as 'an idyllic location with a fascinating heritage for the outdoor enthusiast ... a truly rare and magical offering'. There is a sense of the primordial here. It is hard to imagine how this bleak and peripheral place once constituted the entire world for a few families and now seethes with memory.

AFTER GAINING A sense of Lough Ree's scale and its islands, I want to understand more about its medieval heartbeat and the heritage of its surviving buildings. Harman Murtagh, a local historian, agrees to accompany me on a stroll through the remains of the built heritage. Our walk starts from a farm gate at Rindoon, a small finger of a remote peninsula that projects into Lough Ree from where he fills in the historic background.

'Soon after the Normans reached the Shannon by 1200, they built the castle at Athlone. Then they made another push into Connaught. Most of province was granted to De Burghs and there are still numerous Burkes in Connaught.'

We pass the Medieval Hospital of the Crutched Friars of St John the Baptist, a place that cared for the sick, and walk along the side of a graveyard over to a tall wall. The Rindoon peninsula is of considerable strategic importance and is one of the most impressive Anglo-Norman sites in Ireland. Its eighth-century gilt-bronze Crucifixion plaque – the Rinnagan or Athlone plaque – is regarded as one of the treasures of the National Museum. The ten-metre-high main wall is in a venerable condition given its age. In the 1250s the town walls were built over 500 metres long and ran from shore to shore across the peninsula. Originally the wall had four towers and one gatehouse and replaced an earlier earth-and-timber defence. It was topped by battlements with a large timber-built wall walk behind it.

'The walls served a defensive purpose for the English settlers but were also built to proclaim wealth and status and defined a legal boundary between urban and rural space,' Harman explains. 'The wall was in a terrible condition but there was a great local drive to do something about it. It has recently undergone much-needed conservation and the towers and gatehouse have been renovated.

The remains of Rindoon Castle, completed in 1235, now partially covered with an overcoat of ivy.

The gatehouse would have gone up another storey although you can see just one bit of stone where the portcullis would have come down but the top storey is gone. It requires a full archaeological investigation of the suite of medieval remains and for the buildings to be taken into state care as a national monument.'

We come to the castle, completed by 1235, which overlooks the harbour. Just as in Hayward's time, it is smothered by an overcoat of thick ivy strangling the walls and is closed to the public. He described it as a 'majestic' ruin but said that from a distance it did not look like any castle at all, but like a clump of trees. Today, with the sheer volume of greenery, it is impenetrable.

'Defensively the castle was the last resort for the town,' Harman says. 'A curtain wall was topped by a timber structure that over-sailed the wall top, which allowed defenders to fire down at the besiegers. It all lay in ruins until it was rebuilt in the late sixteenth century as part of Elizabeth I's reconquest of Ireland. A cottage beside it was occupied until the twentieth century.'

This area is one of the best-preserved deserted medieval towns in Ireland and Harman enjoys untangling its meaning. 'Rindoon is the second castle built on the shore of Lough Ree and is very well situated on the water routes because it's exactly halfway between Athlone and Lanesborough. It was strategically important because at the narrowest point of the lake there was a traditional ferry crossing between the east and west banks. You can see that half of the great donjon has collapsed – it was deliberately collapsed by the Irish after the Normans left but the other half has two watchtowers still perched on top. The castle consists of a deep moat and even with all the trees that have fallen into it, it is still impressive.

'The curtain wall was a slightly irregular shape because it's dictated by the contours of the stone ... One part of it looks rickety and is higher than the rest and that's because the castle was taken about 1270 and the fortifications were improved and they used this method of having a narrower wall with an arcade. All this is in a parlous state ... The castle is far too big for the local people to take on, it badly needs work and would be a very skilled job for the OPW. But you feel like crying when you see it.'

Harman talks about the town that developed after the building of the castle and a ditch across the peninsula at Warren Point: this may have been a canal connecting the two harbours. The partly submerged and overgrown remains of the medieval town harbour are just about visible around the edges of the inlet. It is possible to make out a slipway, which was a centre for boat building and repairs in the thirteenth century.

A nearby signboard shows an illustration of how the parish church looked in the late thirteenth century with people walking in single file into the building where mass was said in Latin. The high notes of lark song provide a flighty soundtrack as Harman takes up the story again.

'We have a date for the church of 1251. It's a big nave and a big chancel and all the ivy has been cleared off it ... the stonework has been pointed and is in excellent condition. The sad thing is that at some stage in its history someone took all the dressed stone off it and you just now see the door openings, the chancel arch opening, the window opening but no dressed stone. They probably took the stone to use in some other church.'

All this is in sharp contrast from the church that Hayward saw on his journey when he explored Rindoon. In those days the Board of Works was the authority responsible for preserving National Monuments under legislation from the late nineteenth century. But the Heritage Council of Ireland – the statutory body charged with promoting, educating and encouraging enjoyment in Ireland's national heritage – was not established until 1995. There was no concerted interest in protecting much of the heritage. Rindoon is an example of a much more engaged twenty-first-century interest in the preservation of built heritage, which did not exist in the Ireland of the mid-twentieth century. Hayward was of an antiquarian temper, loving ruins and ancient stone, but when he came here, he was shocked by the crumbling walls he found: 'I have never in my life seen such dilapidation and neglect, and it was not until we had hacked our way through the brambles for fully twenty minutes that, bleeding and torn, we stood inside the four walls of the old church to find that they were completely choked with brambles and undergrowth.'

We walk around the side of St John's Bay, following green and blue waymarked signs through a soaked field. Harman speaks about his implicit communion with the lake and what is so special about it for him.

'This area, especially Newtowncashel, is special to me as my distant ancestors come from there. I like Rathcline, which is a tower house and was turned into a seventeenth-century mansion by Sir George Lane, who developed Lanesborough. I have a strong emotional attachment to the whole area, which takes in four generations of my family, and I've grown very fond of Lough Ree.'

SCORNING THE COMFORTS of modernity, Hayward set up camp at Coosan, erecting a tent for several days, a base to explore the lake as well as Athlone and the surrounding countryside. In early evening I drive out to track down the location. Along a road of fuchsia-filled hedges, this area is where the town edges out into the countryside and is known as the 'Garden of Athlone'.

Three cars are parked outside the Lough Ree Inn beside a signboard stating that in 842 the Shannon provided a route for the longships and the infamous Viking warrior Turgesius and his wife Ota to invade Clonmacnoise. Ninety years later another Viking king from the Limerick fleet also made an appearance in Lough Ree in 933. According to the *Annals of the Four Masters* he was known as Óláfr the Scabbyhead, by all accounts a ferocious character. More than 200 years ago, two large Viking treasure hoards were discovered on Hare Island. They consisted of ten gold arm rings weighing more than five kilos, one of the largest finds of Viking treasure in the world. Along the narrow Lough Ree walking trail I stumble across a twenty-first-century metal curiosity, a railing bristling with lovers' padlocks.

Coosan has not been subsumed by the spread of Athlone. A cruiser, *Take It Easy*, heads out into the channel over to Killinure lough, followed by *Coosan Lady*, while a smaller boat moves into the wider reaches of the lake. From the deck of a stationary cruiser, a young boy plays a mini trumpet, annoying the swans, drakes and mallards. In Hayward's time this area was busy with a wide variety of boats. He saw powerful motor barges operated by the Grand Canal Company, small rowing boats with 'hopeful' anglers, house boats and cabin cruisers all moored amongst the tall reeds at the water margin.

Views stretch over the densely treed Hare Island where the German Nobel Prize-winning novelist, Heinrich Böll, spent time. Since Hayward camped here, the site has been heavily interpreted and is now classified as an 'amenity area', landscaped with walks, nature signage and a playground, and designated a Special Area of Conservation and Special Protection Area for birds. The bays on this south-eastern shoreline of the lough are collectively known as the Inner Lakes and, as well as Coosan lough, include Cleggan, Doonis, Ross and Killinure loughs. It is at this point too where the boundaries of counties Westmeath, Longford and Roscommon all conjoin. The RNLI unveiled a monument here in 2012 dedicated to all those who lost their lives on Lough Ree. Just two years later two fishermen, David Warnock and Daryl Burke from Portadown in Co. Armagh, drowned in the lake. A memorial seat to them states: 'Gone to fish calmer waters'.

In the Lough Ree Inn a few garrulous old salts sit slump-shouldered sipping pints at a corner of the bar. One of the regulars, Diarmuid Mulvihill, talks about his family's deep-rooted connections to the area and shows me a wall display of black-and-white faded photographs hanging in a corridor. One is of the Coosan GAA team from 1936, which includes his father, grandfather and uncle, who all played for them. Diarmuid says matter-of-factly that a relative of his survived the sinking of the *Titanic* in 1912. Bertha Mulvihill was his grandmother's sister and had left Coosan as a young woman and travelled across the Atlantic, moving in with her aunt Kate in Rhode Island. He tells me about her life and although he did not want to be quoted directly, he allowed me to write about his aunt's intriguing story.

Bertha had, it seemed, tried her hand at various jobs in her adopted country and met Henry Noon, an Englishman who worked with her brother-in-law at a local foundry, and they became engaged. Henry gave her three gold treasures: a pocket watch, a bracelet and a cross on a chain. In the summer of 1911, around the age of twenty-two, Bertha boarded the *Lusitania* and returned to Ireland. Her sister Kitty was also engaged and planning her wedding. Bertha stayed with her family back in Coosan for several seasons, and Kitty married early in 1912.

After the wedding, Bertha was anxious to return to her fiancé and her new life in America. She missed Henry and decided to surprise him, secretly buying a third-class ticket for £7 15s. for the maiden voyage of the 'unsinkable' ship. Passengers boarded in Southampton and Cherbourg before the final group of passengers in Cobh, then known as Queenstown, Co. Cork. Most of those embarking at the last port of call on 11 April were Irish immigrants travelling third-class like Bertha. Boarding at Queenstown with Bertha were two friends, Maggie Daly and Eugene Daly from Athlone. Just before midnight on 14 April, about 565 km south-east of Newfoundland, the liner struck an iceberg, which quickly tore through its starboard hull. Bertha, Maggie and Eugene struggled through the chaos and made it up to the deck. Here they witnessed an officer shooting two men as they tried to board a lifeboat. He then shot himself. Bertha and Maggie jumped into a lifeboat. She later likened it to jumping off the roof of a three-storey building. Several of her ribs were broken in the fall. Some others, who also jumped, landed on her and worsened her injuries. The lifeboat became overcrowded, but remained afloat. By 2.30 am, the *Titanic* had disappeared into the deep along with 1522 lives.

Bertha spent the night thirsty, nauseous, horrified, wet, freezing and in pain from her injuries. But both she and Maggie survived. Just after 4 am, the *Carpathia* arrived and rescued 705 survivors. The ship docked in New York on 18 April. Despite her broken ribs, Bertha snuck away from the other passengers and hid amongst the luggage. She then was able to disembark, slipping into the crowd unseen. Finally, she saw Henry and crept up behind him, covered his eyes with her hands and said 'Guess who?', which began their joyful reunion. They travelled to Providence, Rhode Island with a man on the train giving up his berth so she could sleep. Bertha was extremely fortunate since three-quarters of third-class passengers perished. Dozens of Irish citizens working on the ship's crew also died. The story of Bertha's survival had a happy ending since she went on to marry Henry and they had five children.

Darkness and silence has fallen over Coosan Point as I head into Athlone. Hayward had witnessed the *Titanic* departure from Belfast on its maiden voyage and later wrote about it. The location at Coosan inspired in him a romantic and purple prose response:

> The sheer magic of it is impressed for ever on my mind, a magic which started with one of the most gorgeous sunsets I have ever seen and continued through a night made glorious by brilliant starlight, and the awe-inspiring, resplendent spectacle of an aurora borealis of such intensity that it was possible to read a newspaper by the light of its shimmering magnificence. With long, opalescent fingers

it played about the translucent dome of the heavens, so that one might imagine the combined fleets of the world engaged in some gigantic searchlight display just beyond the western lands which came down in their sleeping to meet the nocturnal beauty of the lovely Lough Ree.

7

A Two-faced River

ATHLONE IS A turnstile between the west and east. It is a two-hour drive to the sea either way so on hot days the banks of the river are places for relaxation and the Shannon a significant presence. The town has been bidding for regional city status and local opinion is that it is on the cusp of something special, but then it has been for several years. It is said to have a split personality because of the difference in the two sides glaring at each other across the river. With a population of just over 21,000, it is Westmeath's largest town and since 1995 has been twinned with Châteaubriant in the Pays de la Loire region of western France. Its hotels have the placeless names of international tourism, Radisson and Sheraton, with gleaming glass, steel and concrete edifices dominating the streetscapes. But these apparently soulless corporates have shown an interest in blending into the community, reflecting their locality. In the foyer of the Sheraton, swirling intertwining red and white lines on the plush lobby carpet speak of the river's zigzag path while horizontal lines represent bridges. Public areas feature furnishings with a flowing design and nod to other aspects of the Shannon's heritage.

Lough Ree in particular has inspired watercolourists, poets and authors, as well as a raft of sailor-scribes, travel and nature writers. At the Radisson Hotel, built at the waterfront on the former site of Athlone woollen mills, the Shannon is celebrated with a huge artwork in the shape of a rectangular hand-cut map of its mid-section. Entitled *Sionna*, it was named after the ancient goddess, produced by the Kerry artist Susan Leen and occupies a section of wall of the hotel's quayside lounge where gleaming white cruisers are quadruple-berthed in the marina. A notice states that the Shannon was an important waterway since antiquity, having been first charted by the renowned Graeco-Egyptian geographer Ptolemy in his first-century map of north-west Europe. The Greek version of the name Shannon was *Senos*.

The map consists of a black line snaking through it like the curve of a swan's neck. Parcels of land are identified by squares, rectangular shapes and a network of twisting lanes. The goddess Sionna informs part of a larger body of Susan's work about mapping and I am intrigued to find out how painters represent water. When I discover she lives in Paris, she explains by email that she is interested in lines and connections, and generally works in monochrome using black, white or grey. Her complex map was made on a roll of black Fabriano paper and in one-metre-wide sections representing bog and field boundaries in an abstract way.

Susan traced the river's trajectory and saw it through fresh eyes since she has lived abroad for ten years. It was important for her to emphasize the location of the hotel on the river but also how it has influenced the growth of the settlements along the riverbanks. She was interested in the effect that being close to a river might have on the psychology of the local people as areas of 'blue space' – rivers or lakes – are known to have positive effects on their well-being. While working on it, she reflected on the history of the mid-section of the Shannon and on the relationships between bodies of water and the evolution of the community.

The myth of Sionna being a woman possessing strength was important in making people reflect on ancient stories and in enabling a connection with place to be formed. Susan pictured the goddess as a 'long dark-haired woman who was tall with a powerful physique'. Time was a vital part of her work, allowing her to meditate on the place, slow down, pare back the elements

Statue of
the tenor
John Count
McCormack in
Athlone.

and reduce the form to a line. In recent years, she has become more interested in topography and how a natural border can be formed and influence a region's character. She loves the physicality of maps, using different papers to emphasize their tactile quality and the way knowledge is transferred through touch and materiality. For someone to feel at home, Susan thinks it is important to become familiar with social history and place lore, which can be aided by maps and way-finding tools.

The go-to man for information on the social history of Athlone is the town librarian, Gearoid O'Brien. The modern library is in the newly developed John Count McCormack Square where there is a permanent memorial to the tenor. A large statue on a pedestal by the sculptor Rory Breslin occupies centre stage. McCormack's former house is just a stone's throw away although it is now an Asian street food restaurant. Gearoid is familiar with Hayward's Shannon book. We talk about the fact that Hayward liked to pass judgement on what he saw, and consider what he wrote about the castle: 'A more peculiar-looking conglomeration of styles and shapes it would be difficult to conceive, and the only ancient portion today is the decagonal keep, which contrives to look nothing but absurd in its present surroundings.'

'I suppose it isn't the most impressive castle. Hayward observed it well because it was virtually demolished during the siege of Athlone and when we look at it today and what he would have seen, then it was very much a Napoleonic fortification. The drum towers are like the Martello towers you find around the coastline, so the castle changed over the centuries to keep up with the weaponry that was going to attack it. There was probably very little going on in it at the time apart from a small amount of military activity. It was part of the military barracks – the British garrison ended in 1922 and the Irish army took over but they would have been there in small numbers, perhaps two families living in the castle and some soldiers. It was a drab place then and he reflected that. In 1967 there was a move to knock down the castle and at one stage the urban council voted to demolish it and replace it with a car park, but they had to rescind their decision as locals were against it. At that time there was still a view that it was a symbol of British imperialism. Thanks be to God they saw sense and they've done a great job on it now.'

One of the other landmark buildings in the town that Hayward did not like was the Church of St Peter and St Paul, which had opened in 1937, two years before his visit. He felt it was incongruous to find such a building on the banks of the Shannon:

It looks at once astonishingly lovely and absurdly out of place. If you look at this church from the river it is not in Ireland you will think you are, but on the Continent of Europe. And that is not the way things should be at all. For all great building has sprung from the soil and has expressed the soul and spirt of the nation to which it belongs, and a church in Ireland should reflect the spirit of the people of Ireland, and not the spirit of the people of Italy or Spain or England. This church is usually described as the Church of SS Peter and Paul, an abbreviation which, I consider, is detestable.

Gearoid believes that Hayward was perceptive in what he wrote. 'The architect of the church was Ralph Byrne but the whole story about it was that the man who was responsible for building it, Dean Crowe, had his own ideas. Apparently, he dictated to the architect in many ways and he had travelled a bit himself. He had brought back small photographs from abroad and reputedly said to the architect that he wanted two of those towers and this kind of cupola on top so it's a bit of mongrel … Hayward could be quite outspoken and that is one of the things I admire about him.'

Hayward was never afraid to express a view and was shrewd enough to know that making candid observations about individual places would provoke comment and stimulate sales of his book. He showed his disappointment that there were so few links with the past and wrote that he found 'a dismal lack of knowledge' of the ancient history of Athlone. He felt that people took little interest in the ancient glory of their river fortress, which Gearoid points out is not the case today.

'You have to remember that even at that time there was no public library in Athlone, there was no bookshop, tourist office or museum, so there was no place that people could go to find out the history, apart from talking to older people. Today Hayward could have talked to eight or ten people who would put him right on any aspect of the history. Back then there weren't the resources to check facts but that's not one of the things I would criticize him for. He hadn't the Internet, but he saw the big picture and the context.'

We discuss some of the black-and-white photographs in the book. Hayward wrote about the Dutch General Ginkel, the 1st Earl of Athlone, born in the Netherlands, who lived at the corner of North Street with a doorway bearing the date 1628. The house was demolished and was one of the few remaining relics of old Athlone. Hayward met Mr Simmons, the photographer, who supplied a picture used in the book.

'In his book there are a couple of important photographs, including the beautiful O'Ferralls shopfront in Fry Place with a dated window, as well as doorway by Simmons. Nobody knows where that door is, and Hayward was going to try to find it. Simmons was an important photographer. Apart from recording the people of the town he recorded places as well and the interesting thing is that the work was carried out by a father and son. He came here about 1905 and his son, Jack, was here up to the mid-1970s. Every photograph they had taken over that time was properly indexed and accessible but unfortunately they have all disappeared. He did preserve two significant photos – O'Ferralls was important in Fry Place and is a Regency terrace, which in itself is important. He helped to focus attention on that building because in later years it was taken over, the shopfront was taken down, and in some shape or form preserved by a local businessman. He has since died but his family still have it as far as I know. And the building is now occupied by the Left Bank Bistro. Whether it would be possible to reinstate it I'm not sure but at least it is well recorded.'

While the layout of Athlone with its long main street, and the general character of the place has not changed, some aspects of old Athlone can still be traced. 'Hayward mentions in his book the old town wall and he was probably instrumental in focusing a bit of attention on it but there are portions of it still to be seen and in fact just outside our building here we have preserved a portion of the bastion. We have no town gate left but fortunately two streets, Dublingate and Northgate, have survived, and we have bits and pieces of the town wall here and at Court Devenish House.'

Hayward mentions writers affiliated with the area, but was saddened to find that there was a serious neglect of them, of the houses where they lived, and of their work. His literary reference points included the poet Leo Casey, Anthony Trollope and Oliver Goldsmith, while a thirty-page section of his book is devoted to the life and work of Maria Edgeworth. Nowadays their names are remembered, if nothing else as part of the roads infrastructure, since there is a Leo Casey roundabout on the N4 near Longford while two other floral roundabouts are named after Trollope and Edgeworth. A Trollope trail takes in twenty-seven locations along the Shannon region, including an area known as Flaggy Bottoms, and a Goldsmith international literary festival is held each year. In

Ballymahon a memorial has been erected to Goldsmith and his grave rededicated in 2004. Maria Edgeworth has come sharply back into focus with a society promoting her work, a literary festival and the publication of her letters in 2017. Although Hayward is from a later generation than most of these writers, Gearoid believes that his writing is still valid today.

'Hayward still holds his own as being an important writer and his books are in demand and sought after. He covered all the significant writers and in a lot of detail, but if he was working today, he would be writing about Athlone authors such as Hanna Greally, who was born in 1925. She was admitted to a psychiatric hospital in Mullingar and wrote *Birds' Nest Soup*, which brought her story into the public domain. Perhaps the fiction of John Broderick, who was born in Connaught Street in Athlone in 1924 and died in England in 1989, would be a focus. Broderick was outspoken too and was important in the 1960s although he is rather dated now. There's even a street named after him in the town and a few Broderick commemorative weekends have been held in his honour. He wrote twelve novels, some of which have been reissued, there is a biography on him and a writer residency programme in his name, so his legacy is recognized.'

I mull over what Gearoid had said about Hayward not being able to find out information. The writers of today certainly do not have a problem sourcing details but Hayward was tireless in his pursuit of the past and for his Shannon book he carried out detailed research before setting out. I saunter through town from east to west, wandering down steep and narrow back lanes such as Lloyd's, Payne's and Friary that slope off the main streets to the riverbank. While the shopping centres have succumbed to chain stores, family-run businesses with long connections to the past still operate on the main streets. Burgess department store, for example, reaches back to 1839. Across the water, the twin campanili of the SS Peter and Paul breaks the skyline. Smoke signals come from the chimney of a forest green barge moored near the elegant wrought-iron white bridge across which, almost unnoticed, a train glides.

The bridge – which could benefit from a lick of paint – was designed on the bowstring-and-lattice principle, and has carried trains from Dublin to Galway since 1851. It was built with a central swivel opening span thirty-seven metres long to accommodate tall sailing craft and opened up until the mid-1930s. The engineer was George Willoughby Hemans, the son of the Liverpudlian poet Felicia Dorothea Hemans whose paternal grandfather came from Co. Cork. She is best known for 'Casabianca' with its oft-quoted first four lines: 'The boy stood on the burning deck/ Whence all but he had fled; The flame that lit the battle's wreck / Shone round him o'er the dead.' And is sometimes parodied to read: 'The boy stood on the burning deck / His feet were covered in blisters / He'd burnt the socks right off his feet / And had to wear his sister's.' Poets, writers and singers have eulogized the river too and it has been a muse to many. Vona Groarke's lengthy poem 'Athlones' calls it 'a two-faced river, holding the line between the Pale and Irishtown'.

IN RECENT YEARS Athlone's left bank has taken on a bohemian character. Sheltered underneath the high castle walls are a tight knot of steep streets, a little enclave closed in on itself. It is an architectural chaos with higgledy-piggledy styles and buildings, which in mainland Europe would be called the 'Old Town'. The hub is Main Street and Bastion Street, a concentration of temples to gastronomy with a bracingly continental feel. Three-storey buildings with bright facades line the twisting street before running uphill. There is a tangible atmosphere of regeneration alongside a cosmopolitan vitality. Independent shops proliferate, such as liturgical bookbinders, a second-hand bookshop with ramshackle charm and the funky Bastion craft shop whose claim to fame is that Michael Jackson once visited. Interspersed are a clutch of hair stylists, beauty salons and nail bars, as well as the Divine Mater Centre with a chapel of adoration and a newly established *Titanic* memorial wall plaque.

It is a place with a chequered history of siege, destruction and rebirth. The castle is still an elephantine presence, casting a formidable shadow over the town. The bold and imposing grey thirteenth-century fortifications have been stylishly converted to house exhibitions on the vicious Sieges of Athlone during the War of the Kings. A timeline from 1129, when a bridge and timber castle was built, leads right up to 1969 when the Irish army evacuated the castle and it was taken over as a national monument. In between times the castle has survived burnings, rampages, rebellions and attacks. It has also come through natural disasters such as the Night of the Big Wind in 1839, which damaged most of the town and caused a fire that destroyed many houses. In October 1697 a lightning strike passed into the castle's arsenal and blew up 260 barrels of gunpowder, 1000 hand grenades, 220 musket and pistol balls as well as pickaxes and ironmongery. The explosion was a catastrophic conflagration that demolished the castle and destroyed much of the west town, newly built after the great siege of 1691. Down the centuries the castle has been rebuilt, repaired, expanded and adapted for different uses.

The noises of warring cries and drumbeats mix with the songs of John Count McCormack along a corridor. An elderly woman and her daughter slowly walk and talk their way through the exhibits, which include cups presented to McCormack in the US, his papal chain from meeting the Pope, HMV records and the story of his singing with Dame Nellie Melba on an opera tour in Australia. He is hardwired into Athlone history and his tenor voice rings out through speakers in the hallway with a repertoire of songs on a looped recording. The elderly woman is serenaded with 'I Hear You Calling Me', one of his best-known songs, and her eyes become soft with nostalgia.

The tiny purple flowers of ivy-leafed toadflax spring out from the castle's ancient walls while higher up red valerian flourishes and circular splodges of yellow lichen add colour to the afternoon sunshine. The castle still looks a dark and imposing building that dominates the area; little wonder that authors thought it gloomy. In his *Selected Writings*, John Broderick was quoted as saying that the castle was 'by far the most historical building in the town and certainly the ugliest'. Sitting regally, if

Sean's Bar, which claims to be the oldest pub in the world, is part of Athlone's thriving left bank.

somewhat incongruously, opposite the castle the showy facade of the Church of SS Peter and Paul, which Hayward disliked, far outclasses the older building. With its sparklingly restored walls of Wicklow granite and Portland stone columns, it is a striking ecclesiastical landmark, which many mistakenly think is a cathedral. But it remains a parish church giving an immediate impression of grander pretensions.

It was opened on the feast day of the patron saints, St Peter and St Paul on 29 June 1937. Architecturally it looks as though it has been shipped directly from a sunny city in southern Europe and would be more at home in a Roman or Neapolitan square. It is built in the south European baroque style and comes as a complete surprise rising beside the river. Its twin campanile, with their broken silhouette, open arches and corner Corinthian columns, rise high above rooftops and open at the top, ending in ogee domes – one of the highest points along the Shannon – although not as high as the tower of the Sheraton Hotel.

By way of contrast, my left bank peripateticism ends that night at Sean's Bar, a place of revelry and untamed beards. If any bar represents *ne plus ultra* then it is this one – the oldest in Ireland with turf fires, sawdust floors, candlelit sessions, a beer garden and its very own boat house for private parties. Its documented history dates to 900 AD, leading to an entry in *Guinness World Records* for being not just the oldest bar in Ireland, but the oldest in the world. In those days it was called Luain's Inn, named after the innkeeper who guided people across the river at the Ford of Antiquity. It later became known as the 'Ford of Luain', from which Athlone took its name *Athluain*. During renovations in 1968 the old walls of the bar were found to be made of wattle and wicker dating from the ninth century. Ancient coins, from the same period, which were minted by landlords for barter with their customers, were also found. These are in the National Museum while a section remains on display in the pub.

The bar's present-day walls are carefully curated with slices of Shannon history, framed advertisements, old Wills cigarette signs, heroic stories of rowing events and sepia-tinted images of the flowing river while the pints flow freely at the bar. Navigation charts of the Shannon's lakes line walls in a snug. While the bar may be a time capsule, glass cabinets promote its corporate twenty-first-century merchandise: Sean's Bar sweatshirts, bobble hats and T-shirts share wall space with badges from the California Highway Patrol, Dallas Police and the McKownville Fire Department of Guilderland, New York. The low ceiling is adorned with fishing rods, oars and paddles.

The all-age bar represents Hipsterville central: ripped denim, crop tops, body art, high heels and back-to-front baseball caps. The clientele is a mix of American and French tourists, fishermen and sailors. Fresh from rescuing a German cruiser stranded on rocks on Lough Ree, a lifeboat crew is relaxing. Black T-shirted members of a Harley-Davidson chapter indulge in motorbike power handshakes. Peopled by a diverse coterie of colourful characters and wine-guzzlers, it is a place where the art of conversation thrives along with music. In a corner window, a three-man group, Hickory Wind, seated underneath a framed map of Lough Ree dating from 1808, plays rock 'n' roll hits from the 1960s. Named after a song written by the country rock pioneer Gram Parsons, they blast out folk, rockabilly, bluegrass and country from the era known to some musicians as BCDB: Before Chris de Burgh.

The bar sells its own beer, called Sean's, alongside a house beer on tap via a hand pump saying AD 900. 'How old is it really?' asks an American standing beside me at the counter when his pint is being poured. Quick as a wink, the barman chips in that it was brewed three weeks ago in Carlow. The bar has also launched a limited-edition boxed whiskey set called 'Luain', a blend of grain and malt matured in bourbon casks, said to have a 'caramelized nose feel'. Co-owner Timmy Donovan takes time off from his duties to talk in a quiet snug about its history.

'We have the official certificate stating that it is the oldest bar in the world, which is framed on the wall over there,' Timmy says. 'Over the years it has had different names, including the Three Blackamoor Heads. Then in the 1950s it was owned by Sean O'Brien and in 1968 bought by Sean Fitzsimmons so the name Sean has stuck. The bar was always connected with clubs on Lough Ree. At one stage the sub-aqua club and RNLI operated out of here as we are so central. Because of the slope in the floor the water flooded in and the sawdust was used to soak up the water so we've kept that tradition. In 2016 we had pumps working for four months on the water.'

When I ask about the pull of the river, Timmy's face turns pensive. 'I couldn't live without the river. It's such a part of my life. I'm either in the water or on the water. My kids are involved in sub-aqua, swimming and rowing so we're always dragging them in or out of the water. In fact, I have named two of my children after Inchcleraun island. My son Ciarán is named after Ciarán who went on to found Clonmacnoise, and my daughter Maeve is named in honour of the warrior queen of Connaught, Queen Maeve, who retired with her sister on the same island.'

Anthony Barry, a local businessman, always comes in around 10.30 pm for a nightcap and enjoys the Wednesday evening sessions. I ask him about the theory I had read that Athlone has a split personality.

'It's not really a split personality,' he says. 'The left bank has developed over the last fifteen years and become commercialized, but Athlone has the advantage of being a large town and not a city. The population is 20,000 but within half an hour's drive we have the potential of 250,000. This keeps the shops and restaurants thriving and bolsters tourism although many locals don't really appreciate what they have in the way of history. The river brings people into town and is a focus, but most people here take it for granted.'

As he looks around the bar waiting for another stout to settle, Anthony says that one of the best things about Sean's is the diverse crowd it attracts. 'You don't know who you'll get any night as it's always different. We've had many famous people in here, such as JR and Sue Ellen [from *Dallas*]. One night recently we had two guys from Borneo singing 'Boolavogue' at the bar so you never know what you're going to hear or who'll be playing.'

After two hours of rambunctious musical intensity tonight's performance draws to a close. Two Johnny Cash numbers, 'Ring of Fire' and 'Folsom Prison Blues', are followed by a bravura solo 'Sleepwalking' played by the acoustic guitarist resulting in sustained applause. Last orders are called, the fire is out, candle stubs are crying, and the double bass is zipped up in its huge protective coat. The bar staff disappears, leaving drinkers to finish their dregs. A greasy, hirsute man, dressed in the international uniform of bikers, grunts a few staccato sentences at me through a whiskey haze before releasing a volley of curses. With a raffish grin, he places his arm around me and drains the last of his Powers. A frown of confusion fills his Santa Claus face when I explain my Shannon journey. He launches into a drunken lecture. 'Each to his own, but that river is just one long string of misery. The sooner they get rid of it and pave it over the better. They should put in asphalt, two or three lanes, and there'd be no more flooding.'

The melancholic and sonorous strains of the double bass ring in my ears as I wander through nocturnal Athlone bathed in subtle lustre lending a polish to the air. Its landmarks – the castle, church and road bridge – are flattered by soft lighting, giving them an understated glow beneath the starry Shannon night. There is no glaring neon, the only colour comes from traffic lights, streetlamps, and winking yellow beacons. The night-movers appear from Sean's, the Mother Church of music. Giddy teenagers are on their way to the piano bar, a smoker rolls a Rizla, while boy racers in souped-up cars screech across the bridge. Oblivious of it all 'the long string of misery' is listless, in no hurry anywhere. One moment it is satin, the next it produces a flickering ripple from a breeze as it winds imperceptibly on its slow meander (the word 'meander' is derived from the Menderes River in south-west Turkey) south of town, while all the people in that museum-piece of a bar go their separate ways.

8

Longboat to the Celestial City

THE NEXT STAGE of my Shannon itinerary should take me on a driving route along back roads from Athlone to Clonmacnoise. But I am suffering not so much from a headache after my musical fact-finding night in Sean's as from decision fatigue, trying to work out if I should drive or cycle to what some call the 'celestial city' or walk barefoot or on my knees across bogland like any respectable pilgrim. My quandary is determined by the fact that there is only one proper way to arrive at this ancient site and that is by water. The *Viking* longboat sails at 11 am. I have no time to lose. Fifteen passengers, including a couple of families, are already inside, sheltering from the rain as they make themselves comfortable for the ninety-minute journey to Clonmacnoise.

It is a peaceful counterpoint to last night's west bank revelry; or at least it is until a party of forty noisy Italians clamber on board, taking up every available space, port and starboard, bow and stern. Most are prepared for the weather with anoraks in a rich array of colours, backed up with umbrellas and blankets. Some wear red and black AC Milan football jerseys and white fleeces. Under a slate-grey sky, the oldest operating wooden Viking longboat in the world slips from the docks at St Peter's Port close to the castle walls. There is a short delay at the lock gate before we are given the all-clear, nudging our way through Big Meadow. A team of gulls sits on the pier wall, while a swan watches as we leave behind the sluice gates, apartment blocks and historic buildings. At the old canal on the Connaught side, our presence causes two herons stalking prey to lift off from a field. A cormorant assumes sentry duty on a navigation marker, monitoring our movement with an alert stance as we motor through water the colour of molasses. Mallards head off to the edge of the riverbank. Rivulets of rain create a soft patter running down the plastic covers put up to keep the inside of the boat dry.

From his position at the wheelhouse, our captain, who styles himself 'Viking Mike', provides a running commentary on the journey, starting with a brief history lesson. Steamers have been on the Shannon since 1826, but the full potential of the river, he says, was not realized because of the imperfect state of the navigation. The job of surveying it was carried out by Thomas Rhodes, a relative of Cecil Rhodes of Rhodesia. He submitted detailed plans of the work, which included the building of a new bridge, opened in 1844, the construction of a weir and erection of a new lock. The first stone of the lock was laid in April 1845 and opened for navigation four years later. The sleek Viking longboat dates from 1923 and was brought to Ireland in 1979. Its planks are made of larch and its frames are oak, giving it a mellow feel. The boat is a replica of a Viking *knarr*, the Norse merchant ship used for Atlantic voyages. Longships have sailed around the coasts since 795 and the Vikings arrived by river at Clonmacnoise in 842. The water is dark, Mike explains, because of its peat bottom, which is only about four metres in depth with a maximum of six. We drift along on a straight stretch of opaque water through the townlands of Ballygowlan, Srameen and Buggane. The rain eases and a local man beside me quotes an old proverb: 'A sunshiny Shannon shower never lasts half an hour.'

I move out to the foredeck to enjoy the view beside a large, decorative, red wooden Viking head as Mike announces we have reached the Three Counties Point where the borders of Roscommon, Westmeath and Offaly meet and from where we swing around towards Hall's Point. Cows are lunching with all the appreciative deliberation of Clonmacnoise cattle connoisseurs. I look at my map and ponder over the curiously named townland Bunua Cunna, which sounds like a place name more at home in southern Italy or on an atlas of Indonesia. When I type it into Google on my phone it asks: *Did you mean: buying a gun?*

Mike points out a Bord na Móna bog, part of the Blackwater group, which stirs little interest. The Italians' escort explains that they are touring religious sites in Ireland, exploring paths between tourism and faith.

'Some of my group have already visited such sites in France as Lourdes or Nevers in the footsteps of Bernadette,' she tells me. 'Others have been to the Holy Land, as well as Fatima and Santiago de Compostela. They like to discover new spiritual paths and lands where faith and culture blend into a single entity. Ireland has such a richness and offers a profound experience for a pilgrimage – apart from yesterday when they went to Kylemore Abbey, which was profoundly terrible because of the weather. They are praying it will improve today, at least the rain has stopped. A few of those on this trip have been to Ireland before but for most it is their first time. For them, it is about going deep down to the very roots of their being, about religious vocation and about cultural breathing.'

Two sturdy horses graze silently in a field, breathing heavily, perhaps in sympathy. The landscape takes on a different character. Viking Mike points out the flatland of the callows on either side of the boat where there is no riverbank and the water laps into low fields making it an area that is prone to seasonal flooding. We sit in silence looking across a thinly populated landscape as we skim through an almost secretive countryside. This is a place to appreciate the interplay of physical features and the permanence of the river as an ecclesiastical superhighway that has bound together many centuries of fluctuating history. Horizons are wide and heavy with symbolism. Mike identifies a narrow ridge between undulating fields that we can see clearly from the boat. This is an esker, a natural glacial gravel ridge and one of the most distinctive features of the midlands landscape. The *eiscir riada* was a chain of

Clonmacnoise, seen from the river, is one of the most revered sites on the Shannon.

eskers, which extended most of the way from Dublin across the midlands, marking a significant political boundary line in ancient Ireland. At one time the long, snaking, low ridges, which were raised above wet or wooded landscape, were an important natural line of communication. Many stretches of road still follow the crests of the summit.

As we round a wide bend, there is an air of expectation when the churches come into view. Seen from a watery distance, the grey stone buildings, towers and crosses in a pastoral setting have a timeless uniformity, representing a mélange of colours with blue river, green fields, milky sky and grey limestone. They are best contemplated from the river, the same view as the Vikings would have known, now captured on Italian iPhones and cameras with selfie-sticks held out at acute angles. The Italians' interest peaks when Mike talks about the papal visit in 1979. Pope John Paul II said prayers at the glass-covered papal altar addressing 20,000 people. He had requested the visit, believing the monks from Clonmacnoise brought the Christian faith to Poland. He spent forty-nine minutes at the site, describing it as an emotional moment. After returning to Rome, the Pope said he would never forget the ruins of the churches. For him, they spoke of the life that once pulsated there and he found them charged with a great mission, still constituting a challenge.

My mission is about to start after we tie up at the jetty alongside *Lady Lorraine, Jessica* and pleasure cruisers belonging to Carrickcraft. As we disembark, the party choruses a noisy sing-song clash of *arrivedercis* and *ciaos*. Single file, they make their way along an uphill path that has been etched into the grass and climb a wooden stile. The grass and sky are alive with frenzied larks sprinkling their continuous breathless afternoon warbles as part of their vertical columnar flight beside a path mined with cowpats on all sides. The group sets off on their pilgrimage tour with the guide making the most of the photo-friendly ruins.

There is a softness and clarity in the air. I pause to watch the Viking boat head off, taking in my new surroundings. Rivers are the arteries of the world, a link between the atmosphere and the land, and since time immemorial people have clustered near them. In the monks' case they were taking advantage of a prayerful sanctity as well as the water, fresh land, transport links and plentiful fish. From a natural-history point of view, this part of the Shannon landscape has unique habitats and features. Apart from the river and the remnants of a marl lake fed by springs, it is known for its eskers, callows, raised bogs and a section of limestone pavement.

Many history-sodden sites dot the riverside, but in any age-ranking of the Shannon's 'greatest hits' Clonmacnoise is unquestionably the highest. Of all the buildings sitting cheek by jowl along the river, these are the oldest and hence most visited. One of the most persistently revered sites in the country, it is a place where land- and riverscape, ecclesiastical history and weathered buildings blur into one piece of consecrated ground. The network of stone churches and buildings has been part of the uninterrupted view for 800 years, absorbing the setting, and a place to connect with the natural world. The very name Clonmacnoise whispers saints, scholars and a golden age of learning, as well as history and architecture.

Hayward arrived at Clonmacnoise by car and remarked that the journey by river would have been much more interesting than by road, which he found monotonous and dreary. But when he got here, he confessed that he found it difficult to know what to say about the place and what to leave unsaid, since so much had already been written about it. Nonetheless, he was not stuck for words and managed to write what amounts to a twenty-page history lesson, invoking poetry, work from *The Annals of the Four Masters*, and the writing of his friend Professor R.A.S. Macalister. By the late 1930s the buildings had already been in state care for more than sixty years but there were few, if any, tourists. Hayward was shown around by a local schoolmaster, Mr Molloy, an authority on Clonmacnoise, who 'with the greatest of good humour answered our many tiresome questions'. He found a monastic calm at the site, noting that the monks had 'an eye for beauty', and was impressed particularly by the collection of cross-slabs:

> Despite almost continuous violence and disaster throughout the ninth century, art and learning and religion went steadily forward at Clonmacnoise, and we cannot fail to wonder at the recuperative powers of this place and at its elasticity in the face of almost overwhelming misfortune ... One of my chief delights was the great collection of over two hundred monumental slabs, dating from the eighth to the twelfth centuries, most of them carved with crosses and many of them bearing memorial inscriptions in Irish.

Since Hayward's time three of the main sandstone high crosses have been moved indoors to protect them from the weather and been replaced by replicas. I am struck at the material effort by the skilled craftsmen that went into building the simple churches and carving the designs. There is a sense of the long-vanished pilgrims, of how it captured their imagination, and how over the centuries these pathways echoed to the footsteps that have trodden this way.

There is no set path to explore, nor a definite plan to the buildings, but I am following, not just in Hayward's footsteps, but in those of early medieval travellers and explorers, adventurers and dreamers, merchants and Viking marauders, and all who operated the old commerce of the river in cargo boats. This is a place to ponder over the details of the black-cowled monks who went about their practical and spiritual business here and to think about the skill with which they worked. Numerous plunderings and burnings took place throughout the centuries, yet the significance of the settlement has not diminished. The smallest of the remaining eight churches is Temple Ciarán, traditionally the location of St Ciarán's grave, but whose fragmentary sandstone walls appear to have shifted off plumb.

Twenty-first-century Clonmacnoise is a cultural landscape of national and international importance but it is far from a prayerful sanctuary or a place for those seeking atonement. Like swarms of bees, three separate groups of up to fifty people in each are shown around different parts of the site in what appears to be a normal conveyor belt of tourism. They include the Italian boat pilgrims, a French group vying with them in terms of noise, while out-trumping them all is an American party. Smaller groups and couples walk around on their own, some engaging with the spirt of the place as they listen to the sparkling effervescence of the skylarks. The sculpted crosses with different architectural styles and cross-slabs dating from 700 to 1150, round towers and church remains are all now Instagrammable.

Today's prototypical visitors are not necessarily religious devotees, but some are in search of peace, history or perhaps just a fleeting connection with the mysticism of another time. Others are more concerned with box-ticking, capturing images and social approbation. A ponytailed man with a T-shirt that reads Look After Thy Selfie genuflects at the north doorway of the limestone cathedral before taking a 'sacred selfie' featuring the three carvings of St Dominic, St Patrick and St Francis. Scant attention is paid to the guide's talk. In the car park tourists spill from coaches and minibuses. *The Pilgrim*, a statue of Aedh, son of the chief of Oriel who died on pilgrimage in 606, bows his head near the entrance while a woman holds forth volubly into her phone. The Cross of the Scriptures is regarded as one of Ireland's finest surviving high crosses and attracts much attention because its arms tilt upwards. Figures in the panels are depicted on all sides of it and on the base. Inscriptions refer to a prayer for King Flann, Flann Sinna mac Máelsechnaill was King of Meath and King of Tara who reigned from 879 to 916.

In the eighth and ninth centuries Clonmacnoise had the status of a city and was a settlement of power and influence. It teemed with monks, clerics, scribes, lay workers, craftsmen and students from throughout Ireland and the continent. Fifteen hundred years on, the word 'pilgrimage' somehow seems archaic in twenty-first-century secular Ireland. I have often thought a pilgrimage should be an intensely private act rather than a communal one of being bussed or shipped in as part of a large group, which dissipates the site's tranquillity. In terms of tourist visitors, Clonmacnoise was a world away from all this in the late 1930s, but even thirty-five years later nothing much had changed by the time Tom Moore took over as custodian of the site in the early 1970s. Tom, who is now the centre manager, may not have the pedigree of the oldest site on the Shannon, but his guardianship of it is still long, stretching back forty-five years. In those days, as he explains over a coffee, the business of the place was dealt with through a small caravan. 'Looking back, 1973 was the first year that guide information service was introduced and it was seasonal then. I started in June and it was supposed to run only to the end of September but the OPW who managed the site asked me to stay on with them. They didn't have an awful lot of work but they needed a presence here over the winter.'

In those days visitors numbered no more than 10,000 each year and were delighted to have someone who could provide them with basic information about the site. By 2016 numbers had shot up to 171,000. The technology has changed, Tom says, and people are now much more informed before they arrive but that can cause problems for the staff. 'We have our interpretation of the site based on facts and dates but it's always difficult to know where people have got their information from, what they have read, how accurate it is, and sometimes they might be looking at the guide and saying I didn't read that or maybe it differs to what they expected.'

Tourism is now Ireland's largest indigenous industry, creating annual foreign earnings of nearly €6 billion. Clearly a visit to Clonmacnoise stitches itself into the minds of visitors but the curious thing is that it continues to exert such a strong pull in a world where many have given up on organized religion, having outgrown its dogma. The monk's life is a far cry from the pilgrimage industry of today.

'Some companies deal mainly in pilgrimage tourism and focus on certain places. We have a service at the site or a mass although we don't get involved in organizing that. A lot of German, Italian, French and American groups request a prayer service.' It costs €8 to get into the site and I wonder if the Clonmacnoise 'commodity' is now somewhere you bring your faith and leave your money, and if visitors feel they are gaining a proper spiritual experience. Tom's view is that religion has, to a certain degree, become a business and most people are not bothered by the sheer numbers the site attracts.

Many changes have been wrought by the passage of the years. He speaks about some of them and about the historic link of the site to the river. 'Historically the Shannon was part of the reason why the monastery was founded as St Ciarán arrived by river. In the sixth century there were no major roadways, so they used the eskers or higher ground going east–west to travel overland because most of the landscape was bogs and it was a safer route that way and the river was used to move north–south. In later years, right up into the nineteenth and twentieth centuries, the river was a huge means of transport for goods and the canals linked into it. In the early 1960s there was no docking at Clonmacnoise as there wasn't a jetty – people could view the site from the river but you had to use a smaller boat to get in. When you look at some of the old photographs you had the gentry from Athlone having their picnic, so it was always a place to visit, whether people arrived by river or by road. Now the whole waterways system has opened up and visitors are not confined to the mid-Shannon. We have a regular visit by the *Hotel Princess*, which stops off every week in a luxury cruise as part of an all-in price at the high end of the market.'

To escape the crowds, Tom recommends I visit the Nuns' Church, dating back to the eleventh century, which is a ten-minute walk away. He adds: 'There's very little traffic, it's a beautiful setting and it's the best place to go for what we might call pure peace.'

I follow his advice and, in the evening, after the crowds have gone, walk over to the Nuns' Church in a small field beside the Pilgrim's Way. The colours are fading to monochrome as dusk gathers. Apart from the gentle soughing of wind through the trees it is sepulchrally quiet, calling to mind Gray's 'Elegy': 'And all the air a solemn stillness holds.' The impressive building comprises the remains of a Romanesque church with nave and chancel built for the nuns in 1167. I admire the architecture of the arches and the decoration, which includes animal heads and an exhibitionist female figure on one of the voussoirs, the wedge-shaped stones of the arch. For whatever reason, someone has placed eight small black and grey pebbles on one of the shelf's arches. The chancel arch, which had been in a precarious state, fell in 1838 and was rebuilt in 1865 under the auspices of the Royal Society of Antiquaries of Ireland. It supports a hood mould with hollowed chevrons, some with decorated lozenges and ornamented capitals.

Evening light pours in over the river, silhouetting the remains of the strangely contorted shape of King John's Castle. Its south-west corner is balanced precariously, apparently defying gravity. Hayward described this as a site that 'jarred incongruously'. But he rhapsodized about the Hiberno-Romanesque style of the Nuns' Church and 'its unspeakable lovely doorway and chancel arch … executed with the most loving care and minute elaboration'. This was a place where a convent of Arrouaisian nuns worshipped quietly with a vespers hush and worked a short distance from the main settlement, once one of the most famous monastic cities in Europe. Tonight, with the disappearance of the bum-bag brigade, there is a remarkable timelessness about twenty-first-century Clonmacnoise: it is imbued with a spiritual significance of solemnity, a holy silence and a strange numen where history oozes from its epic buildings.

THE FIRST THING that I am aware of early the next morning is the wind blustering against the Velux window followed by rain slamming down on it. It is 7 am in Kajon House B & B, a few kilometres south of Clonmacnoise, my base for several days. In her breakfast room, the owner Kate Brennan has assembled scores of colourful baseball caps on walls and on curtain poles. Her collection spans many parts of the world and runs to 140. Originally from Dublin, Kate and her husband John opened the guest house in the early 1990s. Breakfast is served at a table overlooking the callows, which are shrouded in a vichyssoise of lingering mist flattening the land. A family of six Spaniards appears from upstairs and occupies the next table. They puzzle over the breakfast menu, trying to work out what to choose and how to pronounce it. 'Sconnon ... sconneee ... skan ... how you call it?' the father asks.

'Bon dias,' Kate greets them. 'Scones, we call them, scones, you can have plain or fruit. Would you like some melon?'

'Mell ... on,' the father repeats the word. 'For breakfast? Never, not possible?'

'It is possible, and we have it for breakfast in Ireland. Vive la différence.'

Kate outlines to them the bewildering topographical jigsaw of the local landscape.

'We are in Offaly – west Offaly to be accurate – and looking into Roscommon, which is just over the bridge in Shannonbridge. A short distance after that is Galway, over to the right of us is Westmeath, so we've four counties beside us covering two provinces, is that clear? Offaly is separated from its seven neighbouring counties by no fewer than ten rivers.'

They are bemused, not only by the breakfasts and the geographical facts, but also the roads and the weather. 'I tell my guests if you're not lost, you're not having a good time.'

After the dishes are cleared, Kate talks about her business, the people who come, and the river.

'In the summertime you don't see the river, just the boats, while in the winter with the floods it's all river but this is a crossroads with a huge amount of history. In Dublin they call the country people culchies, so because I'm a mongrel-culchie it means I'm therefore a mulchie, which is an old Dublin term. I was called that by my sister who thought she was insulting me, but I thanked her for the compliment. It's a very tight-knit community but there are a lot of good people who live around here and support one another. The house next to here is Anderson, the next one after it is Anderson, and the next one, and the one across the road is Anderson and I call that Andersonville. Then you go a bit further down the road and round the bend at Clonmacnoise, I call that Duffystown as there's three Duffys built there. Everybody knows everyone else and they're all related – they might be a second cousin or two, but they are intermarried and keeping the land together.'

Some of those who stay at Kajon come to explore the area, wishing to see the wildlife on the river. 'You watch the swans, chicks and birdlife and I sometimes look at hawks going overhead here. We also have a man from France who stays with us for five weeks. He's called Pierre-Jean but when he's here he's known as Peadar John and he just loves the place. We're a small country but everywhere is different and there's so much to see. We're in the middle of a working bog and I apologize sometimes for the black dust when the weather is bad.'

By 10.30 am the mist clears and there is a quicksilver beauty to the rest of the morning. I have been invited to make a return trip to Clonmacoise as my visit coincides with a Sunday afternoon church service. Some commentators have referred to a twenty-first-century retro-religiosity but in the 1930s Ireland was a devoutly religious country. I have often been told how people periodically turned their back on the river and how over the years it has experienced what Harry Rice in his River Shannon book, *Thanks for the Memory*, classifies as a 'resurgam': 'I shall come into my own again.' Now, as a parallel, much of the country has turned its back on organized religion and the Catholic church is struggling. Yet when I read the local notes in the weekly papers, I get the impression of a place that still holds strongly to beliefs and traditions. In between stories about open darts tournaments and line-dancing classes, some of the headings show Catholicism is flourishing, at least in rural areas: Fatima statue visit, divine mercy devotions, Faithcast (a weekly podcast from catholicnews.ie), all-Ireland rosary rally, triduum to St Anthony ...

The Church of Ireland, meantime, is concentrating on whist drives, the Mothers' Union annual outing and its 'Big Sing'. The church is holding its open-air service at Temple Connor, a plain rectangular stone church that sits low by the river beside the polygonal wall, squeezed in between O'Rourke's Tower and McCarthy's Tower. The service, described as an annual jamboree, has run for more than fifty years and I have been invited to it by Trevor Sullivan, a retired canon. The service is held underneath a canopy with a makeshift stage, just a stone's throw from the glass-covered papal altar.

The river-worshippers arrive in twos and threes, dividing into optimists and pessimists. Optimists are armed with folding chairs, sunhats and sunglasses, while the pessimists carry umbrellas, waterproofs and tartan blankets. Some spread themselves out, leaning against shafts of crosses or early medieval sandstone grave-slabs decorated with uneven carvings of allegorical themes and animals. Behind them a flag-waving guide talks a group of forty Spaniards through the significance of the buildings, pointing animatedly at a repertoire of human figures on crosses and an archway. As I take a seat on a cold stone wall furred with patches of pale-yellow lichen, a woman hands me a two-sided order of service. About seventy people are assembled, along with a large youth group in electric blue tracksuits, the Clonmacnoise Warriors, who swell the numbers. On stage a guitarist and keyboard player tune up. Canon Sullivan, master of ceremonies, conductor of the music and speechmaker, welcomes everyone and asks them not to retreat if it rains. 'We can go inside the church as the door is open and all are welcome.' A choir takes their seats as the preachers arrive, clad in liturgical vestments of black cassocks, white surplices and blue stole. After a mumbling start, the first hymn, 'Shall We Gather at the River?', rouses the singers and is invigorated by the Warriors adding to the mood music.

> *Shall we gather at the river,*
> *Where bright angel feet have trod,*
> *With its crystal tide forever*
> *Flowing by the throne of God?*

On the margins of the river, half a dozen cattle appear at the stone wall separating the church from the water. Two curious whiteface Herefords swivel their heads as the sacred refrain ricochets off slabs, towers, churches and walls. Tourists stroll around, intrigued by the veneration of the Shannon, a few sitting and tapping their feet to the beat. A couple of white cruisers putter past. The air is filled with benediction. The main preacher, the Bishop of Limerick, the Rt Rev. Dr Kenneth Kearon, speaks about coming to the service as a child with his parents from Dublin and how he always remembered it as a sunny day. The church, he says, sits naturally in the landscape by the river.

Suddenly the rain and a breeze sweeps in. Known to some as St Ciarán's wind, it forces worshippers to huddle under umbrellas while others hunker behind tall stone crosses, although it quickly passes. After the service, picnickers gather in a field with baskets of that particular mix of Church of Ireland high-energy sandwiches featuring cucumber, Mars bar and apple, cheese and crystallized ginger, and chicken and red onion, along with sponge cake and pastries. I fall into conversation with members of the congregation. A farmer from Longford and his wife come every year, enjoying the atmosphere and describing it as a 'socially required' outing. He has been attending for nearly five decades and says that many years ago hundreds of people took part, but numbers have been dwindling although he is delighted at the multigenerational aspect of the service. He also mentions that the skylarks are deeply embedded in the place and have even been known to sing in a Shannon dialect – although how this is recognized is not clear. There is still something that stirs deeply with many people and that is why they like to come. The connection to the water, the man tells me, is expressed in a profound quotation from Ecclesiastes 1:7: 'All the rivers run into the sea; yet the sea is not full; unto the place from whence the rivers come, thither they return again.'

THAT NIGHT I arrive in Shannonbridge in failing light and make for the brightness of Killeen's grocery shop and bar. In Hayward's time this would have been referred to as a place selling general merchandise. In the intervening eighty years nothing much has changed. Today it is a veritable Aladdin's cave where you can buy everything from coal, jam and cornflakes to packets of porridge, fishing tackle and Clonmacnoise rhubarb. On the shop counter a bacon slicer sits beside a wooden trolley laden with white sliced bread and rolls. Posters advertise Champion coal alongside fire log specials and hot-water bottles. A large glass cabinet contains scores of baits for fishing. Locals mix with visitors in a spirit of inquisitive friendliness. The house speciality is rum and hot chocolate served with a toasted black pudding sandwich. The pub is packed with drinkers and diners. The sessioners arrive in the form of two guitarists who have just taken the stage in the main bar. With a seen-it-all gaze, they play well-known numbers such as 'Galway Shawl', 'City of Chicago' and the 'Galtee Mountain Boy', which do little to stir the drinkers.

The premises are made up of numerous different rooms: a well-stocked grocery shop and bar to the front left where customers sit quietly at the counter, a main bar to the right, a kitchen bar area, a pool room and darts area, a smoking room, and other cubby holes. On the ceiling and walls hundreds of business cards, postcards and currency notes jostle for space.

The owner of the bar, Derry Killeen, explains that the premises have been in the family name since 1928, although the building can trace its origins to the Battle of Aughrim in 1691.

'It was a bloody and decisive battle in which more than 7000 people were killed and it meant the effective end of Jacobitism in Ireland, although Limerick held out until the autumn of that year. There's a memorial cross at the site now and a visitors' centre with a film, artefacts and displays, so they haven't forgotten about it as memories tend to be long here.'

The two-man band strikes up again with 'The Maid of the Sweet Brown Knowe', 'Kilkelly', 'Ordinary Man', and a selection of jigs. Derry talks over the music about the importance of the river to the village.

'The Shannon was huge here thirty or forty years ago, especially with English anglers coming for bream and buying bags of dried bread and mixing them with the maggots. You might have had several hundred fishermen here in the 1980s for competitions and we had many pike anglers from Germany.'

The national card game of Ireland, twenty-five, is taking place at one end of the bar with eight serious gamers in action, although the rules are explained slowly to an Arizona couple who join in but lose track. The card school is synonymous with rural Ireland and popular in places along the Shannon. In many ways Killeen's bar and nearby Clonmacnoise have their similarities. Derry likens his premises to another form of religion.

'People come in for ladies' and gents' habits. Sometimes there's a bit of run on them. You could get a knock on the hall door at three or four in the morning to waken you from your slumbers. Somebody would say, "My granny is dying and I want to get a habit – can you help me?" The gas thing was that the granny might have lived for another eight or ten years – she just had a heavy cold and thought she was going to die but decided that she didn't want to die.'

The singers take to the stage again. One heats up the musical tempo to such an extent that the doors are opened and a couple of dogs wander in, which leads to the singing of 'I'm a Rover'. This is followed by several slow ballads, 'The Parting Glass' and 'The Lonesome Boatman'. The evening reaches a rousing climax with a classic riverside song in which drinkers spring to their feet, clap their hands and punch the air, swaying in tribute to 'The Broad Majestic Shannon'.

9

Crossing the Callows

MOST PEOPLE WHO visit the midlands, south of Clonmacnoise, rarely build in time to walk across the callows, a trelliswork of fields that flood in the winter and are rich with a diverse assemblage of wild flora and flowering grasses. One of the reasons for this is that they have trouble finding their exact location as no road runs parallel to the river for any length of time. The callows (from the Irish *caladh*), flank the river but for many visitors they are obscure, invisible, or at best flat and monotonous, which is why most do not take the trouble to stop. They characterize a sprawling area stretching from south of Lough Ree to north of Lough Derg, covering over 4000 hectares. It may lack the drama of the mountains of the west, and no hills disturb the illimitable distance, but its wide horizons draw me in through its abstraction. Over several days of walking, cycling and driving I discover a fluid landscape with shifting tones of water and light, a realm with its own individualistic imprint on the land, but still difficult to pin down.

The ecologist Stephen Heery came to this area in 1979. Birds and grassland are his forte and he has studied the meadows intently. It is a hot early afternoon when we set off on a leisurely examination of fields in different parts of the callows.

'People sometimes ask where the callows are, and they are standing in fields right in the middle of them. They are difficult to access and are spread over both sides of the river. There are only four bridges to cross between Athlone and Portumna, so if you're standing on one side and you want to look at the callows on the other, this might involve a 32-km journey. The farmers know their own callow lands as they provide grass in the spring and hay in later summer and autumn. In some places the river would be two metres below the bank so parts of it are hidden while in other places the water is lapping against it, so there is a difference of elevation on them. The low-lying land that floods often has a different vegetation species composition; you find dry fields and wet fields with sedges.'

Hectare by hectare, the callows support a large web of life that links grasses, sedges, flowers and invertebrates, including insect communities, as well as birds and cattle. On a minor road north of Banagher, we pull over and open a gate leading into a dry meadow owned by different farmers and cut into strips, which we explore at close quarters. Agricultural grasses, which often go unnoticed, are a dominant feature and an ethereal presence. Timothy grass, with pale green smooth and hairless leaves, short-stalked spikelets and a cylindrical flowerhead grow in tall, crisp clumps. The flora of the callows is a riot of colourful common, unusual and rare plants, all part of the grassland crop. Poking around the graceful beauty of thigh-deep grass, we find pink clusters of wild valerian, the tall, pink flowering spikes of willowherb and crush small aromatic water mint with its lilac-blue globular heads; the air fills instantly with a sharp green minty scent, a distinctive callows summer smell. Bog thistle, hogweed and the shiny bright yellow flowers of the buttercup-like lesser spearwort are prominent. Large heart-shaped colonies of yellow marsh marigold, regarded as the emblem of the callows, carpet another patch, interwoven with marsh ragwort and deep purple statuesque marsh orchids. Stephen sinks to his knees to identify the pink mist-like clusters of meadow rue, red clover and silverweed speckling the ground. He points out that part of the reason for the extraordinary diversity of wildflowers is because of different soils.

'We have the alluvium soils that are low-lying, then the peat bogs and the white marl, which is almost pure lime and is a creamy white clay found in drainage ditches, so it's no wonder that it is a diverse place. You also have to consider the fact that the environmental conditions mean it is the last part of the farm to be cut and is difficult land to manage as it is fairly un-intensive but sometimes you see a big tractor careering around the meadow.'

Although the word 'callow' was used in the nineteenth century for lands liable to flood beside the Shannon, it was not a term that was in use when Hayward visited in the 1930s but it came back into more general use in the late 1960s. On his travels around Ireland, he loved hills and high places but on his Shannon journey he found this area 'flat, uninteresting and rather dreary country', a description with which Stephen disagrees.

'There's more to a country than elevation and if you kneel down into the meadow as we are doing it is anything but uninteresting. Quite apart from the twelve different sorts of grasses and more than fifty different species of flowers on the whole callows, there are unlimited and unseen invertebrates, which have only recently begun to be studied. A recent survey on the marsh flies showed that one third of all species in the country were present in the callows. The place that Hayward saw would have been equally species-rich, and of course, there were no tractors, whereas today a contractor will shoot around a field in two hours. What is so special about the callows is that anywhere you go, you are looking at different natural landscape features … They are the largest continuous expanse of floodplain grasslands in either Ireland or Britain. If you come here on a November day and there are floods and no birds around, and the pubs are closed, then I would call it bleak. But bleakness is not necessarily a bad thing these days.'

We drive a few kilometres across to a major watery junction with the meeting of the Shannon and Big Brosna River. The area looks out to Bullock Island with its traditional hay meadows, which in 1991 became the location of the first nature reserve on the callows. Today, it is bereft of traffic but busy with wildlife and the delectable aroma of coumarin, the smell of newly cut hay. We scan the horizons. A chorus line of straight-trunked, tall, slender poplars show-dance in a light breeze at the edge of a field, bringing a formal touch to the natural surroundings. Along an old backwater, bumblebees are feeding on handsome marsh thistle while blue damselflies vie with white wood and green-veined butterflies on reeds. Tall bunchgrass, known as reed canary grass, grows breast-high in large clumps, as well as rare meadow barley. The afternoon sunlight has an astringency to it. Pinks and purples dominate the colour palette and the ground vibrates with a teeming mass of plant life. In one meadow we come across the oval-shaped leaves of marsh pea, a relative of sweet pea, the eye-catching purple knapweed – a key food source for butterflies – while the conspicuous magenta spikes of purple loosestrife loom large on the riverbanks. There is a sense of long continuity in the luxurious dry meadowland. The callows is a four-season thoroughfare for birds, thanks to its feeding and breeding opportunities. Winter is the best time to see wildfowl, when the area is also the haunt of large concentrations of lapwing and golden plover. Because it is devoid of disturbance it is regarded as an ideal habitat for ground-nesting birds. Stephen has an ornithological claim to fame in that he once saw a lesser yellowlegs, a slender long-legged shorebird. He claims the distinction of being the first person in Offaly to have seen the bird.

'It is an American bird, like a redshank with yellow legs, and it is sometimes called a yellowshank. Unusual birds occasionally get lost. Over the past twenty-five years we have counted a fair number of rare vagrant species and we still get them, but of course a lot pass by without anyone seeing them. The writer J.A. Baker, author of a book on the peregrine, said that the hardest thing of all to see is what is really there.'

Stephen describes the callows, in Irish terms, as a huge ecosystem. 'It's all connected land, linked to the floods, the meadows, the pasture and because about 500 farmers own the callow land that is one of the reasons for its diversity. Hay cutting generally takes place on different strips at different times, and there is some fertilizer used but not much. The hay operations on the callows tend to be the last thing they do on the farm. A callows hay meadow strip will include dry meadow and wet meadow with plants that are equally at home with their feet in the water. The farmers have been very supportive of protection measures in relation to the corncrake as they worked hard in adhering to their methods.'

Visitors who make their way to the callows are frequently astounded by what they find. While these wetlands may not be on the scale of African grasslands, local folklore records the story of two tourists who came from Botswana in the early 1990s. They thought the scene from their B & B in Shannonbridge, looking north to the expansive Clonburren callows, lacked only giraffe to remind them of home on the Okavango delta. For forty years Stephen has come to know these sinuous and narrow wetlands, their hidden secrets and sequestered backwaters. He has seen how nature, farming and tourism can exist in harmony in the twenty-first century.

'My favourite time of the year is June because you see almost every plant species that is going to be here in their young stage. If you take Bullock Island, that would make an unusual patch of nature on its own. But that's only 200 hectares out of 4000. Apart from the corncrake, we used to have breeding lapwing, redshank and curlew – we had forty-eight pairs of curlew in 1987 along the callows and in the hay meadows. As long as these species don't become extinct on earth then there is always hope they will return. There is a danger that we forget about what it could be like – that creeping change is something that has to be guarded against.'

THROUGHOUT MY travels I have seen the river in different lights, becoming familiar with its many paradoxes as Ireland's most famous watercourse. Slow and ponderous, the Shannon is laden with memories, powerful in symbolism, prone to running rampant through fields and swamping houses, sometimes impeccably well-behaved and relaxed, at other times tempestuously alive, unpredictable, twisting and turning, eroding and evolving, secluded, capricious, languorous, glimpsed yet neglected, at times frustratingly unget-at-able, filled with religious and cultural significance and, according to Celtic mythology, possessor of wisdom. Shannonsiders are amongst the greatest talkers in the world, possibly since the Greeks. And people who love rivers love to talk about them. When I reach Shannonbridge, Basil Mannion, who is closely attuned to the needs of river-users, outlines his role. As a community water officer for Westmeath, Offaly and Laois, his job is to help refocus people to place more value on their natural waters such as lakes, streams, rivers, canals, wetlands, waterfalls and bogs.

'The idea,' he says, 'is to make people think more about the rivers: if they put more value on it they will be less inclined to pollute, more inclined to get involved, and they'll try to understand it a bit more. We still have this idea that Ireland is a country of blue-green pristine waters and to a certain extent we are, but it's dropping all the time, so we want to reverse that and bring it up to at least good quality.'

Basil explains that quality is broken down into five categories: high, good, moderate, poor and bad.

'Forty-three per cent of all Ireland's rivers are less than good status so we have high quality beautiful waters, then good status ones, moderate status, poor status and then not great. At the moment nearly half our waters are less than good. The idea is to get communities to realize what is on their doorstep. Even if it's only a little stream over a bridge at the corner of the village, it's important to make them aware that it flows into a bigger stream or lake. For some people the river is like wallpaper and is in the background. They don't really notice it unless something happens and then it stands out.'

Rivers shape landscapes and provide a focus for local identity, but Basil has discovered that in the towns and villages of this part of Offaly people have more affinity with the smaller rivers than with the Shannon.

'It's so big that people can't get their arms around it the way that they would embrace a small stream, and it overwhelms them.

The sixteen-arch bridge that spans Shannonbridge was a strategic river-crossing point.

Of course, the boaters and fishermen put a huge value into it but there is a negative outlook over the flooding. There are people who think the Shannon should be turned into a canal. The main problem is that the rivers are being channelized and the water is flying into the bigger rivers, leading to the flooding. Rivers aren't canals, they have a personality and should meander and find their own course … The feedback we get is that there are too many government agencies involved and we want to reverse that negative thinking.'

The sixteen-arch bridge, a strategic crossing point on the Shannon, links Roscommon with Offaly, and was completed in 1757. It was restored and strengthened in recent years, and now operates a one-way system controlled by lights. House martins skim under the bridge while kayakers from the local primary school learn the ropes on the water. A solitary swan preens on the grass on Lamb Island. Two tractors trundle over the bridge, followed by a livestock transporter, haulage trucks and a tailback of cars, vans and motorbikes. The fortress at one end of the bridge looks forbidding but is now a café from which a small party of

Germans emerges, loading bicycles on to a cabin cruiser. Luker's pub, at one end of the bridge, has been renovated but the authentic old bar is still in its original state. Once the traffic noise subsides, Basil picks up a point about a collective sense of ownership of the river by the local community and connecting people back to it.

'We'd love to see a number of river trusts set up whereby the river or lake, the local farmers, anglers, boaters and yachters and speedboat people come together to form a trust to look after this body of water ... We're a talkative bunch, we like to communicate with each other and talk about the environment and I think that has helped us a little bit to take stock of what is around us.'

Basil's infectious exuberance comes across as he outlines how people learn to read a river. 'Individual bits of it have a character of their own. I try to read the people who are able to read the river whether they are anglers, people living on the shore, trying to see it through their eyes. You would notice the rise in the Shannon in places but it's never overly choppy. Mostly it's just there and you can't hear it, it's not a noisy river. Of the different groups I've dealt with, it's the anglers who are taking it all in. They're in the waders, spending time out there. They're very passionate about looking after it and spend a lot of money themselves looking after it.'

Our talk turns to how people revere rivers and what Basil sees as the pull of the riverscape. 'People like the history of the river and what their parents might have said about it, or they may talk about angling, paddling, birdwatching or walking along a stretch. It comes from childhood and they want to try to protect the river and can get very emotional about it ... the river is telling a story as it moves along and is part of our history and heritage.'

After our chat I wander along the riverbank. The emblems of solidity are all around. The main fortress, a three-storey block house known as the Shannonbridge *tête-de-pont*, dates from the Napoleonic era, its purpose to prevent a French invasion expected to land on the west coast of Ireland. At the derelict Watch House, I snack on a sandwich in the sunshine amongst a splatter of buttercups, dandelion heads and dock leaves. At one time this small building was connected to the main structure by linear earthworks, a ditch and a bank, which featured a timber palisade and protected the flank of the river. Hayward called the barracks, which was then used as a warehouse for Messrs Moran Bros, 'a magnificent example of the builder's craft'. He found the old gun emplacements were still quite perfect. Today it is the River Café with outdoor tables and flower boxes attracting passing visitors. But the main street, a sad procession of distressed and derelict properties, has just benefited from €90,000 for a village renewal scheme, which may help revitalize its appearance.

JOHN DONOHOE, owner of the second-hand bookshop in Athlone, had mentioned a Shannon connection to Flann O'Brien's *At Swim-Two-Birds*, one of the funniest books ever written. John believes the title comes from a ford on the river south of Clonmacnoise. As a long-standing 'Flannorak', my curiosity is piqued. O'Brien's book was published in 1939, the same year Hayward set off on his Shannon journey, although it is unlikely the two ever met. A strange and anarchic novel, it was written in the strain of dark humour, long a feature of the Irish style from Swift to Beckett. The plot involves a university student whose effort to write three separate stories gets wildly out of hand. The novel is regarded as his masterpiece, but its appearance was badly timed since most copies were destroyed at the publisher's warehouse during the London Blitz and it did not attract much attention because of the war. 'Hitler, the literary critic,' O'Brien said, 'bombed the publisher's warehouse and burnt the stock.'

The Ordnance Survey Map 47 covers parts of Offaly, Roscommon and Westmeath but has no mention of a place name resembling At Swim-Two-Birds, in either English or Irish. Other maps show Carrick O'Brien, a hill south of Golden Island near Athlone, and O'Briensbridge, a village in south-east Clare, named after Turlough O'Brien in 1506. I consult references in my book bag, but they give no firm answers. Then I turn up a Rambler's Guide to the Shannon Valley, a colour map with delightful illustrations, and in small letters on a bend of the river, I find marked 'Curley's Island' and underneath it the words 'Swim-Two-Birds' close to Devenish Island. Devenish Island, in Irish *Snámh-dá-Ean* (literally 'Swim-Two-Birds'), was one of Mad King Sweeney's resting places in the original Sweeney cycle and one of the most famous fords on the river between Clonmacnoise and Shannonbridge. It was said to have been visited by the Mad King who appears amongst other phantasmagoric characters in the novel. In the Anglo-Norman era, Curley's Island was guarded by the castle of Clonburren on the west side of the river. Some accounts also state that St Patrick crossed the river into Connaught at this point.

In his biography of O'Brien, *No Laughing Matter*, Anthony Cronin states that the author did not like the title and suggested to his publishers, Longman's, that it should be called *Sweeney in the Trees*. O'Brien said he liked *At Swim-Two-Birds* less and less, and although he had no objection to it being retained, he suggested, 'I do not fancy it much except as a title for a slim book of poetry.' However, the title was chosen, as well as the pseudonym Flann O'Brien for the author. He later decided that he would prefer the less evocative 'John Hackett' because he had used 'Flann O'Brien' in his letters to *The Irish Times* attacking Seán Ó Faoláin and Frank O'Connor. Although the novel did not receive much coverage in Ireland or elsewhere, it came to the notice of James Joyce in Zurich, who described it as a very funny book, an assessment that did not please the author. Joyce was almost blind and it was one of the last books he read.

In the community-run tourist office in Shannonbridge – the former bridge-keeper's house – the man in charge is prominently displaying a copy of *At Swim-Two-Birds*. He is unaware of the author's connection to the area and admits to not having read it. O'Brien was born Brian Ó Nualláin (Brian O'Nolan) in Strabane, Co. Tyrone in 1911. When he was nine, the family moved to the midlands and part of his childhood was spent in the flat landscape near Tullamore, not far from this part of the Shannon. O'Brien is attributed with the quote: 'Hell looks much like Tullamore.' With exquisite timing for a comic writer, he died on All Fools' Day,

A cabin cruiser makes its way between Curley's Island and Devenish Island, which translates as 'Swim-Two-Birds' (*Snámh-dá-Éan*) and provided the inspiration for Flann O'Brien's novel *At Swim-Two-Birds*.

1 April 1966, aged fifty-four. The date has now been acquired as Mylesday as part of the Dublin literary calendar.

'Head across the bridge to the west side of the river,' the tourist office man says. 'Take the narrow back road to Athlone, follow signs for Clonburren cemetery and veer off to Cappaleitrim. There's tractors and trucks flyin' around there, so you'd need to be careful but keep goin' till you run outta road.'

As a tribute to the man himself I decide the best way of approaching the subject's topography is to increase my Shannon bike-print on a humble velocipede, a Claud Butler, which I have owned for twenty years, although I have forgotten my bicycle clips. The road follows hedges overflowing with cow parsley and bright yellow gorse. At the flat expanse of Clonburren bog, a blue tractor moves slowly up and down, corduroying it with tracks and throwing out a mini brown dust storm. Along an edge of the bog runs a bumpy metre–wide railway track. Clucking blackbirds dance on hedge tops; two hares leap up in a field, pelting away at speed; a bushy-tailed squirrel, followed by a second one, saunters blithely across my path; a pair of pheasants dart into roadside vegetation.

Chattering birds flit from tree to tree while bumblebees whirr past. I wallow in the glorious aimlessness of an afternoon of easy-going pedalling across a flat landscape. Three kilometres along, the road leads up an incline, testing my leg muscles. Two chestnut horses stand statue-like by the roadside. A highland terrier greets me outside a cottage while a sheepdog snaps at my wheels at a farmhouse with outbuildings and a caravan. Across fields, cuckoos signal their presence, punctuating the air with loud repeated calls.

Few coaches or motorhomes frequent the area and it is mercifully empty of tourists. The tarmac road turns into a lane, then a grass-carpeted tendril, petering out 200 metres from the riverbank. When I reach the meadowland by the river's edge, I wander over knee-high grass. The fields are filled with a sea of buttercups, dandelions, pignut, plantain, gleaming cowslip, bobbing heads of bog cotton and cuckoo flower, its tips dipped in pale lipstick pink, starring the grass. The river is low-lying here, but it is clear there are a couple of islands that appear to be made up mostly of grass and stone. A motorboat slips past on its way south. A skylark sings vigorously while the chirping and cheeping of other birds rocket from the reeds.

On a stroll around, I come across a fellow cyclist and dog-walker. When I explain my search to him, he introduces himself by the name of Flan – a serendipitous encounter that the author himself would have enjoyed, even though he spells his name only with one 'n'. Flan Barnwell is exercising his dog, Guy, a cross between a golden Labrador and a retriever who reconnoitres the ground with the careful nose of a detection dog sniffing for marijuana.

'Guy's a real beaut,' says Flan, giving me an affable greeting. 'Just eighteen months old, very docile and passive. I had a golden Labrador retriever for ten years and he died from cancer of the lining of his stomach, and I felt that I would like to get a dog of a similar type. He's an affectionate dog, goes everywhere with me, and I confine myself to places where it's safe to bring him.'

We talk about the title of the O'Brien book. Flan is immediately interested and joins me for a tour of the fields to see if we can track down any sign of a connection to it. When I was at Clonmacnoise I had seen the Cross of the Scriptures, one of the most important Celtic crosses in Ireland, which is also known as King Flann's Cross and is mentioned twice in *The Annals of the Four Masters* from 957. The name Flann, or Flan, means 'red' or 'ruddy' and has much historical resonance. 'It was originally a Birr name, and Birr is in the diocese of Killaloe where the patron saint is Flannan, so I shared the name. If I'm ever asked for identity it's easy because there are not too many people of that name.'

Flan does not claim to know much about his namesake's famous parody but has read some of his work and has a fondness for the writer since he is a cyclist. As a young boy growing up in the area, he has been a strong advocate of the benefits of a bike.

'I grew up outside Birr and there were six of us in the family. My mother had to buy a bike when my eldest sister started secondary school. In those days there was only one bike per household, and it was a question of "where's *the* bike?" not "where's *my* bike?" so things have changed a lot. Of course, years ago people saw the Shannon as a slop heap and up to the early 1970s it was the main dump. There was no recycling then, people didn't know any better and everything was dumped on to the riverbank.'

We walk through the meadow to get as close as we can to the edge of both islands. Curley's Island is a thin strip of grass and sand of six acres to the north of Devenish Island, which is much larger. There is an architectural grandeur to the lofty, tottering reed beds, which rise with a towering palisade of stems up to six metres from the edge. When we reach the river we can make out the division, with one part falling down like a finger to Devenish.

'Curley is a common name, more so in south Roscommon, along with the Mannions where in the old graveyards a lot of those names are buried. The ford meant that the water was so shallow that you could literally walk across it. You'd be walking through water up to your ankles perhaps and Devenish Island was likely dug out or drained to make it navigable. Once they dug that then there was an island in the middle. There was a small ford here that would have been used by people to cross the river and salmon would have loved it too.'

Flan explains that a considerable number of walkways and new cycle trails have been developed in recent years. He wants to see a cycle trail continuing from Athlone down to Clonmacnoise.

'It would really make sense because the N62 road to Ballinahowen is a very busy, narrow road, and there is absolutely no way you could cycle on that because of the volume of coach traffic. I have no business or commercial interest but am involved in trying to link a cycle path between the two places. It's part of a pan-European programme of cycleways. The one going through Athlone is called Euro Velo 2 and when it's completed you will be able to cycle from Galway to Moscow and go through all the capitals. The Wild Atlantic Way is Euro Velo 1, which starts up in northern Norway and comes down to Bergen, then into Scotland over to Northern Ireland and is roughly ten thousand kilometres – and 2500 kilometres of it is in Ireland before it goes on to France, Spain and Portugal.'

The refurbished Green Heartland Cycle route in mid and south Roscommon is gaining popularity and Flan enthuses about the newly opened Old Rail Trail linking Athlone and Mullingar. Bike weeks are held to encourage all ages and groups. And there's a group from Banagher known as WOW: Women on Wheels, who take part in challenge events.

As we look over my vintage Claud Butler, I recall a quotation from *The Third Policeman* celebrating the romance and mysticism of cycling: 'How can I convey the perfection of my comfort on the bicycle, the completeness of my union with her, the sweet responses she gave me at every particle of her frame? I felt that I had known her for many years and that she had known me and that we understood each other utterly.' I also mention to Flan about O'Brien's molecular theory, which stated that bike and rider eventually become one through 'arse-saddle symbiosis' meaning that you are not sure whether you are talking to a bike or its rider. Much of his writing is tricky to understand and almost all of it is not about bicycles. But it posits the theory that if you spend too much time in the saddle then by some unscientific process of energetic exchange, you will find yourself becoming a bit mechanical. O'Brien sums it up: 'You would be surprised at the number of people in these parts who are nearly half people and half bicycle.' As we go our separate ways, a light shower begins to fall, and I cycle back into town, a spring in my pedalling. With the music of stream and spoke in my ear, I call to mind another quotation from *The Third Policeman*: 'What could be more exquisite than a countryside swept lightly by cool rain?'

TEN KILOMETRES SOUTH, tucked away in a quiet corner, Shannon Harbour straddles the Grand Canal. It is a village that is not on most people's radar, apart from the boating cognoscenti who have arrived with their shiny vintage vessels for the annual heritage barge festival. More than forty boats, some dating as far back as 1846, have made their way along the canal to take part in a rally. But they have also come to help in the celebration of another significant event: a bar which opens only once a year. The Canal Bar – beside the humpbacked limestone Griffith road bridge with its handsome elliptical arch – will open its doors in the afternoon to its first visitors in 364 days. At the rally nerve centre, just outside the Harbour Master's House where I have secured the last bedroom, barges nudge each other lying four-deep across the canal. This means visitors are able to jump from one to the other with ease, explore the living quarters and talk to the owners. Festooned with bunting, flags and lights, there is a party atmosphere to the boats. A bouncy castle and events such as face-painting, a sack race and model-boat building make it a place where children let off steam.

Up and down the canal, energetic skippers busy themselves applying a new coat of paint, hanging up lights, polishing, varnishing and erecting signboards on their distinctive boats. Evocative names are being touched up: *Realt na Móna* (Star of the Bog), *Gortmore Belle*, *Pearl B*, *4 Winds* and *72 M*. Many are in pristine condition, given their age. A sign on one reads: 'We are not old – we are recycled teenagers.' An enormous St Bernard paws the glass door of one boat with a look that means 'Please

The handsome single-arch Griffith humpbacked road bridge at Shannon Harbour.

open.' The place is alive with dogs big and small, terriers, poodles, bulldogs, boxers and a basset hound. The animals clearly enhance the barge owners' mental and physical well-being although a few boaters enjoy a more solitary life. One woman sits playing solitaire on her iPad while another is deep in a novel.

The Shannon, Brosna and Grand Canal all meet at or near Shannon Harbour. The length of the canal at this point stretches for two kilometres. It is lively with pleasure craft of all ages and has become a place of assembly for floating homeowners. The towpath along either side is now part of the Grand Canal Way. The water is mirror calm without so much as a gurgle.

Across the other side from the Griffith bridge, several corroded barges are long past their sail-by date. Some appear to have been simply abandoned and left to rot in the water. Buckled bows, torn canopies, broken windows, flaking and crumbling paint exemplify the wear and tear, while others are no more than ancient rusting shells lying docile. Taken as a whole, this aspect of Ireland's floating heritage, which includes barges and narrowboats at the far end of the canal, is an unsightly mess.

Aquatic splashes of colour lie all around with many flowers in the yellow spectrum. Golden waterlilies enrich the water, and around the towpath, hawkbit, the closely-knit bird's foot trefoil and a few withering flag irises make a show. Banks are crowded with masses of the fluffy heads of the conspicuous meadowsweet with its marzipan scent, while purple thistles, oxeye daisies and clover are mixed in with the invasive seeds of rosebay willow herb, bracken and grasses. Tiny water mint with hair-purple stalks grows close to the canal's edge. Thickets of willow, ash and oak line one side of the bank. The path is also a conduit for bird and insect life. Birds and bees zoom past like rush-hour traffic. Hoverflies hum their monotone refrain. Robin, stonechat and wren are in full voice; a grey wagtail flirts its yellow underbelly while a heron uses the path as a runway. In the trees, willow warblers and tits are active. Beside the bridge, a goldfinch skirmish involves two males picking a fight, locked in battle over their new beau. The rally-fest is organized by the Inland Waterways Association of Ireland and their blue flag flies from barges, more correctly called canal boats. The canal is a safe and secure berth.

Gerry Burke, who coordinates the event, owns one of the boats and shows me round. This is the 23rd annual rally he has organized in Shannon Harbour but at one stage its future was in doubt.

'This year the event was cancelled, but three weeks ago a group of us got together and felt we should try to do something to keep it running,' he says. 'We pulled it all together and formed the Heritage Boat Association in 2001, which is made up of heritage boats and barges from throughout Ireland.'

Plaques on the walls of his boat testify to Gerry's interest in inland waterway-based events. This year's rally has attracted forty boats, although frequently they have between fifty and sixty.

'The Grand Canal Company originally had horse-drawn boats,' Gerry says, 'and then towards the end of World War I they started motorizing them. In the early 1920s they began putting engines in old horse boats and there are a few here that were converted to motorized boats. They started with *1M* and it went up to *30M*. Then they designed and built a new fleet of boats with motors. The design of *33M* was the best design and that is it outside. *Chang Sha* is the oldest of all the boats here.'

The association is interested in preserving many different kinds of wooden boats, barges, lighters, tenders, steam tugs, yachts and ferries that have ended up on Irish inland waterways. These vessels provide a window into the past and a direct link with the people who worked on them. Gerry speaks about the history of his barge, *68M* (the M stands for 'motorized').

'My boat is one of the newer ones since it was built in 1936 and worked until 1960. We probably have the names of twenty people who worked on it in the 1940s and '50s along the Grand Canal Company, which was a public company owned by the state and integrated into CIE. The boat was going for twenty-four hours a day, six days a week with a four-man crew. The youngest, who was perhaps twelve, was called 'the greaser' and he might have been the son of the skipper, the engine man or one of the other men on board. When they were unloading, he was expected to carry twenty-stone sacks of corn and it was heavy manual labour. Then in 1946 it went from a four-man to a three-man crew, eighteen hours a day, six days a week. When the men loaded the Guinness in Dublin to go to Limerick, they had four days, but if they did it in three, they had a day off.'

Many of these barges, representing living history, were the juggernauts of their day when the canals were commercial waterways. They fell out of favour in the 1950s when road and rail took over, destroying the traditional transport network, leading to many becoming neglected. Some barges were converted into houseboats or cruisers. Gerry admits that the sight of old boats lying unloved in the water is a problem.

'Waterways Ireland do a clean-up every couple of years but effectively each one of those boats is somebody's dream. Technically if they're not paying their permit and are blocking the navigation then they could be removed, but they have to tread carefully because you're dealing with somebody's love affair, their hopes and aspirations. Those people did not buy it as it was — it started off as something else and they had grand designs for it on the waterway. Perhaps because of sickness, or for some other reason such as lack of time or interest, they couldn't take on the magnitude of the task that was required as it was a big job and the boats were left to the elements.'

For Gerry, the spirit of camaraderie about the weekend is important, even though there is a train-spotter mentality about the boating fraternity. 'A lot of us are into the history of the barges because we are real anoraks. It's also a community and a family event. Everyone knows everyone else and the boating community operates what we used to class as collective parenting, which you probably can't do anymore. If our kids were with others and if they were without a lifejacket, some other parents might ask them to get them so we all look out for each other. We could be here this weekend while on Monday we can pull into the canal bank and spend a week there and not see another person so you really are in step with nature. Unlike England, the canals in Ireland are very quiet, if not dead. Some people liken this to bringing their barge to a birthday party to celebrate.'

The traditional craft ownership clearly runs in the DNA of his family. Gerry and his brother have a barge, his daughter has a barge, and his son has one, and he likes to say that he has a couple of spare ones as well.

Next to Gerry's barge, Colin Becker owns one of the star names in the heritage barge world. *Chang Sha* dates from 1846, a time when Ireland was being ravaged by the Great Famine. For Colin and his fellow enthusiasts, it is a whole way of life.

'There is no rational explanation for what we do,' he says. 'If you tried to put a cost justification on what we do, it's an insane thing. Nobody owns seventy tons of steel that rusts faster than you can paint it. My boat is a hell of an age so it's about the history, heritage and the social interaction of the people. We might not meet each other for six months, but when we do, we just pick it up and carry on so it's that kind of a relationship. If somebody tries to justify owning a barge in terms of saving on foreign holidays it just doesn't work but there is something about turning up in Shannon Harbour where we have people photographing us on every pier. We've also got some young people who are catching what we call the barging disease.'

Beth O'Loughlin, who owns the boat next to Colin's, says the rally is partly about keeping the canals open. 'If we don't use them, we're definitely going to lose them,' she says. 'We've seen bits of it go into disrepair so that's part of the reason for the rally.'

Our talk turns to the perennial appeal of the river and the canal, and books written about the waterways. Through the years, the river has been documented from many different perspectives. Beth recently came across Hayward's Shannon book.

'I inherited a bunch of books from a man called Jimmy Dillon who many years ago was one of the first people to refurbish these old boats. And one of those books included *Where the River Shannon Flows*. I was fascinated by it as it gives a wonderful snapshot of the Ireland of the time. It is very much a period piece and is so interesting. I'm not sure what I learnt from it, but Hayward is of his time clearly, and I particularly loved the black-and-white hand-drawn map at the back of the book.'

The mid-century authors on the Shannon fed off each other in their writing but have since suffered neglect, with many titles becoming obscure. Colin feels that some of their work is stuck in a particular period.

'People reading Hayward's book would feel it a bit dated and maybe even a little bit pompous but then if you read *Green and Silver* by L.T.C. Rolt, which was published in 1949, it's the same, which is the way that authors wrote in those days.'

Gerry too has a copy of Hayward's book. 'It's probably at least twenty years since I read his journey down the Shannon but most of the barge owners would know of it and of the other books too, such as Harry Rice's *Thanks for the Memory* or *Voyage in a Bowler Hat* in which Hugh Malet cruised through Ireland and Britain in a sixteen-foot dory. Then in later years, Dick Warner and Ruth Delany wrote memorable books enhancing the long literary tradition. Most of us would have a good library of Shannon books and Hayward is as much a part of it as the others. It's important that the vignettes of their time are taken as he did.

The Georgian Harbour Master's House at Shannon Harbour is now run as a guest house.

We all have memories but our oral history is never going to get passed on like the previous generations. Whatever is ahead of the Internet – and no one knows that – oral history is just going to get lost and that's a shame.'

Beside the boats, the history-infused Harbour Master's House, a compact yet imposing grey and black Georgian guest house, is strategically placed at the waterfront. Built in 1806, it has three bays over a basement, single-storey wings with blind arches and windows, and retains its railings while a flight of steps sweeps up to the front door. The canal predates the house by fifty years since it began operation in 1756 with water traffic through Shannon Harbour and on to the River Shannon. It was a purpose-built village, designed and operated as a trans-shipping centre, and became a place of storage meeting the canal's requirements. I have checked into what might be termed the 'east wing' of the house, all of which feels agreeably lived in. The hall and staircase come with cream wainscoting and unexpected nooks, corridors and stairs leading in many directions. Framed photographs show the house in summer sunshine and iced with snow. The work of taxidermists is also on display. A stuffed fox catching a chicken in its jaws stands near stairs. A startlingly large black tiger's head is a commanding presence above the lounge fireplace, baring sharp white canine teeth. Gráinne Kirwan, who runs the guesthouse, was born in it. Her father, Eugene Byrne, was the last harbour master and she recalls where the tiger's head came from.

'My father was from the North Circular Road in Dublin and my mother was a nurse from Galway. The tiger's head was in his house and he brought it when he came here. It is stuffed and preserved, and as far as I know, came from Africa. It is quite a feature of the house. My father came here because he was doing relief work for the canal company and was positioned in different places, so whenever there was a harbour master on holiday, he would stand in. Eventually, in the late 1940s, the manager's position became vacant in Shannon Harbour so when he got that they moved in to live here. His job involved a lot of paperwork and hiring people. At that time all the barges that came from Dublin were laden with freight, feed, grain and alcohol and they were all checked off in the store. I can remember the barges coming in and big sliding doors with rails coming out of the shed on to the canal. They would unload a lot of stuff and he'd have to check it all, especially the alcohol.'

In 1999, after her parents had died, Gráinne decided to renovate the property and within a year had turned it into a guesthouse. She has become used to living in a place so full of history and heritage.

'The harbour master before my father was called Larkin — a well-known family in Tullamore. They had nine or ten children. Some of them have called occasionally to look at the house and to meet me. They would have known my father. We had electricity and the luxury of having a toilet.'

Today Gráinne's family uses the basement as a living area. In her father's time it was his domain and where he made oars. 'It's perfect for us, although the view is better from upstairs. At the back we look out on the restored walled garden and on to the callows while the canal is at the front. The view changes regularly with different boats coming in and out and we have a new view, day and night. We get to know the boaters as well as a lot of fishermen, walkers and cyclists so it's an interesting place to live.'

We look out at dozens of barges on a busy canal. Someone is making a megaphone announcement about an imminent barbeque. Gráinne talks about how the rally started forty-seven years ago.

'My father and the local headmaster, John Moore, and a Dublin barrister, a friend of my father, Gerry Brady, as well as a forester, Joe Deasy, were all involved. It started off as the Queen of Shannon Harbour but I don't think there were too many queens to be found, so it evolved into a boat festival. The people running it wanted to bring life to the harbour and that was the early 1970s and it's still going.'

There are other living animals running around the house too, including a white cat. It answers to the name of Hitler because of his short black philtrum-like moustache, below his lip rather than above it, unlike the Führer's. The cat cohabits with the stuffed animals and has become well known to visitors.

'Hitler strayed in about eight years ago, starving. She's a common everyday cat, but she's a bit nicer now with lovely fur and enjoys running around the place. But you have to remember that there wouldn't be Shannon Harbour without the boats, without the dogs, and of course without the cats running about the village.'

Next door to the Harbour Master's House, the Grand Canal Hotel, built in 1806, stands as a roofless, windowless three-storey ruin although the seven-bay Palladian facade and its shell are in good condition, a testament to the work of the stonemasons. The former hotel was built to a high specification with cut-stone detailing, rusticated quoins and eaves cornicing. It recalls the days 200 years ago when it provided shelter for more than 1000 people who lived in Shannon Harbour. These days, crows hover around the rafters. A low front wall is covered in a soft yellow moss alongside masses of sprouting wall rue. Most passers-by do not give it a second glance. The remnants of other stone buildings, such as warehouses, grain stores, a customs and excise post, RIC barracks with holding cells, as well as boat and barge repair dockyards and a drydocks are still to be seen.

Across the road, the Canal Bar is open for its once-a-year moment in the sun. The bar is on the ground floor of a large two-storey house, painted red, white and black. The top half of the external wall is splattered with shards of deep lapis lazuli blue glass mixed in with green and brown glass, pebbles and delft to produce a stunning effect. It is known to architects as dry dash, although some refer to it as spatter dash. It is everyone's idea of what an old bar should be: a half-door and a stone floor, low ceiling and dim lighting, cushioned benches beside a turf fire, red wainscoting with black trim. Beside the window, three musicians, calling themselves 'The Banksmen', enter into the spirit of the drinking theme on acoustic guitar, fiddle and a cajón drum with 'Whiskey in the Jar' and 'The Rare Old Mountain Dew'.

Despite not having been in use for 364 days, the bar is spotlessly clean and remarkably dust free. On a high shelf, china cups and saucers vie for space with pewter jugs, blue-and-white milk jugs and other curios. A large framed picture of Jerusalem hangs over the fireplace and elsewhere mirrors from Perry's Ale reflect the name of a once-famous brewery in neighbouring Laois. On a poster, a handwritten cocktail, 'Grandad's Dentures', made with pink gin, grenadine, lime juice and milk teeth, is advertised for €8. Nothing draws a crowd like a bar that opens once a year. Tonight, boaters and half-boaters, bussers, visitors, back-to-earthers, drinkers and tinkers are all quenching their thirst. A minibus on a pub tour of Offaly drops off twenty people stopping for their annual nightcap. One of their party tells me the bus is filled with 'buffalos', an acronym for 'big ugly fellas from around Laois & Offaly'.

A break in the revelry is announced for some mischief-making across the road. More than forty people have come to enjoy a game of strength, which involves rolling an empty beer keg up the incline of a car park to see who can achieve the longest distance. The idea is to keep the keg in a straight line, avoiding the kerb, if possible, and the spectators. After watching a few participants, I queue up taking my place and with a Herculean effort achieve three-quarters of the distance, being outpaced by two burly farmers showing off their muscles and dexterity. They become involved in a play-off for first place. The winner is presented with the Pat Henry Mischief Cup awarded in memory of a man with a love of Shannon Harbour. For the past four years various games such as welly throwing, footin' turf and skittles have been part of the festival fun. Back in the Canal Bar, the man in charge, Gerard, talks about running the premises on behalf of his aunt, Teresa Mann.

'She's in a back room and doesn't really like the crowds and the noise,' he says. 'It's a bit like a pop-up bar, but it's not, as most people believe, anything to do with the licence. My aunt doesn't need to open up for the licence but she likes to tie in the opening of it with the weekend heritage rally. In my opinion, the Irish pub has largely descended into self-parody. What we're providing is something more genuine but it's not a museum as it's still a lively working pub. We are without pretence – for example, we don't serve gin in fishbowl glasses.'

Two pawky men with beards of pre-Raphaelite bushiness contemplate the proceedings. 'We like to support the reopening of the bar,' one says. 'It's not very difficult to put your hand in your pocket once a year to keep it alive. There's nuttin' like it anywhere else in the country as far as we are aware and when it's tied in with the rally you get a decent crowd. If you got barred last year though, I'm not sure whether you're allowed back in this year.'

The other man talks about the difficulty of running a rural pub. 'It would be hard in a small place like this to keep it open all year round as there's a limited amount of sightseeing around here. The population of Shannon Harbour is only thirty-nine so you could have ten times as many people passing through this bar for the duration of its annual opening. They also like the turf fire and since many bogs are closing down, you'll find that more turf is cut in here than out on the bog itself. We have all these Blueways and Greenways nowadays and I don't know why we can't have Brownways running across the bogland.'

The bristle of gossip flows as freely as the taps. Sitting by the fire, an elderly man tells me that Offaly is known for the rhyming nature of its weather. It is, he quips, splashy, rainy and misty, other times foggy, haily and floody, and always muddy, soggy and boggy. A deluge of grievances follows about Offaly's broken infrastructure, its potholed roads, the lack of political will to develop the area or to clean up the canal of its ramshackle boats.

'They call it slow tourism,' a woman says, 'but it's so bloody slow that the whole place is dying. You might find it hard to credit this but Fáilte Ireland don't have a single tourist office in the entire county. They don't care about one-tractor towns so I don't know how they're planning to promote the hidden gems.'

Last orders are called for another year, and a disorderly queue forms three-deep at the counter. The musicians end with a rendition of some well-known songs and the community singing of 'Roll out the Barrel', leading to some high-stepping Shannon Harbour dance moves, resulting in a barrel load of fun. A bar in the midlands is not just a bar – it is music, theatre, drink-fuelled talk and original one-liners. The short opening has moved a customer to proclaim on his T-shirt: The drink in here is on me tomorrow.

10

Let the Bird Find You

FROM EARLY ON Sunday morning, horses, ponies and donkeys are being driven into Banagher's main street. The annual horse fair is a place of arrival for more than eighty animals along with hundreds of visitors. Road checks on the way into town are operated by gardaí and every truck and trailer is inspected. Warm winds blow up from the river and the sky is clearing. One of Ireland's oldest traditional horse fairs, it is an ancient if controversial gathering. In recent years the authorities have tried to move the organizers to a site at a new bypass on the outskirts, but those running the fair insisted that it be kept in the town centre. More than half of the long main street that runs uphill has been cordoned off to allow trading to take place.

It is already densely packed by the time I arrive and there is a raffish air. Horse boxes, lorries, trailers, tractors, transit vans and trucks fill both sides of the street. The central thoroughfare is a free-for-all. Heavy-bodied mares and kid goats compete for space with pigeon sellers and hens, all alongside families and shifty-looking tricksters in an easy-going camaraderie. Tweed-capped and wellington-clad farmers lean on long ash plants, scrutinizing animals. A drove of donkeys is tied up to a trailer's bars with blue bailing twine. Along one section of the street, thirty horses corralled at railings line up like supermodels on a catwalk. Amidst much whinnying, head-swivelling, champing at the bit, ear-twitching and scraping of hooves along the ground, they attract considerable interest from potential buyers.

A variety of equestrian paraphernalia is on sale. Stalls display second-hand saddles for €50, bridles for €20, lead ropes €10, bits and head collars €5, and what all best-dressed horses are wearing for the season: the 'must-have' Mustang two-tone, breathable, waterproof turnout rugs for €50. After wriggling through the crowds, I join a queue for coffee at Bob's catering wagon. A bristly man, moustachioed like a Mexican bandit, who has come to look rather than buy, says dealers are from all over Ireland and farther afield.

'Most of the horses here are half-bred or purebred and there's a few good quality hunters,' he says. 'You'll find a lot of cobs such as Connemara cross or Welsh cross, as well as a few sturdy Clydes, hunt horses and the Irish draught horse, but there are no thoroughbreds. It has always had a name for being a lucky place to buy or sell. Although it's not on the same scale as Ballinasloe, it still draws a big crowd and has survived against the odds.'

As he bites into a bacon butty, he advises me to be careful walking up the street. 'You could get a kick easily from an animal moving suddenly, and you'd need to look out for horse hooey on the ground, which can be a bit slippery.'

Across the street an owner leads his newly purchased pony away with an animated smile. Two pot-bellied men amble slowly down the footpath with small trays of chips. By 11 am horse trading is underway, although most deals appear to be furtive or out of the public eye. Softly-spoken buyers and sellers shuffle behind tractors or trailers. Wads of €50 notes pass through big coarse hands ending with a firm handshake. A tall dealer, restraining a jet-black Friesian horse of the type often used for pulling traps or carriages, says his animal is selling for €2500.

'You could pick up a sturdy Connemara pony here for €1100 or thereabouts but the prices go up and down, so you have to shop around,' he tells me.

On the stroke of midday, the Angelus bell signals a hush over the crowd as a minute's silence is observed in memory of Tom Moran, a horse trader revered throughout the country who died the previous week. At the Crescent, dull-eyed ponies are tethered, scratching themselves against the rusting white railings surrounding a carved limestone Celtic cross. At one corner of the monument, Dermot Moran stands beside a framed photograph of his father Tom. This year's fair is being held as a tribute to him for having run it through difficult times in the 1960s.

'He came from Lusmagh, just out the road, and was one of Ireland's most widely respected horsemen,' Dermot says. 'He was a stalwart here, knew everybody and was proud of the fair. One year he brought fifty horses and sold twenty-four of them, which I think was a record. Each year he had a regular spot on Church Street above Market Square. He was a great stockman. He could judge a beast through the bars of a gate from a distance. He had a natural eye for that and the experience to go with it.'

Dermot does not trade in horses but follows the action and knows what dealers are looking for. 'Buyers want to know about the animal's bone, the limbs and the body, and they like compact horses with a good back. They also want a horse with kind eyes and a placid temperament. If you see white in their eyes that could be a bit freaky. The legs are important too, and the way the animals are shod. Their teeth show their age and must be well looked after, so there's a lot to think about if you are buying. Many horses bought here are for hunting or riding schools and some go abroad. It's well organized and regulated these days, not like years ago. All horses, ponies and donkeys must have a valid passport. A microchip is injected into their neck for identification purposes and the information is on databases. If you're on welfare and you turn up here with ten horses the authorities will want to know where you got the money from.

'It was all different in my father's time. They used to have a weighing machine in the square and it was a big family occasion. The fair covered a much bigger area and ran right down to the

Shannon where horses washed in the river by a slipway. There were separate days for horses, cattle and pigs, and children were given three days off school. My father had a lot of time for horses but used to say that you should never fall in love with a horse; if you do, you'll never sell it.'

Dermot laughs at the mess of the street and footpaths. 'The simple fact is if you've got horses, you've got manure, and it shows they're healthy. There's an old saying, "shit luck is good luck". It all gets cleaned up and the women love it for their gardens as it's good for composting and helps the roses grow.'

Parishioners emerging from St Rynagh's Church across the street pause at the spectacle. The air is thick with the perfume of horse sweat and leather mixed with frying chips. A woman frowns like a Mother Superior. 'Jesus, Mary and Holy St Joseph,' she cries, crinkling her nose at the cheval shit on the footpath, hurrying off when a pure-white horse snorts at her. Looking on in benediction is the bearded and belted figure of Padre Pio, his right hand raised as though approving of the Sunday morning horsey business. Farther along, a group has gathered in a huddle around the magician and hypnotist Keith Barry who has turned up out of nowhere. He weaves a spell, shuffling card tricks, thrilling those present with his fast-talking comedy and magic and melting into the crowd as quickly as he has come.

Four teenagers, with hurls and a sliotar, organize an impromptu game in a front garden. A row of late-Georgian houses runs down to the riverside where a sweeping bridge links Offaly with Roscommon and Galway. The bridge is fortified on the west side by a small circular fort built against possible invasion by the French during the Napoleonic Wars. At the entrance to the marina, *The Musician*, a wooden sculpture of Johnny McEvoy, a famous musical son born here in 1945, has pride of place. 'Banagher you'll be my town until the day I die' proclaims a sign. McEvoy's most famous song was 'Mursheen Durkin', the story of an Irish emigrant who went off to mine for gold in California in 1849. His recording of it reached number one in Ireland in 1966.

Banagher marina in a late afternoon torpor.

THE SUN MOVES slowly in its arc. Piles of creamy cumulus clouds drift overhead high in a blue sky and the weather holds. Jackdaws, crows and starlings all circle the airspace while sand martins, which enjoy flying low over the water, nest in the old stone harbour walls beside the disused Waller's mill. Large and ebullient red admirals show off, busying themselves jinking a figure of eight along the listless riverbank where *Happy Ours*, *Paddy's Dream* and *Lady Lydia* are moored peaceably. Bumblebees crisscross the grass in an urgent manner seeking a nectar fix. Damselflies settle on waterside vegetation while dainty banded demoiselles come and go and dust motes drift in the air. Banagher marina is drowsing in a late afternoon torpor. Tiny whirlpools of water form and reform. A terrier sits on its haunches on the roof of a cabin beside collapsible bicycles lying strapped on deck. Some owners sunbathe, enjoying the quietness of a horse-free zone. The six-arch masonry span of the cut-stone bridge, completed in 1843, forms the county boundary between Offaly and Galway, and between Leinster and Connaught.

Proud and placid, the Shannon slumbers like a river of noble pedigree – which is more than can be said for the some of the buildings. The arrival experience into Banagher is not a pretty one. The bow-fronted and mustard-coloured Royal Shannon Hotel is an unsightly derelict property for a town badly in need of somewhere to attract visitors. There is a strong literary and historic connection to the boarded-up hotel since it is where the novelist Anthony Trollope, inventor of the pillar post box, was stationed when he worked for the post office, and in 1843 wrote *The Macdermotts of Ballycloran*. Trollope arrived in 1841, just in time to witness the Great Fair of Banagher, a four-day festival of horses. His chief work at Banagher was as post office surveyor investigating letters of complaint. In the 1960s James Pope-Hennessy, who wrote a compelling biography of Trollope, stayed in the hotel. It has been left to ruin and comes with rotting window frames, missing glass in the windows and peeling paint. Clumps of ivy and weeds grow from the roof and the garden is choked with dead plants. This first view of Banagher from boat users is a shame on the town.

Back at the fair, the crowd is thinning out. A teenager breaks in a chestnut foal by riding helter-skelter through the street, shouting as he careers between the remaining stalls. Turning a rising foxtrot into a canter, he causes commotion, scaring horses and leading to cries of 'Whoa! Whoa!' A man snorts, 'He's having trouble finding the handbrake.' Panicky screeching breaks out amongst a group of young girls. Two dun-coloured animals with light brown muzzles give a buck leap, throwing their hind ends upwards, keeping their feet planted on the ground. At the side of a lorry a piebald mare stamps, while three horses indulge in crow-hopping, another form of mild bucking. A donkey, ears erect, shies behind the back of a trailer. By 5.30 pm the day's bartering and haggling is done. Horse manure and hay is flattened, bins overflow and the street is a mess of polystyrene boxes, plastic bottles and cans. Horses are led into trailers, clumping up reluctantly. Some have second thoughts but are quickly shooed in again with hurley sticks.

The fabric of the town has not changed for many years. When he came here, Hayward noted that Banagher was famous for its fairs, distillery and old bridge, which had stood for over 500 years. The town was a *locus amoenus*, a place of safety and comfort, and added to his cosy and non-threatening portrayal of an older Ireland. He invoked the tagline 'That bangs Banagher and Banagher bangs the band' and tried to find out something about the slogan. Some people he met had never heard of the phrase, which moved him to expatiate:

> The more I saw of these Shannon towns the more I was convinced that the pleasant people who inhabit them have not the faintest interest in their past, and when you come to think of the preoccupation of the Irish people with political thought fiercely and immovably rooted in a past which they would be happier to forget, this is most strange.

The creeping vine tree growing outside Hough's bar in Main Street is a good reason to find out if anyone is aware of the old saying about Banagher. The tree reminds me of a quote from Frank Lloyd Wright: 'A doctor can bury his mistakes, but an architect can only advise his clients to plant vines.' Inside, owner Mick Hough is pulling two pints of Heineken.

'That vine has been growing at the front for nearly forty years,' he says. 'My wife planted it to make it bright. We cut it back every spring and it sprouts again but people like it and it brings curious visitors like yourself.'

A glowing fire burns to one side of the counter. I ask Mick about the Banagher phrase, but he says no one uses it today, although there is an annual weekend summer festival called 'That Beats Banagher'.

'It's a bit of a catchphrase really. Mind you, there was a landlord called Banagher. But as regards the town it's a place that is off the beaten track and this part of Offaly is under-visited. It's not a town that you come to by chance, it's a destination place and out on a limb. Banagher has not been fully exploited. It's a perfect location but the closure of the hotel is an awful loss. There's no accommodation, apart from a few B&Bs. The far side, Eyrecourt, is dead as well. There's not enough to hold people here. You need a good hotel and restaurant.'

Ancient teapots, kettles and lamps dangle from the ceiling. A naked red bulb burns, but the place is still dim. Two young musicians entertain the growing crowd with a run of jigs. Mick enjoys explaining the bar's history and how his family acquired it.

'My father bought it in 1949 from people called Bracken and we've owned it since then. Charlie Bracken died prematurely so the family left and emigrated to America and their offspring come back to the pub. There was one of them here last night. I took it over about 1977 and I've been serving full on fifty-five years or more. It hasn't changed much – we knocked out a couple of walls, the ceilings are the same. The original counter has moved. The women went into the snug and did not appear in the bar at all. This was one of the first pubs to have music on a regular basis when the folk scene took off in the late fifties. Then everything became a lounge bar. I remember going to Dublin when I started driving in '62 and I'd go into Mooney's and see the lovely marble top counter and the barmen all in white and there was no spitting, swearing or singing – there was no music allowed anywhere as it was counted rowdy.'

Times have changed. Music is an integral part of Hough's pub and an attraction for tourists. A series of reels spill out through speakers. Mick walks over to their corner and, accompanied by the musicians, holding the microphone close to his lips, launches into 'Love is Teasing' and a couple of Munster songs, 'Any Tipperary Town' and 'The Galtee Mountain Boy'. Chalked up on a blackboard is the day's special, the Salty Dog Cocktail, made up of Havana Club rum, Jamaican ginger beer and fresh lime with angostura bitters and ice. Two women at the bar order the house special, Shakalaka Boom shots, a mix of Irish whiskey and Bailey's cream liqueur. Mick takes up duties again and while he is waiting for four pints to settle, talks about the visitors who come to the area.

Mick Hough pictured with the vine growing outside his bar in Banagher, County Offaly.

'We get repeat German business coming for more than forty years and they also bring their friends. But the smoking ban ten years ago killed off an awful lotta people. There's some I've never seen since it, although maybe they're dead. But then again, I'm alive now but maybe I wouldn't be alive if the ban hadn't come in because the smoke wasn't good for you. I enjoy talking to people and meeting them, and people meet each other here too.'

Not only does Mick enjoy talking to people, he also enjoys performing. After he slips from behind the bar again, more songs pour forth in a rich baritone, including 'The Lonely Woods of Upton' and 'Down by the Salley Gardens'. He joins the musicians on the bodhrán for 'Toss the Feathers', while 'Aggie's Waltz' rouses several drinkers on to the small dance floor. They negotiate their way around old sherry barrels repurposed as tables with empty wax-covered bottles of Jameson and Rabbit Island, a slow-distilled Irish gin. Mick moves at lightning speed behind the bar, pulling pints and shooting the Shannon breeze about horse prices. He speaks about the self-belief that the fair brings to the town.

'There used to be a lot of caravans, it was caravan after caravan in the 1950s – there would be a big crowd of farmers and the horses would be from the hill to the bridge about a mile long. They took over the whole town and you'd a week's holidays from school. My mother had a draper's shop up the town and sometimes a cow would smash a window in it. There would have been working horses and the Irish draught. The horses were used in World War I and in earlier European wars. I was never really a horseman, but my wife bought draught mares. They've been trying their best to stop the fair and there are restrictions on everything from diesels to donkeys. You even have to have official papers for a donkey – isn't that going a bit far? I paid 80 euro to get a foal microchipped yesterday. The best thing about the fair is that there is no committee, it just happens with a few people organizing it. But there are heavy checks from the guards, customs and revenue who like to target fair-goers, and then there's the passport-for-horses brigade.'

Mick breaks off to say he can feel another song, or three, coming on. He takes up his perch again beside the piano with the toe-tapping evergreens 'The Leaving of Liverpool', 'The Last Thing on My Mind' and a shimmy into 'Streets of London', before he stills the bar with the haunting 'Red River Valley'. Speaking in a rapid-fire Offaly accent, a feisty man at the bar wheezes with a smoker's lungs about his old job. He was, he said, head butler at the hotel many years ago. When I query the aspect of a hotel having a butler, he corrects me with a wicked horse laugh: 'Head bottler … I washed the bottles.' Mick re-joins the chatter, talking about the Ireland of today and how, in his opinion, it has changed for the worse.

'My view is that for Ireland the European Union was a bad choice. This country was different, and we should have kept our individuality, which has been completely lost. We've gone into this legalistic thing of a law for this and a law for that … If you can't take two pints and drive out a back road there's something wrong. It's down to responsibility. I'm not arguing for the pubs as most people are responsible and you don't drive when you're drunk. I remember bringing patients to the hospital in Tullamore and back then there were thousands working, especially in Bord na Móna. Every farmer employed a farm labourer. We had factories here and there and still there was never a backlog in the hospital. And it was free to all intents and purposes. You could get a doctor or a taxi any hour of the night. Now it's a merry-go-round of gay marriage, abortion and euthanasia, all going the same way as Europe. We've gone overboard to be liberal and we have thrown away an awful lot.'

The fiery duo brings the exhilarating entertainment to a brisk-paced end, their tunes embellished with occasional yelps and yee-haws from the appreciative audience. Mick could well have a one-man stage show but prefers to alternate his musicianship with his bartending. By early morning his voice is reduced to that of a horse-whisperer. He has by no means exhausted his extensive song collection, but the burning embers are fading, the lights turned off and the front door is locked. He shakes hands with me.

'You've come on a good day. From what you've seen at the fair, you can tell all your friends that on a day like this Banagher is certainly not a one-horse town and tomorrow it'll be a no-horse town.'

THE PHYSIOGNOMY OF the Shannon has long interested scientists and rheologists. In the mid-1950s an American army engineer was brought in by the Irish government following severe flooding of the river. Colonel Louis Rydell, of the US Army Corps of Engineers, had experience of taming the Mississippi down to New Orleans and was regarded as an expert on flood control. He spent considerable time working out the channels to be dredged in the Shannon and its tributaries and suggested an 'aggressive approach'. His report reflected the complexities of the situation: 'Drainage improvements on one of the tributaries … might solve the problem, but by accelerating the flood run-off might create another problem on the main stem.' He conceded that the difficulties were immense, needing much further study, before he moved on to tackle the Indus in Pakistan. But he emphasized the navigation, fisheries, recreation and wildlife potential of the Shannon, which he considered to be 'one of the world's great rivers'.

This accolade stands alongside many epithets that have been applied to the Shannon by writers, travellers, poets, musicians and other chroniclers. The most overused adjective is 'majestic', but it is also frequently referred to as 'lordly', 'mighty', 'spacious', 'noble', 'slumbering' or 'stately'. Hayward classified it as 'the great mother river of Ireland'. The Kerry novelist Maurice Walsh, who wrote the foreword to Hayward's book, called the river 'immense'. He said it once separated the Pale from Hell – 'though there was a small dispute as to which side Hell lay'. The elegist of the Irish midlands, John Broderick, was less flattering, referring in *The Waking of Willie Ryan* to the river's 'silent, menacing presence'. Writing in his autobiography *Nostos*, the Kerry-born poet, mystic and philosopher John Moriarty described the estuary from Tarmons Hill near Tarbert as: 'A grandeur of water ... the Shannon flowing through it with a landscape that had in it a remembrance of Paradise.' In the final passage of his short story 'The Dead', Joyce writes of the 'dark mutinous Shannon waves'.

Rivers are not permanent features of the landscape. They expand and flood, they silt up, erode and change course, adapting to the weather. The Shannon is referred to by scientists as 'water-rich' because it drains a fifth of the island of Ireland. Astonishingly, more than 1600 lakes, rivers and tributaries feed into it. By far the biggest problem in recent years has been its susceptibility to flooding, although as those who live alongside it are aware, it has flooded for centuries. On my journey I have heard about these inundations in Carrick-on-Shannon (which became known as Shannon-on-Carrick), Athlone and other towns. Online pictures show how the river rose inexorably to record levels, looking like a Cajun swampland with roads submerged and pastures and bogs turned into paddy fields. Heavy rainfall caused the river to bloat, overflowing sewers creating havoc and confusion. The water had nowhere to go, overloading drains and setting off floods.

Amongst older Shannonsiders, the specific years of the never-ending battle of flooding are embedded deep in their collective cerebellum. The winter of 1954/45 (when Col Rydell came to try to solve the problems) saw the worst ever flooding with the Shannon Valley declared a disaster area and hundreds of families forced to leave their homes. Other serious periods included 1965/66, 1985, 1990, 1999, 2002, 2009/10, 2015/16 and February 2020. In 1928 the area from Athlone to Portumna turned into a vast chain of lakes, and in the winter of 1924/25 it reached what were then record levels. Several years earlier, in January 1916, many villagers were swamped when floodwater rose up to four metres above the normal level and southerly gales swept away cattle, hens and geese. In 1911 and 1913 a semi-biblical deluge meant that people had to resort to boats for shopping and the postman used a boat to deliver the mail, while 'abnormal' flooding was reported in 1910.

A litany of 'worst' water surge dates harks back to the nineteenth century and earlier. After the devastating floods of November 2009, Met Éireann described the rainfall during the month as a 'once-in-a-500-year event'. Their prediction was wide of the mark by 494 years since just six years later, during the winter of 2015/16, a similar inundation took place and still the problems persisted. In February 2020 three major storms with record levels of rainfall caused grief for landowners and severe hardship in homes and businesses, swallowing up gardens and driveways in parts of Leitrim, Westmeath, Roscommon, Offaly and Clare. Much of the flooding down the decades has been caused by bad planning and allowing houses to be built on river flood plains. The intensity of the storms has worsened, creating a terrifying experience for locals with a dangerous and destructive potential. One woman well versed in the river's cantankerous force of nature is Maura Flannery, who runs Dún Cromáin B&B just outside Banagher. The scale of the floods remain long in her memory due to the amphibious nature of it creating a stubborn wall of water, which left her isolated for weeks on end on her road.

'Many people who stay here love the view of the river, but others don't realize it's there and that we are adjacent to it as it's just on the other side of Crank road. In November 2009 it flooded for three weeks but when it happened in 2015 it flooded in December for three weeks before Christmas and then for three weeks after into mid-January. We were completely marooned and the only way we could get in or out was by a tractor and even that was dodgy at times. The road was flooded up to our thighs and we had to wear waders. If it had been any higher, we wouldn't have been able to use the tractor. It was crazy, we had swans floating around because they hadn't a clue and were all confused wondering what was going on.'

During this deluge hundreds of homes in different parts of the midlands suffered devastating damage with up to 600 people evacuated and others cut off by rising water levels. In one estate in Banagher, suction tankers were brought in to clear the floodwater with additional sandbags.

'The house escaped, so from that point of view we were lucky, but we could not get in or out and the tractor ferried people into town. Our cars were brought in on a low-loader but we couldn't use them and they had to remain parked in town. I had some people booked in and had to cancel them but a couple from England insisted on coming even though I explained the situation. They got a lift back here at night and we used a transport box attached to the back of it, which of course is normally used for animals. They absolutely loved it as it was great fun but at the same time it was a horrendous pain in the ass and frustrating to have to live through that for six weeks. My two daughters have children and they were both coming to me for Christmas that particular year so Santa had to come on the back of the tractor. At the time they said everybody would get compensation if they were affected. I lost some business and had insurance and applied but because the house wasn't flooded, and I don't pay rates, they wouldn't cough up.'

As a result of excessive floodwaters the cumbersomely entitled Shannon Flood Risk State Agency Coordination Working Group was established by the government in 2016 as a single authority to include all agencies and to prevent any further flooding. The Mid Shannon Flood Relief Group, made up of people living in the area from Athlone to Portumna who were adversely affected by the floods of 2009 and 2015 and 2020, called for drastic action to redress the situation, even threatening to block cruisers from using the river. In 2018 the national Catchment Flood Risk Assessment and Management Study (CFRAM) for the Shannon River Basin proposed a €10m programme of concrete-and-glass defence walls, flood gates and drainage work to protect 550 properties. As far back as 1979 there were calls for an overall plan. A major blueprint to drain the river was produced with a deputation to government seeking to have the Shannon treated as a single entity rather than development taking place on an ad hoc basis, but still nothing came from it. In 2000 an inter-party committee found a lack of integrated management. Overlapping, sometimes contradictory roles have been held by different organizations. There is a certain Shannon stoicism about it all – those not directly affected call it 'Shannon-freude' – but many still live in fear of the next weather forecast. According to Maura, the single biggest problem is that there is still no holistic or cohesive multi-agency approach to the management of the river.

'There are so many vested interests with the ESB, the OPW, Bord na Móna, local councils, the farmers, the fisheries, wildlife people, the cruisers, Inland Waterways, Irish Water, the heritage service, and they're all pulling in different directions. If the river becomes too low then the boats aren't able to travel along it. We have to look after the fishermen as we get a lot of business from them during the year with several festivals. After the last flooding there was great talk of a plan to have one body in charge of the Shannon but it never happened.'

During 2017 a series of what are known as Shannon 'pinch points' were highlighted to be removed with the aim of improving the river's conveyance capacity. There are eighteen pinch points between Athlone and Meelick and their removal will reduce water levels by up to 45 cm. Many proposals have been mooted to try to solve the crisis, such as siltation, dredging the riverbeds and draining or widening the river. But despite it all, red tape has slowed down the process and there is still a sense of uneasiness about the river. Taming the Shannon is difficult, and the levels are at the mercy of the weather. Many people believe the tributaries need to be cleaned and Maura says serious work has still to be done to allow local people to cope with their intractable predicament during extreme weather.

'Pinch points, where the river narrows, may help. And there are an awful lot of overhanging branches along the river and if a lot of them could be cut back it would improve the situation and allow the water to flow more freely. Other people feel that dredging the river would help but I'm not sure about that. The ESB let the water off and when they do that up here Limerick could be flooded as there seems to be a knock-on in other places. It always has flooded, and it probably always will, so we have to live with that. I can remember girls out here taking off their shoes and stockings and walking in through the floods to go to the dance hall. It would be great to have a footpath and lights here leading into the town as it's narrow for people walking at night, although it's not a busy road.'

An element of resignation is palpable about living so close to the river but Maura feels that the town itself is in a sorry state and needs to improve its image, especially in relation to the hotel.

'Banagher is one of the worst towns in Offaly as regards closed-up businesses. It suits me, to a degree, that if you come here you have to stay in a B&B as there is no hotel. But I would prefer if the hotel was hopping and I was getting a spin-off from that. Back in the Celtic Tiger years, you could build a house anywhere you wanted. There's an estate near the bridge just before the old hotel and that was always a swamp and yet they built houses on it. They just about escaped in the last flooding, but the sewerage came up everywhere and people had to be evacuated out of it for a few days. At least the houses weren't destroyed, but it was an awful mess.'

ORNITHOLOGY CHRISTENS it *Alcedo atthis*, and in Irish it is called *cruidín*, but most recognize it by its common name, the kingfisher. It is also known in Irish as *biorra an uisce*, meaning 'water-spear'. On my journey so far, the bird's image has haunted me on signposts, sculpted in wood and framed in portrait; prior to this I had only ever come across the bird in Ireland on calendars, crockery and postcards along with some sightings on foreign travel.

In the offices of BirdWatch Ireland in Banagher I seek advice from Brian Caffrey about the Shannon population of the bird. His office, shared with several others, is a veritable birding library. Piles of folded Ordnance Survey maps sit on a shelf and a tower of books holds bird reports and atlases, as well as monographs and studies of different species. Boxes are filled with back copies of *Wings*, BirdWatch Ireland's magazine, with its motto 'protecting birds and biodiversity'. Resplendent on the most recent issue is a stunning photograph of a kingfisher. The bird has just ambushed a minnow and is captured jumping out of the river, the fish clasped in its beak, a wheel of spray droplets of water sprinkling from the architecture of its feathers. Brian has carried out studies on the kingfisher, one of the shortest-lived of all birds.

'They are a pretty difficult species to survey because they are small, fairly secretive, and not terribly easy to see. One of the ways that we work is through the large-scale surveys such as the bird atlas. The most recent one gives a snapshot of how all our bird species are faring over that period and whether numbers are increasing or declining. If we want more in-depth knowledge as to how kingfishers are faring, we need to do specialized surveys. This means walking along riverbanks and has involved canoeing downriver looking for territories and trying to figure out the numbers, so it is very intensive.'

The population of the kingfisher waxes and wanes with cold and mild years. One of the things that is known to affect the birds adversely is bad winter weather, when a cold snap or severe flooding has a big impact on them.

'The latest atlas shows that in Ireland generally over the last forty years the population of the kingfisher has dropped nationally by about one quarter. You can have local impacts on the birds, such as river pollution, but overall the decline of roughly 25 per cent would be similar for the Shannon. It is not a perfect science but the imperfection is consistent over time so we repeat the same methods every twenty years because it is a tried and trusted system. It is the consistencies of the imperfections that make it repeatable and therefore the data can be compared, which gives a good snapshot of the change that has taken place.'

Brian came to work in Banagher in 2003 on a six-month contract and has remained ever since. He says that the favourite habitat of the kingfisher is slow-moving rivers.

'The Shannon is a large wide river and, from the kingfisher point of view, fairly deep and they like relatively slow-moving and shallow areas which they can dive into for their prey. You have fantastic backwaters, which are islands in the middle of the main river. You also have back channels where cattle have gone down to the river's edge and that is where sticklebacks or minnows go. If there is a branch out over the edge or a reed for the bird to perch on, that's often where I see them.'

According to the most recent bird report, *Birds in Central Ireland 2012–2016*, kingfishers are 'widespread on rivers and streams' and I am interested in finding out where I can see them on the Shannon.

'One of the best spots is on the Little Brosna where there is a bird hide on Ashton's callow. There is a drainage ditch and you might find it there. Victoria Lock, not far from here, is also one of my favourites spots. In the past there were kingfishers' nests in the old stonework of the building itself. Traditionally they burrow into the back of stonework and there are records of them in man-made structures. In Shannonbridge too there is a record in recent years of a bird nesting in the stonework of one of the historic sights next to the river.'

Although they may be widespread, the birds are extremely difficult to spot and luck and patience play a part. Ninety per cent of people see only a blue blur going past. Brian has watched them in flight and describes the best approach to spotting them.

'Nine times out of ten their flight path is always a dart along the river. But from time to time I have been lucky enough and just by chance when standing still one will come fairly close to you. It's a matter of trying to pin down the site, and if you go for a walk along the riverbank you are increasing your chance of seeing them but you might be flushing them off a perch and you might just see a dart in the distance. They are superb fishermen and dive to take minnows and insects but the flow of the river is really key because they can only dive to a certain depth and they need a level of clarity in the water to see their prey. During a high flood level they would move well off the middle channel and go to the edges for shallower water.'

Brian says their best estimate is still the *New Atlas of Breeding Birds in Britain and Ireland 1988–91*, which shows the Irish population at between 1300 and 2100 birds. He speaks about how other birds, specifically the corncrake and the curlew, have fared. The latter is nearing extinction and experts reckon that its bubbling and haunting call may soon be lost.

'It's scary how the curlew is disappearing so quickly. The last count that we had on the callows is somewhere between twelve and fifteen pairs at the most between Athlone and Portumna. Huge efforts are needed to try to save it as nationally only about 130 pairs are left so it really is on the brink and will take a very big effort to pull it back. As for the corncrake, it has gone from this area but fifteen years ago when I came here, there were up to thirty calling males and ten years before that perhaps up to eighty but they were dwindling continually.'

Brian feels that because the kingfisher is not celebrated enough, schoolchildren may not recognize it. He makes some suggestions about how I may see it.

'You have to remember their basic hunting strategy is stillness. Your search for the kingfisher is similar to my quest for killer whales. I've gone to many countries and spent hundreds of hours looking for orcas and never seen them. If you just keep trying then it will happen and at the time you least expect it. You have to wait for the bird to turn up, you can't force it, so let the bird find you.'

Following Brian's advice, I drive out the Crank road to Victoria Lock. It passes a disused canal, ancient bridges, a long-forgotten derelict lock, and throws up mysterious and largely unseen watery worlds. For the length of its ten-kilometre course, the road bends, kinks and weaves with offshoots leading down inviting boreens. It starts in a narrow fashion at the Liffey Mills in Banagher. Three kilometres later the road shrinks to a single track and degenerates into potholed tarmac with a grassy central strip. In the 'olden days' of the 1970s, drivers referred to them as potholes, but the new prosaic term is roads with 'severe structural distress' consisting of deep craters, crumbling surfaces and in some cases roads that are undriveable because of a plague of potholes. In a survey of the network of roads falling apart in all counties, Offaly notched up 14 per cent and came second worst (after Monaghan with 15 per cent). Shortage of money and bad weather have all played their part. With careful negotiation, I pull over at a gate opening to let a 'Classy Massey' pass, followed by two vans and a 4x4. When I step outside, all around is movement and restlessness. There is an energizing chill to the air, which is fizzing with courtship and saturated in birdsong.

The grey and green countryside colours are transformed by more than twenty large pink-wrapped circular silage bales piled high at a farmyard. The purpose of the bright eye-catching bales is to raise funds for the Irish Cancer Society through a rural campaign called 'Wrap it Pink'.

The abandoned remnants of Hamilton Lock, dating from pre-1840, are tucked away beside a disused canal across the road from the original white lock-keeper's house from 1755, which is maintained in excellent condition, although unoccupied. The wooden struts of the rickety bridge are not secure enough to walk across while other pieces of timber structure are discoloured and lie mildewed with broken gates. Stone steps lead to what was the Clonaheenoge Canal. I gaze down into the dilapidated lock and although stone walls are intact there is no sign of any birdlife until a couple of wood pigeons start their soft cooing. Following a sign for Victoria Lock, the road crosses a narrow bridge and cattle grid. I scan a large body of water across a bridge but to my chagrin the kingfisher still continues to play hide-and-seek. This wide stretch of waterway, which I mistakenly believe to be the Shannon, is called the New Cut. The river itself, although nearby, seems secluded and remote.

The single-storey Victoria Lock from the 1840s replaced Hamilton Lock and is an impressive example of canal architecture. It was built to accommodate large Shannon steamers carrying passengers in the mid-nineteenth century. The old stone building is undergoing repair and the area is cordoned off with railings while tools lie against its walls. It is now used as a canteen and for storage while offices were built in 1991. Stephen McGarry, the full-time lock-keeper, is a softly spoken man with a navy jumper proclaiming Waterways Ireland. New main gates, he says, are replacing the old ones, which are rotten. He agrees there is a mysterious allure about Crank road, which he says is 'lost in time'. Stephen talks about the New Cut, a man-made spur leading off the Shannon with sluice gates controlling the level of water in winter and summer.

'This is my cockpit, and my job involves opening the gates, lifting the lock gently and letting the boats into the lock. I check the names and numbers of the boats, log the times and enter the details into a book. Every morning I check the levels of water and the rainfall and bring that into the ESB.'

The same position has presided in his family for more than four generations. 'My great-grandfather came down from Leitrim in 1906. He was a lock-keeper and his son took over from him, and in turn his son passed it on to myself, so I'm here twenty-three years. In many ways, the job is similar as we have always helped and guided boats through the lock, but they have changed from working barges to tourism cruisers. These started in the last fifty years or so although there would have been some here earlier than that but it really kicked-off in the 1970s. There's still some fishing but it's not as good as it used to be.'

The days of the sturdy, dependable barges carrying cargo have long gone. Luxurious cabin cruisers and canal boats built for comfort now ply the waters but the reassuring figure of a lock-keeper is still important to many sailors. Apart from the outdoor nature of Stephen's job, in which he revels, one of his pleasures is in coming across people from different countries.

'Some are terrified, they panic about the lock and I have to calm them down, talk them through it and point them in the right direction. After that they're happy and go on to enjoy their holidays. For some, it's their first time hiring a boat and they haven't got a clue. They are so frightened that sometimes I bring the boat in for them and let them out again, but it's better that they learn how to do it for themselves. The main visitors these days are Austrians and Americans, but the Irish are using it more too. The Dubs love to escape from the traffic and chaos of the city. People who come here are not in a rush, they're getting away from the rat race. They often don't understand how quiet it is and then they might see a swan, which comes in with them, keeping them company.'

Apart from looking after the boat-owners' demands, Stephen is a wildlife-watcher and speaks about the birds he has seen diving for aquatic insects or small fish. 'Many's a time I've seen kingfishers, not so much on the main channel but on the back canals where it's quieter with fewer boats, so that would be your best bet to find them. Sometimes they're on trees but they could be perched anywhere. They're in and out, opening their wings on impact with the water, zooming around with a flash of blue, but you can see all sorts of ducks and waders such as golden plover here.'

On cue, in the distance, we transfer our gaze to a fast-flying, tight-knit party of over one hundred *Pluvialis apricaria* caught in the morning sunlight, rising, twisting, turning and hurtling in synchrony over the water like fragments of silver foil, a mesmerizing spectacle.

'Nature is mighty, and I love to watch such a great sight, but once you see it every day you tend to take it for granted. The plovers are on the callows and you see them quite a bit of the time. We have a lot of different species of ducks during the winter and you'll hear most of the smaller birds although you may not see them all. I've had glimpses of otters around here too but they are also elusive.'

The sun hits large rocks on the water. Stephen points out that this feature marks the three counties rock where Tipperary, Offaly and Galway meet. It has also another unusual topographic claim to fame since it is the tripoint of Connaught, Munster and Leinster. He is uncertain about the longer-term future of the keepers of the locks. Smart cards have recently been introduced at Athlone lock as part of the rollout of a new testing system on the Shannon. It is already being used along the river for services such as showers, toilets, pump-outs and electricity. I ask if he thinks his job will exist in years to come.

'They're trying to introduce it by a do-it-yourself system, which is a bit too fast for people who come in a hire boat. There mightn't be a lock-keeper in fifty or a hundred years' time but people still want the personal touch and need the help we provide. My son has not committed yet as he is only thirteen. A lot of the full-time lock-keepers have recently retired and been replaced by seasonal staff. There were fourteen and now it is down to about seven or eight full-time ones, but no one can predict what the future will bring.'

On his journey, in the upper reaches of the Shannon, Hayward too met a lock-keeper, making observations about the pace of life in the late 1930s: 'There's a dreadful amount of meaningless hurry in the world, and with the growth of the Machine Age it is rapidly getting the better of us. To think more and hurry less was clearly the philosophy of this old lock-keeper, and the more I ponder it the more I like it.'

With the passing of eighty years his words still resonate, reflecting a similar outlook on life by Stephen McGarry, a latter-day guardian of powerful lineage holding down a job which has survived, against the odds, into the twenty-first century. His 'office' on this stretch of river ranks as one of the Shannon's pockets of bucolic peace, an atmospheric enclave of land and water.

PART III

Lower Shannon

'A road map is the printed lyrics to a siren's song where highways and rivers are like stanzas, and the little circles indicating towns are notes – some flat, some sharp, a few off-key.'

William Least Heat-Moon,
Here, There, Elsewhere:
Stories from the Road

11

Holy War on Holy Island

BY EARLY SEPTEMBER 1939 Hayward's party reached Portumna. After enjoying a meal in Keary's Hotel they were given advice about a camping site and directed to the grounds of a deer park at the Belle Isle Sports Hotel, the former mansion of Lord Avonmore near the head of Lough Derg. Hayward was full of *joie de vivre* and his party was anticipating the final stages of their Shannon journey. The date was Sunday 3 September, a day that has been imprinted into history and which would stay long in his memory:

> I shall never forget that breathless moonlit night in the quiet little town as, walking up the main street, we heard coming through an open window serious news of the European situation given out in a special radio bulletin. We stopped dead in our tracks outside that open window, tense and silent as we listened to the ominous words. The little town lay quiet and peaceful all around us, looking strange and unearthly as the bright, silvery light of the moon transmuted the ordinary things of day into magic things of the night … we found it hard to credit the black news which was coming to us, telling us that within a few days Europe must once again be plunged into the red ruin of bloody war.

Worldwide events had now suddenly become instant. The announcement by Neville Chamberlain that Britain was at war with Germany occupied the minds of Hayward's party that evening. More than two-thirds of the way through their Shannon odyssey, they were preparing to explore Lough Derg, as well as Limerick and its estuary, and were determined to complete their trip. When they returned to the Belle Isle camping grounds, the grim news of the impending war was put to one side when they discovered that a mare with a foal in the deer park had run amok, biting several corners off their caravan and tearing a long strip from the canvas hood of their Austin car. 'It seemed,' Hayward recounted, 'that the war in Belle Isle had started already,' and they speedily moved to another part of the demesne where they were separated with high fences from further animal attacks. The next day they explored Portumna, which he described as 'the cleanest and most cheerful-looking town in the West'. With its flowers, spick-and-span house fronts and fresh paint, it was a contrast to many shabby towns through which he had often passed in Ireland.

Fast-forward eight decades and there are few flower boxes around Portumna. Withered weeds sprout through the pavement. Salons and shops specializing in beauty, hairstyling, health and nutrition are lined up along the main street in between supermarkets, a Polish shop and farm and dairy services, along with the statutory immobilized petrol pumps outside Martin's pub. Portumna manages to squeeze itself into south-east Galway and enjoys a relationship with the Shannon, as well as sites at the mouth of Lough Derg. It is a major nexus with no fewer than eight roads converging on it from different directions, while the bridge is a historic crossing point. It takes some time to get my bearings, although just thirty minutes to walk its two main streets and a cross street – but to *really* get to know it takes years.

One man who has spent five years on meticulous research is John Joe Conwell, a retired teacher who has produced the definitive book on the parish – which weighs three kilos, runs to 860 pages and contains 1000 photographs. We meet outside St Brigid's Church for a tour of the town.

'In the early seventeenth century the Norman de Burgh family moved their seat of power to Portumna and built the castle between 1610 and 1618. At that time the Shannon was the highway through Ireland, equivalent to the M6 and M7. All livestock, grain, butter, eggs and other produce left from Connaught Harbour. Large boats would go around the various harbours on Lough Derg and collect cattle and bring them here and then they would go on to smaller boats and upriver.'

Historically, John Joe says, Portumna always punched above its weight. It came into existence as a market town granted by charter to the Clanricardes, a powerful family connected to royalty.

'The 14th earl built a new street and a fair green in the 1930s. Everything was laid out around the green and it was terribly important for a town to have one. The Irish state acquired the private farm and demesne of the Clanricardes in 1948 but years earlier, in 1929, we had a very engaged parish priest, Monsignor Timothy Joyce, who applied to the council to have all the streets renamed so old main street was divided up into Abbey Street and Dominick Street. There was a little cross street that became Patrick Street and the new street became Brendan Street.'

In his book, John Joe has written about Hayward's visit to Portumna and quoted from his romantic view of the town:

'The Portumna that he saw would not have had too many cars. Monsignor Joyce would have had a car and possibly the doctor for his calls. He used to travel to Switzerland and other places and brought back ideas. He immersed himself in all aspects of the parish and encouraged people to create flower boxes, dressed up the town square and laid it out in a floral arrangement. This was long before the tidy towns competition was introduced and Portumna was held up as a model town largely due to his work. Any travellers who came here during that period were hugely impressed about how clean the town was. Belle Isle House, where Hayward camped, was owned by Lord Avonmore for a period and at that time it was a sports hotel. Keary's Hotel, which he also mentions, was right in the middle and was very much involved in the land war in the 1880s where the rent was collected from the people. The hotel changed hands quite a few times and is now Ashe's pub.

'Portumna is one of those towns that has what they like to call "potential". This region can capitalize on many things such as the old railways, grand houses and the hills or waterways. The future is going to be amenity-driven, with the Slieve Aughty mountains and Lough Derg on our doorstep and the river. The Shannon is no longer a trade route, it is now a leisure route … But to fully appreciate what's around needs a team of people who understand it, are able to interpret it, and to impart it authentically and accurately, and that's the challenge for the future.'

John Joe believes that a new generation of Portumna people are taking an interest in their past and although many are scattered worldwide as part of the diaspora, he detects a greater interest in history.

'In the past, people were not much interested in their history, which Hayward writes about in his book. They did not care much about what had gone before. Our past has, of course, been very sad. It is conquest and colonization when you go back to the Vikings and the Normans, and the various plantations of Laois and Offaly, so people wanted to forget about the pain of that.'

We soak up the architecture of the town through its historic buildings. Solid and substantial structures such as the courthouse and the former RIC barracks are closed, seeking a new purpose. Our tour ends on St Brigid's Road at the nineteenth-century Irish Workhouse Centre, a relic of post-Famine Ireland. The building is a complete workhouse with all four wings in place although more work is being carried out on its restoration. Like many small towns in the midlands, Portumna has been blighted over the years by emigration with young people leaving due to a lack of opportunity and jobs.

'It is somewhat of a retirement place,' the man in charge, Steve Dolan, says, 'and the age profile and demographics aren't brilliant. Some refer to it as "the town of the Golden Girls" as there are people with more time on their hands because they're not working full-time. But it's important to say that the women are the powerhouses and very often they have come from other parts of the county, or even of this country or abroad, and they drive a lot of the societies and groups within the town. These are the people we need and whose skills we can leverage. One of the women is an accomplished US politician who brings her experience, and we've a Vietnam veteran who volunteers at the Workhouse. He's brilliant, as is his wife who works in marketing and advertising.'

Down at the long steel bridge on the outskirts of the town past Connaught Harbour, a sign declares Portumna 'Gateway to the West'. A boarded-up tollhouse detracts from the view while traffic trundles across. In the distance lies Belle Isle House and its grounds in north Tipperary where Hayward and his party camped. Portumna boasts Ireland's first urbanized glamping centre, the Pod Umna Village in Dominick Street, part of the eco-tourism drive, where I check in for the night.

The owner, Dick Ridge, shows me around a range of small wooden cabins. 'They're designed on the concept of the Gallarus Oratory,' he says, 'which is a humble stone church on the Dingle peninsula and resembles the arch-shape of an upturned boat.'

The well-spaced cabins, made of red deal timber with roofs of composite metal, are insulated throughout with Earthwool insulation for extra warmth.

'I'm told that it's very therapeutic to sleep in timber as there's great energy from it,' Dick says. He is well aware of the work involved in running the pods. 'We've had lean times but any money we have made we reinvested back in, continually improving the appearance of the place. People love coming to stay in them. Trip Advisor is an honest way of getting feedback from guests and we've been awarded a certificate for a Centre of Excellence for the last four years.'

Later that night, the fairy lights dangling around the front door of the pods and decking transforms the area. My pint-size cabin, Pod Cúpla, is known as the baby of the pod family. It is almost entirely taken up by a double mattress (with a proper platform), duvet, pillows and cushions. Although facilities are basic — a lamp, double socket, electric oil heater and a mirror, it is comfortable, if minimalist, but extremely difficult to remove my shoes and clothes. It is like experiencing the world having shrunk to hobbit proportions. There is a pleasing simplicity and contentment to spending a night in a miniature house. Birdsong is part of the package and even though it starts from 5 am with a wake-up call of wood pigeons and feisty magpies, for those who like to capture the embrace of the natural world, it is a perfect bolthole.

'YOU'RE LUCKY,' Ger Madden smiles, pointing out that there is not even a hint of what local fishermen call the Scariff breeze as we sail the next morning across the open fresh waters of Lough Derg. 'It's a fierce wind and you get it up to 300 days in the year. It blows up as a south-west breeze and is annoying. The pier on Holy Island is placed the wrong way so you can't land there because of the breeze on those days. It's fine in Mountshannon as we're in a sheltered bay but the breeze has eight miles to pick up momentum and by the time you get into Garrykennedy it's become a strong wind and you don't get many days in the year like this.'

We are on a boat from Mountshannon harbour to Holy Island, also known as Inis Cealtra, following Hayward's aquatic path. Surrounded by stately hills, Lough Derg is flat calm without so much as a ripple or breath of wind scudding across its surface. Ger's vessel, *Irene*, is an eight-metre sea-going matador that he has converted into a ferry boat with a new diesel engine. As well as a fount of knowledge on weather lore, Ger is a charismatic boatman, an expert on wildlife, the cultural history of the island and his patch of the lower Shannon. On the way across Scariff Bay, he points out topographical highlights. Slieve Bernagh, or the Clare Hills, rise on the east Clare side of the lake, while Tountinna on the opposite is in north Tipperary. An English couple, three Germans and a two-year-old asleep in a pushchair share the ten-minute journey with us. The silence is broken only by the call of birds or waterfowl with mallard, the *tsip* of the coot or little grebe dunking and foraging in the reed beds. In hope rather than expectation, I question Ger about the possibility of seeing kingfishers on the lake or island.

'I've seen kingfishers on Holy Island. The colours are amazing and beautiful on them, especially in the sunshine, but they're very shy. I've seen them on the shore, picking up insects and then they're gone before you know it. There are so few people to bother them so you might be lucky and see them.'

Ger is the author of several books on Lough Derg and the surrounding area, including the Slieve Aughty mountains. Holy Island was part of the geographical terrain of Hayward's trip and Ger is familiar with his writing on the lake and the river.

'Not a single thing has changed on Holy Island since Hayward was here. The narcissi were out then and now there's two acres of it on the island … A lot of what he's written on Holy Island is repetitive and taken straight out of books by the antiquarian R.A.S. Macalister. But we found a stone spiral staircase underneath the root of a big ash tree. It needs to be excavated since it's never been noticed before.'

Ger drops us at a small jetty and will return later to collect us. We enter a different realm, stepping into a place associated with an early Christian settlement that has been a centre of pilgrimage for over a thousand years. A dozen cattle graze contentedly amongst the medieval masonry. Holy Island is a monastic site believed to have been founded in the seventh century. The physical remains on the island consist of the ruins of four churches, as well as a round tower, holy well and a network of earthworks. There are also smaller rectangular buildings for which the purpose is unknown. The monastery suffered badly from Viking attacks from 836 and was rebuilt by King Brian Boru around the year 1000. His brother, Marcan, was the abbot but the island is mainly associated with St Caimin, who died in 653.

We walk along the pilgrim's path to St Caimin's Church with its elegant Romanesque doorway and chancel. The only church on the island with a roof, it is thought to date from the twelfth century. Early Christian gravestones date from the tenth to the

The monastic settlement of Holy Island, or Inis Cealtra, was founded in the seventh century and consists of church ruins, a round tower and holy well.

twelfth century with most belonging to the latter. There are more than eighty carved stones. Some have a cross-base, others are free-standing and inside St Caimin's Church are cross-slabs. Many are recumbent, while others lean at odd angles. Funerals still take place on the island and two of the churchyards are in use. Modern graves reflect items such as small wooden boats marking an angling or boating link. The lettering on some is semi-obliterated while others are higgledy-piggledy. Using a technique I learnt from an archaeologist, I produce a small tub of talcum powder, sprinkling it on the chiselled headstones and rubbing it with a sponge to reveal the matter-of-factness and terseness of the words: *Thy will be done / Always Remembered / Too dearly loved to be forgotten / Sweet Jesus give them eternal rest.*

With perfectly aligned spelling, the families' names represent a local selection: Keenan, Woods, Lyons, Hogan, Keane, Waterstone, Higgins, Delaney, Carolan, McNamara, Dooley.

A succession of writers, painters, antiquarians and archaeologists have long been fascinated by the ecclesiastical history they have found here. Wakeman, Petrie and Macalister have come on quests to try to capture the spirit of the place or to unlock a little of the mystery of this sacred landscape. They have puzzled over specific aspects of the built heritage and the rich vein of folklore and legend reflected in the story of the enigmatic Lough Derg monster. When he came here, Hayward had gone looking for a boat to take his party out but could not find one. However, Jessops of Maryboro' stepped in and brought them across in a dinghy. Hayward toured the churches and round tower and wrote about the architectural detail. What intrigued him most was a curious small rectangular building, known as the confessional, divided into two parts by two standing stones leaning towards each other and behind which are two more stones. Hayward again invoked the research and work of Macalister:

> Professor Macalister has pointed out that this could not have been a confessional, for the simple reason that no structure would be made for such a solemn rite into which the priest could not make his way without a fatal loss of dignity. He concluded that it was more like the home of a hermit, or *inclusus*, who submitted himself to a peculiarly rigid form of self-mortification of those who came to consult the holy men, who was himself literally built up with the four standing stones.

Standing to the west of the church, the roofless tenth-century pencil-thin round tower dominates the skyline. Given its age, the tower is well preserved. According to tradition it never had a conical roof because an old witch refused to bless the mason's work. The angry mason hurled his hammer at her and the witch was turned to stone but was unable to finish the roof. Wandering around through shoulder-high purple thistles and tall dandelions, I stumble across bullaun stones, natural boulders with large, round man-made depressions. In pagan times they were used for mixing ritual herbs and spices, and later for grinding corn. Five of these distinctive stones can be found on the island and are in good condition.

Inis Cealtra is a place to experience the localization of the holy in an intense way. Ruins of several other churches including St Brigid's, St Mary's and St Michael's Oratory and 'The Church of the Wounded Men' – although no one knows who the wounded men were – as well as monastic cells and the remains of high crosses, are all preserved. In the early days an annual pilgrimage was held in March and corresponded with St Caimin's feast day on 24 March. A penance of several circuits of the monastery earned absolution for sinners. An annual pilgrimage and day of reflection is held on the island each June.

Back on the mainland we repair to Ger's one-stop shop, which offers a tourism service, local history books and maps, boat trips and weather forecasting. The importance of the natural world and the names of many birds and animals are immortalized in the islands: Cowpasture Island, Cormorant Islands, Rabbit Island, Hare Island, Goat Island, Crane Island, Duck Island, Scald Crow Island, Cow Island, Horse Islands, Sloe Island, Goose Island. Other names reflect the topography, such as Stony Island, The Pig and Sow Rocks. The Henhouse is a cluster of rocks off the Buggane Islands in Urrahill. Few could resist discovering place names such as Jude's Snuff, Lickmolassy Point, Illaunnaskirtaun and Garraunfadda.

I have switched my ornithological focus from the kingfisher to a much bigger species of rare bird – sea eagles, which had been thriving on Cribby Island – but sadly the female has just died. Clare's famous pair of white-tailed sea eagles, Saoirse and Caimin, made history in 2013 when they reared the first-born chicks to fledge from a nest in Ireland for more than a century. They welcomed an addition to their family after eagles hatched on the shores of Lough Derg in April 2017. Such was the excitement that a viewing point had been set up at Mountshannon harbour with spotting telescopes trained on a nest on Cribby.

Ger explains the background to their arrival and demise. 'The eagles came here a hundred years ago, the whole way from

Kerry to Mountshannon, and they hatched out, which was some achievement. 'Twas a wonderful idea and they helped the economy – many people used to come to see them and it increased the footfall. Unfortunately, the female eagle, who was called Shannon, died of avian flu. The male is out there on his own on Cribby so there is no hatch but hopefully he will find a mate before too long and they'll be back again. Although one chick has died the other is still there. They had set up a small centre giving out information and it brought in many bird watchers and they helped put the place on the map to a certain extent. They even had a sign on the main street for the sea eagles but no sign for Holy Island, which is amazing.'

The bird is believed to have died from suspected lead poisoning. Their disappearance is a huge loss to Lough Derg and a further example of Ger's disappointment in how the town has suffered serious decline.

'Twenty years ago there might have been ten hire boats, which meant eighty people had to be fed and wined here. Boatloads of Germans used to come here but now they're going to the canals of Europe, which are cheaper. Mountshannon is the only harbour on the western side of Lough Derg that is actually on the lake, while every other village is a mile or two inland. But for the past few years it's been going downhill along with other towns on the west side of the Shannon. They're all on their knees and are getting no support.'

The Lough Derg Blueway has just been launched, a place which the tourism authorities suggests is where 'timelessness meets time of your life in 13,000 hectares of clear water, surrounded by beautiful and dramatic countryside, providing a scenic perspective into the heart of the Irish landscape'. But Ger is sceptical.

'Five years ago, the Labour-Fine Gael government gave €5 million to promote Lough Derg. Most of it went on infrastructural projects for the local county councils. Then in the past year they spent €200,000 promoting the new Blueway and all I see out of it are photographs of politicians at launches and functions, but I've not seen one tourist that has come to Mountshannon as a result.

'The bottom line is that they're not bringing in the tourists. We never see a tour coach here on this side of the lake. If you see a bus, you stand up and look at it since they don't come to the western shore of Lough Derg. We had twenty people for a while on a FÁS scheme keeping the place going. The two pubs are now open at 5 pm, we had no restaurant for a year, and this year a small café has opened and the best of luck to it, but you cannot get a proper lunch or evening meal in Mountshannon. Clare County Council spent €50,000 doing a tourism and development plan, which was the usual baloney about building a €3 million interpretative centre, getting 250-seater ferries, limiting the numbers to 500 people a day, and here we are – we can't even get 500 people a year. It's a cash-register mentality that they have in Clare with the Cliffs of Moher getting all the exposure and bringing in the money.'

A new concern is about a controversial proposal to extract water from the Shannon and pipe it to Dublin to help meet the city's increasing demand. The plan, by Irish Water, involves putting in place a 170 km pipeline and has raised disquietude locally. Several organizations, such as Fight the Pipe and the River Shannon Protection Alliance, have mounted strong campaigns of opposition, claiming it will be enormously disruptive, degrade land and lead to a loss of income.

'The big fight is bringing the water to Dublin but we're not going to give them a bucketful and that's certain. There'll be holy war on Holy Island if they do, since we have to keep the levels on Lough Derg as they are. You can fish Lough Neagh the whole year round every year for the last 300 years and fish it properly, and Lough Derg is nearly as big as that and there's not an eel to be caught in it. They fish for pike now and they are being released when caught and most of that is being done by Poles and Italians.'

As a literary man, Ger is interested in the success of a local author, also called O'Brien, whom he knows well. She has had a much-publicized Clare background and is world-renowned for her fiction, which includes *The Country Girls* (1960) and *The Lonely Girl* (1962).

'Edna O'Brien has her grave marked out on Holy Island and wants to be buried there. She was born in Tuamgraney in December 1930 and her grandparents were Clearys from Mountshannon. Herself and her father never got on so she doesn't want to be buried with him, but with her grandparents. She's so famous that she knows people will want to go out to visit her grave and she has her funeral ceremony organized.

'A few months ago, she was here after winning an award. She's so sharp. She looked up at the two hills overlooking us and said they reminded her of a young woman's breasts. Now I've been looking at them for forty years but I've never seen that, and every time I look now, I can see them. The one to the right is Caher Hill and the other is Eel Hill, and in between them are two smaller ones. All her life she was always complaining about money because she said she never had any, but she has had an amazing life. There's no doubt that she always had a soft spot for this area and every time she comes home, she gives me a copy of her latest book.'

While the Ireland of the middle decades of the twentieth century had privations and repressions, O'Brien's rural childhood in Clare was filled with primroses and cowslip, ferns and stalks of ragwort, and the cry of the curlew. She loved cycling around the countryside amongst oak and ash trees, while her mother was the hub of the house. As an author she rose to prominence when *The Country Girls* appeared on a banned books list, which also featured work by Samuel Beckett, Seán Ó Faoláin and Frank O'Connor. The book made an impact for different reasons, but according to Ger it was never burnt in public, as many believe.

'The first book was never burnt by the people. The priest burnt it. But there were no books being sold in Tuamgraney then anyway. This was 1960 and there were few people in country areas reading in Ireland. And the mass burning of books that people talk about in the grounds of the church or outside the building did not happen.'

Along the main street, two cats and a dog doze in the sun, a child cycles down an alley on a bike and two workmen beside scaffolding pour tea from a flask. If Mountshannon is not the quietest town on the river, it is certainly in the top one! Along its long, tree-lined, moribund street it could be 1939 or even 1869. There is little sign of modernity. Hayward described it as 'a neat place nestling comfortably at the foot of Knockeven'. Mountshannon does not appear in any guidebooks, but if it did it would be classified as a frozen-in-aspic village.

That night I drift a few miles inland to Feakle where a venue has become celebrated for its music. When I arrive in Shortt's bar the place is throbbing, not so much with traditional music, but with hymns. Choir practice for a forthcoming mass is underway in a small room off the main lounge bar. However, the bar is best known for its traditional sessions. One by one the musicians arrive, taking their place in a corner of the lounge. The bar holds what it regards as the world record for the longest-running traditional session, which has been running every Thursday night for nigh on fifty years.

Once a week, come sunshine or snow, musicians find their way to the bar. Gerard Shortt, who plays the guitar and is learning the fiddle, has been running the pub for a quarter of a century, but the sessions have been held continuously since 1970. Tonight's group is made up of no fewer than fourteen musicians, comprising four fiddlers, three box players, two guitarists, two concert flautists, two on banjo and bodhrán and a digital pianist. Gerard explains how the session was started by the previous owner, Lena Hanraghan, in 1970.

'All the greats from the east Clare music circles started playing here,' he says. 'They used to come along after mass on a Sunday morning and would play for a couple of hours in the small adjoining bar. The pubs had to close in the afternoon for the holy hour, which was two hours. At the same time there was a factory in Scariff called Chipboard and somebody suggested to Lena that she should have a session on a Thursday night because that was payday. So that's how it started and it was so successful that people came from all over and they're still coming.'

The group shows an innate musicality, reflecting an alchemy of imaginative songs and tunes, with, at one stage, more companionable musicians than drinkers in the bar. Bouncing rhythms include 'The Bellharbour Reel', 'Austin Tierney's', 'I'm Waiting For You', 'The Woman of the House' and 'Molly Brannigan'. Gerard says some of Ireland's leading musicians began their playing days in the bar.

'There was one night we had seventeen different nationalities playing. The founders of the Tulla Ceili band played here regularly with Paddy O'Donoghue, then we had P.J. Hayes, and the Donnans and many others on pipes and fiddle … *The New York Times* has done a series of articles on it and each time they would phone me up and ask questions such as 'What happens if Christmas Day falls on a Thursday?' The answer is that if that does happen, we simply move the session to the Wednesday night and play on until 2 am so that ticks the box for Thursday and means that we haven't missed a beat.'

Guinness World Records have been in contact with him about including the bar as hosting the longest-running music session in the world but 'It was too expensive to bring someone over to authenticate it. The cost factor at over €5000 was just too big and why would we pay such a figure to bring them over to investigate something we already know?'

At the bar an overcoated elderly farmer on a low stool with his back to the audience spontaneously bursts into 'The Old Rustic Bridge', and another man, eyes closed and hands clasped firmly to his knees, squeezes every syllable out of 'On Raglan Road'. Set dances activates four couples, intertwining with their partners in intricate foot-stepping to fast-rippling tunes while several rousing reels lead to another high-spirited Thursday night finale.

12

Shannonlanders

OF ALL THE villages along the Shannon, the twin townships of Killaloe and Ballina, linked by a long bridge, appear to have been marketed and exploited more than anywhere in Ireland. 'Easy to Reach, Impossible to Leave.' The latter sentiment of the sales pitch is certainly true if you are caught up, as I am, in an accident near the traffic lights, possibly the slowest in the country. When I reach the Clare end, the traffic is snarled up after a van hit the wall of the bridge leading to a lengthy tailback.

'That bridge is lethal,' says the woman in the tourist office and Brian Boru Centre. 'They're supposed to be building a new one to bypass Killaloe. Plans are in progress but there's been rows over compulsory land purchase. If it takes them three months to fix a water pipe, who knows how long it'll take to build a new bridge? It's not fit for purpose and hasn't been for years. It was built for a horse and trap after all, not for juggernauts and wide tour coaches.'

The thirteen-arch old stone bridge is also perilously narrow for foot traffic. Pedestrians are forced to squeeze to one side to cross. The river here is broad and venerable. Several boats are tied up along the quay on the Ballina side although the main marina is at Kincora on the outskirts of town. Pausing on the bridge, I contemplate ripples unfolding and breaking apart. *The Spirit of Killaloe*, a tour boat, is about to head out up into the waters of

Lough Derg. The square tower-like spire of St Flannan's Cathedral sticks up through the trees: at midday its rippling peel of bells pours out 'Ode to Joy' and 'Morning has Broken' reverberating around the streets and across the river. Under the bridge the mahogany *Romaris* is trying to get through the narrow passage but is too big to make it under the arch. The water is lumpy and the wind pushes it against yellow and black booms before the skipper decides to give up and returns to the quayside.

Persistent birdsong rings out from the trees, mingling with the screams of children at a carousel enjoying the Brian Boru weekend festival. The bridge has a commanding view and is a place to reflect on the age-old artery, providing you avoid being hit by the wing mirrors of vans, coaches and lorries. The alluring set pieces are here for the painter's luminist composition: a stone bridge, bobbing boats, the curvature of the Shannon, and trees in harmony with the panorama as though in communion with the flow of the river itself. Overhead, a drone captures some of the activities. The operator tells me that it was once mistaken for a gull and attacked by a buzzard. Along a riverside walk that follows the path of the old Killaloe railway and beside the Washerwoman's bridge, a ladies' group enjoys some Saturday morning dynamic stretching beside the river. The bridge once crossed the railway line when it was extended towards the Lakeside Hotel, allowing access to the river for women to do their washing. The bridge was not provided for in the original plans to extend the line: as a result, the extension to the railway line cut off the right of way to the river, which the women had previously used. As part of their protest they lay across the new railway line and refused to move, resulting in the building of the new bridge and serving the women of the twenty-first century with a different activity.

The librarian in Killaloe admits that they are Clare-centric. 'We wouldn't have any books on Tipperary. If you want anything on that county you would have to go to the library in Nenagh.' In McGeough's supermarket in Ballina, the cashier expresses surprise when I ask about *The Clare Champion*. 'Clare, is it? That's over the bridge, we don't stock those papers here.' Across the bridge, in Whelan's, the woman in charge says the two tribes are learning the tricky art of coexistence. She describes those living across the river on the Tipperary side as 'traitors'.

'If a Clareman marries a Tipp woman it could be ten years before we forgive them and get over the shock of that, but eventually we do,' she twinkles. 'But we don't care and here you'll see the *Nenagh Guardian* and the *Tipperary Star* – business is business after all. Sporting fixtures you'd get a bit of rivalry, especially in the hurling. But, of course, we're the best county. Mind you, if Tipp were playing Mayo, for example, we'd support the Tipp team so we're not all that bad.'

There has always been a healthy rivalry between the two towns. In 1939 Killaloe had a much larger population than Ballina. Hayward was impressed with Killaloe's past but largely ignored Ballina. He described the river as 'running like a silver band under its pleasant bridge and draining the comely Loch Derg'. Goods trains were still running to Ballina up until 1954, although the last passenger trains ended in 1931. Eighty years on and there has been a reversal of fortunes, at least in population terms, between the towns. The most recent statistics show that Killaloe's population was 1292 while Ballina was double that at 2442. The main reason for this population explosion on the Tipperary side stems from 2002, when the council released more land for house building, encouraging people to move to the area as part of the rollercoaster Celtic Tiger years when it expanded beyond recognition. Both towns are filled with craft shops, art galleries and cafés, although Ballina has a preponderance of restaurants and bars while Killaloe has slipped behind in the culinary stakes. Killaloe is a straggle running uphill and around a square with streets shooting off in all directions. Some of the decorative shopfronts Hayward saw still have handsome examples on their facades including John Crotty's Italian Warehouse, which was a general store, hardware, bakery and pub all rolled into one. The building also has the original Victorian shopfront lettering moulded in porcelain to imitate white marble for W.A. Gilbey, who were major wine importers.

The narrow thirteen-arch stone bridge linking Ballina in Tipperary with Killaloe in Clare.

The route uphill along the Aillebaun path runs from near the bridge on the Killaloe side towards Lough Derg while the forested hills of the Slieve Bernagh hummocks lie inland sheltering the place. Smoke rises from a small pile of rubble. A couple with a doe-eyed Labrador nods a greeting, commenting on the sunshine, as their walking facilitator leads the way, pausing to exchange scents with a retriever. Fuchsia, tormentil and the trumpet-like hedge bindweed line the path, a place to appreciate the scale of new housing in Ballina, which is creeping ever upwards behind the houses and appears to be taking over the landscape. Looming over all this development are the Tipperary hills and Tountinna at 465 metres, which house the graves of the Leinstermen, a cluster of 3000-year-old stone slabs. Stretching from the river and its tree-lined banks into Lough Derg, then up into the fields and hills, the view is a harmonious subtlety of colour. The sun has reappeared with a faint rainbow arcing over the hills. More than twenty pleasure craft are tied up in single file along the jetty that leads out to what used to be known as the canal lock and is now called the flow control gates. A couple of hooded crows strut around the canal bank beside the cruisers. Some of the boats are linked to electricity charging poles and come with evocative names such as *Chill Out*, *Tír na Nog*, *Mistral*, *Sea Claire*, *Wanda*, *Time Out II*, and *Eurydice*.

Hayward set up camp near the historic Lakeside Hotel where he arranged to meet two friends from Limerick, Mick Gleeson and Canty Burke. Gleeson had been associated with him in two of his films about Ireland in the early 1930s. They revived memories, but also planned the next stage of their trip, which would take them to Limerick. A pencil sketch of the original timber building from the 1890s hangs alongside a gallery of black-and-white photographs. One image shows a man water-skiing while standing on a wooden chair. The year of the hotel's founding is memorialized today in the Wi-Fi code: 1894. With the war now underway, Hayward called with the postmistress to make phone connections to both London and Belfast. In Killaloe the disruption led to restricted steamship services to England while British army reservists were preparing to leave in obedience of mobilization orders.

On the road out of Ballina, Barry Holloway, originally from London, runs the Kingfisher Lodge B & B. He says it is a good place to see the eponymous bird. 'You can often get several thousand young fish in the channel and frequently you would see a flash of blue.' I peer through binoculars down into the small channel, which this morning is bereft of both fish and birds but alive with plant life.

THE SHANNON HAS lured hobos, vagabonds, desperadoes and Traveling Wilburys. Donal Boland may not fit any of these categories but as a water gypsy he has carved out an existence for himself on the river for more than twenty years. A retired underwater archaeologist and a former technician, he has reinvented himself as an artist and cartographer. His houseboat is on the Killaloe canal, part of the Limerick Navigation, a man-made stretch from Killaloe to Limerick that meets the Shannon at Ballina. The river runs parallel with his stationary position. His barge, a Humber Keel Sheffield Class, dates from 1949. Donal bought it from a businessman and art dealer Victor Waddington, whom he describes as a 'reluctant millionaire', and named it *James and Mary* in honour of his parents. He lovingly restored it, converting it in Shannon Harbour and refitting it to a high standard. Below deck is open plan with a bathroom, kitchen, study or living area, and sleeping quarters. Upstairs is a small kitchen with 360-degree glass and a lounge with comfortable seats. We sit at a table with views stretching across the long bridge.

'The whole concept of this boat is that your horizon is as far as you can see, and the amount of light is great. People might look in – they're called gongoozlers, which is a word you don't hear very often but it defines them well: they look in on others on canals but do not actively participate themselves. Life on the river moves between summer and winter. There is the season where the water level is quiescent and you can travel, and the season whereby the Shannon goes into flood and the river is essentially a drain in the centre of Ireland.'

We talk about what the river means to people such as him. 'I have asked that question of myself over the last five years – what does the river give me? And I answered it by asking other people why they are on the river. On one occasion I met a Welshman who died in 2016. He came to the Shannon four times a year for twenty-five years. There is a group of people who come every year, or as often as they can afford to come, rather than the people who come once. You can come from anywhere in Europe and be what I call a Shannoner. The main reason people come is for the pubs and the lifestyle as the Shannon is a place of tranquillity. I met a man who owned a taxi company in Berlin and his head is running twenty-four hours a day but he comes to the Shannon and within hours he's sitting on a boat and has forgotten about it. Another man from Dublin, with a German wife, sails Formula One racing yachts and the only place that he comes to relax is the Shannon. I met him recently and he was complaining that he had to go to the Bahamas to collect a yacht and didn't want to do it because he'd rather be on the Shannon. All this is why I coined the term "Shannonland".'

My ears prick up at the term and I ask Donal to define where exactly it lies in relation to the rest of Ireland.

'Ireland is out there,' he points to the footpath, 'and where we are on the boat and water is Shannonland. It's not just a physical place – it's also a mental place. Once I step on my boat I've emigrated, as it's a completely different place.

'The project I've been working on for the last couple of years is to develop and define tranquillity as an entity that is important to the Shannon and to show where these quiet sites are to be found. I've spent time mapping out the places and in the mid-Shannon have listed twenty. You could include hundreds of places along the river that people can come to visit with magnificent views, and with flora and fauna, but tranquillity is what many want. It depends, of course, where your head is. If you look around, we have a cathedral, trees with hundreds of birds – off the bow is a magnificent view of the canal. Being on the water is totally different to looking at it. River people understand the river – no matter which section. People in the estuary, for example, would have a very good understanding of the estuaries and the parameters of wind and tide. There are people who will only boat within a very small area because they know it well. That's changing because we're moving away from the traditional wooden or fibreglass lake boat towards lighter aluminium ones. Fish now are caught for sport rather than for food, so you have this massive husbandry where fish are being caught, measured, photographed and returned, which is a great thing to see. I don't fish because I like to say that I don't interfere with my neighbours.'

Mapping the Shannon, its people and places, is important to Donal. 'In the mid-Shannon flooding is a norm and this is because during the Tiger era people built in areas there they shouldn't have. You might experience a high flood once every twenty years and then you get some nut head who has never seen the flood and gives permission to build houses on a floodplain and along comes the flood and all of a sudden, the Shannon needs to get back to where it belongs – that's the problem. It's always a situation of "Let's change the river but never change what we're doing around the river." The river needs to breathe.'

Donal is familiar with Hayward's writing about the Shannon. 'Hayward was an adventurer, he was like the first man up the Nile, and here he was coming along to talk and write about the Shannon and meet people. These were people who hadn't changed their relationship with the river in probably thousands of years … Shannonland hasn't changed and Hayward wouldn't recognize it if he came back today – not because the river or river people have changed but because Ireland has changed and there are probably fewer river people today. The ordinary people who had a relationship with the river, and the people on the other side of it, don't need to have that link anymore because they get information and communication about what's happening on that side of the river from a different source. It's been provided to them – they don't have to seek it.

'In Hayward's day there was a linear community of river people. But it was a total community in the sense that all the people around the river had a relationship with the river and didn't work in Dublin. Those people no longer have a relationship with it. They drive across, and that's a fundamental difference.'

With his flowing speech, Donal strikes me as the type of erudite person Hayward had in mind when he described the people of the Shannon as 'friendly, hospitable, and good natured to an unimaginable degree … and with that quiet philosophy about them and deep content of the Irish countryside'. I ask if he regards himself as a water gypsy and what he sees as the biggest change.

'The proper term is "aqua knacker",' he says with a philosophical flourish, 'and I think that, no more than the Irish Traveller has got recognition as a separate ethnic entity, then aqua knackers should have the same, but we don't have the critical mass … for me the Shannon retains its peace of mind and the ability to give people wellness, therapy and recovery. The people that come to the river find they can get away from their busyness and can't get it anywhere else.'

Donal's three canine companions are becoming restless. Oscar is a terrier, Coco is a springer and both are rescue dogs, while Mr Pugs is a Jack Russell. He says some visitors who call on him spend time playing with the dogs but have no interest in him.

'Mr Pugs is a bit like the river and has two personalities. He has a personality that is completely docile and gentle but let him smell a mouse, rat or a cat, and it's kill. That's the way they are bred, a psychological switch is part of their nature. There's no question that a dog is a bond between strangers. What I find on the river is that people come on their holidays and leave their own dog at home so they converse with my dog. I've seen a woman from Israel at a remote quay spend the whole day playing with Daisy, God bless her, because she had left her dog at home but she could play with my dog and get exactly the same enjoyment. If you get to the stage with a dog where you're not looking at the dog as a dog but as an individual personality, and you allow the dog to come into your life, that you understand it and it understands you, then those type of people will do that with your dog. I converse with the dogs … but I don't converse in the spoken word – it's a mental understanding.'

I ask him if the dogs recognize Shannonland.

'One thing they do recognize very much is aspects of your personality and how your personality is at a particular time. They'll sense if you're stressed or ill. They'll also sense if someone walks in this door that I've a problem with.'

As regards the future of the river and what lies ahead, Donal feels more needs to be done to promote the core of the river itself. 'People who are making decisions about the Shannon and how it should be utilized for other people or tourists need to be on the river but unfortunately they are not. … And they are right to promote it but they could get more bang for their buck doing that than promoting being on the river. My concept is to have areas on and around the river defined as Special Areas of Tranquillity (SAT) and within those you have Sites of Intense Tranquillity (SIT): SAT and SIT are two terms I've coined, which could, of course, equally apply as very good dog terms.'

EARLY AUTUMN COLOUR is invading the countryside as I drive to the Falls of Doonass. The road to O'Briensbridge is tunnelled with the fan-vaulted branches of trees knitting together in their giddy finery, a riot of browns, auburns and ochres forming part of the multicoloured leaf canopy. The sun causes visual flickers through trees and glimpses of the sky. The writer Paul Theroux describes sunny country roads such as this as having a 'sense of purification'.

Fields of cobs, piebald and Irish sports horses are embedded in the local nomenclature while a handwritten sign attached to a tree trunk advertises a 'Horsey hoedown', a cowboy night on Saturday. For ten minutes I'm stuck behind a horsebox, which in turn is stuck behind a New Holland tractor in creep-speed gear. A hand-painted sign on the horsebox's back door lights up in a starburst of reflected sun bearing the words *Only Foals and Horses*.

At one time O'Briensbridge was an important port on the Lower Shannon where canals were used to bypass the shallow reaches of the river. Nowadays looped walks follow the banks of the river, the Errina canal and the Headrace canal, linking up with the Lough Derg Way. An elderly man relaxing on a bench watches me making notes. He comments on the laziness of the river, which is a brown gold with barely a lick of foam. 'You look like a man with too much time on your hands,' he says.

Although it is autumn, there is no dramatic fall in temperature. School buses are on the roads again and the hedges are bursting with blackberries. Visitors, like the swifts, have gone, but magpies and jackdaws are omnipresent while the sonorous oboe notes of wood pigeons lend a gloomy tone. There is a melancholy feel. Linked by the Shannon, the villages are little-known pitstops to all but those who live in them. Castleconnell is on the Limerick side of the river but when I ask in several shops about the best way to the Falls of Doonass, my query draws blank stares. Eventually, a woman at a filling station tells me I need to retrace my journey back to O'Briensbridge and head for Clonlara in Clare, which is just a crossroads with two pubs and a shop. I am trying to find out if the Anglers Rest, which Hayward visited, is still in business. The Internet is no help and soon I reach Clonlara and a couple of kilometres beyond, arrive at Doonass, which appears to be a road junction. A man in a red van pulls up alongside me outside a cemetery and I ask about the Anglers Rest. He said it closed some years ago and the building has now been turned into an apartment block.

The man has come to tend his burial plot, although he says he's not thinking of departing this life just yet. He adds, 'I'm better than I was but not nearly as good as I'm going to be.' He tells me the story of a priest who lost the details of his plot forty years earlier, and for which he had paid a large sum of money.

'The priest was an obnoxious oul' fella and he just drank the money I'd paid him for my plot and a new path as well. But I wasn't the worst, another one of my friends paid the money twice and never saw it, so basically he had no records of who was to be buried where – 'twas a complete bloody shambles.'

The newly built apartment block is roped off at the front, but a path leads to the river, which sprawls in a wide stretch. The rocks across it are blanketed by theatrical drapes of a matrix of rich moss interspersed with clumps of greenery. The sparklingly clear white foamy river cascades freely, webbing the stones, the sunshine catching the water with a glitter of gold flashiness. Before the nearby Ardnacrusha system was put in place in the 1920s, the entire force of the river came down past Doonass. In the late nineteenth century, the rapids were a famous natural landmark for people from Clare, Limerick and farther afield. By the time Hayward got here, they were still an impressive sight, but the volume of water was much reduced. He called it 'a plain unassuming little place where good Irish country fun and diversion are the order of the day'. Given the surroundings of overhanging branches and the flow of the river, reflecting a clarity and purity, it strikes me as prime kingfisher habitat. For thirty minutes, sitting on a large stone, spyglass poised, I feel becalmed and at ease with the intimacy of the Shannon. As I commune with the riverscape, there is an appreciation of the healing balm of river song, while running through my head are the words of Brian Caffrey in Banagher: 'Let the bird find you.'

IN THE EARLY 1920s, with the exception of Dublin and Cork, Ireland was almost untouched by electric power, but within a few years the situation would change. The Shannon Hydroelectric Scheme involved harnessing the power of the river to generate electricity. It was a huge project, undertaken by a German firm, Siemens-Schuckert, and involved 4000 local men, plus 1000 Germans, working three shifts a day for four years. Many of the locals were underpaid and poorly treated. Construction had begun in August 1925, just two years after the end of the divisive wounds of the Civil War and four years after the Anglo-Irish Treaty was signed. It was a period in which there was still an unsettled political atmosphere and a generally dispirited outlook. The ESB, the first of the Irish state-sponsored companies, was set up in 1927 to manage the project, which was completed in August 1929. The work involved damming the river at O'Briensbridge, carving a twelve-kilometre-long headrace canal through the landscape to a barrage and power station, and a tailrace to return the water to the river. Ardnacrusha became the nerve centre for the electrification of Ireland. Building work led to the construction of a concrete weir at Parteen where the river was dammed, the creation of a purpose-built canal between Parteen and Ardnacrusha, a high concrete dam and the commission of three turbo-generator units.

For such a fledgling state in the formative years of nation-building, this was regarded as progress on a heroic scale. A need was recognized to develop and use natural resources to modernize Ireland. But there was little enthusiasm and much pessimism about the scheme. Hayward said that no project in Ireland was ever so strongly opposed in a country deeply suspicious of technology. A large section of the government condemned the idea, the press was largely hostile, and the leading technical men, with a few exceptions, were entirely antagonistic. It was, he wrote, largely the romance of one man, Dr Thomas McLaughlin, in whose mind the scheme first took shape in 1923. A young Irish engineer, McLaughlin, who was just twenty-six, had spent time working for Siemens in Germany and Poland. Hayward pointed out that many people believed it was an anti-English feeling in Ireland that sent the contract to Germany, saying this was untrue. The Germans got the contract because they had the enterprise to go after it and to spend several thousand pounds in survey and investigation.

On his arrival at the plant, Hayward said he was most courteously received and an official was placed at their disposal to guide them round and explain the workings. He was awestruck by the scheme, how it came about and how it worked. After touring the buildings and speaking to engineers, he wrote about it in detail, as well as including it in his accompanying film. He was impressed with the view, which looked down on the artificial purpose-built canal of the headrace:

> We climbed to the gallery above the great intake building, and from this dizzy height saw the headrace as it entered the four immense penstocks, which are at present in commission. Each of these penstocks, great metal pipes twenty feet in diameter, carries a hundred tons of good Shannon water every second down a head of 110 feet to drive a turbine which develops 40,000 horsepower – 160,000 horsepower which for countless centuries has gone to waste but now serves the needs of the Irish people. And we saw two sluices, like gaps left by missing teeth and awaiting the ministrations of mechanical dentistry ... My head started to swim. Not from the altitude, for I was always a great climber of mountains, but from figures and power and statistics. For I was never a great one for the likes of that, God help me!

The huge penstocks at Ardnacrusha Power Station.

They toured the intake building where the absence of any noise surprised Hayward: 'From this assemblage of mighty machines there came only a great humming sound, as though bees were swarming in lime trees – albeit the bees and the trees would be above the average size!' At the control room, the nerve centre of it all, he found 'an exquisite sense of order and simplicity [about it]', which had an instant appeal for him. He felt that the Germans had done it all with great efficiency and praised the perfection of the workmanship: they were organized to such an extent that they imported German food and beer, and virtually transplanted a German town, all of which meant that very little money was being spent locally in Limerick or other areas. The Germans, though, were not popular around Limerick and he launches into a lengthy description of their national characteristics, which he said were 'poles apart' from those of the Irish. Quoting a local publican, Hayward said if the British had built Ardnacrusha 'they'd have drunk the town dry every Saturday, for they're the lads know how to spend money'.

In his film, which was shown as a travelogue at cinemas in Ireland, Hayward called the scheme 'a dream made manifest', describing it as a progressive piece of national planning and a courageous enterprise. When it was completed on 22 July 1929, Ardnacrusha was the largest hydroelectric station in the world, while a national (110 kv) voltage grid – also a world first – was constructed at the same time, bringing light to Ireland's major towns and cities. The total cost of the groundbreaking scheme was €5.2m, about one-fifth of Irish government revenue in 1925. It quickly garnered acclaim and became a model for large-scale electrification schemes worldwide, taking a seminal place in Irish architecture. Since those early days, it has gone on to win civil engineering awards, as well as architectural awards, from the American Society of Civil Engineers for its excellence as an international landmark: other recipients of this include the Eiffel Tower and the Golden Gate Bridge.

At the time, the work attracted Irish artists to the banks of the Shannon. The company bought some of Seán Keating's pictures which reflected the construction of the plant. The artist was never commissioned but over several years carried out the work independently, executing a series of twenty-six paintings as a result of his fascination with the subject and because of his personal political convictions. Keating lived with the workmen on the building site and enjoyed painting the heavy engineering. His figures are often dwarfed by the machinery. His series encompassed drawings and oil paintings, showing the progress of the work until completion. Amongst the titles are *Night's Candles Are Burnt Out*, *Excavations for Headrace with Steam Shovel*, *Building Site from Top of Barrage* and *Excavator at Work*. Keating described *Lubecker with Stone Wagon and Wagon Train* as an allegory representing the dawn of a new Ireland and the death of the stage Irishman, who is seen hanging on one of the power standards in the corner of the picture. Keating was born in Limerick in 1889 and educated at St Munchin's College. He was not a good attender and spent hours playing truant on the city's docks, drawing and scribbling. His father was a bookkeeper at a bakery company. He moved away from the city and later became president of the Royal Hibernian Academy. In 1948 he was admitted an Honorary Freeman of the City of Limerick, but the appointment was in danger some years later when on an RTÉ programme he described his native city in his day as 'a medieval dung heap'.

When the building opened, the ESB began facilitating tours for the public and welcomed 85,000 visitors within the first nine months in the late 1920s. It quickly became a tourist draw, attracting nearly 200,000 people between 1928 and 1932. To mark its 90th anniversary the company revived the tradition and began running dedicated school and public tours during 2017 when the newly refurbished visitor centre opened with a free tour called the Ardnacrusha Experience. Information panels display key facts and technical data related to the building, as well as photographs on its history and timescale, which includes Phase 1 from 1925 to 1929 and Phase 2 from 1933 to 1934. Our party of twenty fix on yellow hard hats and yellow jackets and are led around the building on a ninety-minute tour by the plant manager Alan Bane. Workplace risk assessment notices read *Safety is everybody's responsibility*. CCTV cameras track our progress.

'This workplace is an important historic site in Ireland's development and it has been a source of great pride to everyone to open the gate to the public,' Alan says. 'The four turbines are still humming, supplying the same eighty-six megawatts of renewable electricity as when they were first installed. In 1929 the station met 100 per cent of the country's electricity needs. But in the meantime, development has been such that the power station now represents about 2 per cent of the total installed capacity, supplying electricity to more than 46,000 homes.'

We are led along narrow corridors past the generator hall and brought into the heart of the station with a visit to the original control room, which Hayward classified as 'living heritage'. One of the main changes since his visit has been to the turbine hall, which was altered in the 1990s with the installation of a digital control room, although the original analogue clock still hangs over the new construction. We move outside to view the headrace canal, locks and tailrace. The four large cylindrical steel structures, known as penstocks, through which water is delivered to the turbines and which Hayward wrote about in detail, are still firmly in place. Each penstock is forty-one kilometres long, six metres in diameter and can deliver around 100 tons of water per second. From a viewing area we stand beside a railing and look across to where the river was dammed at Parteen Weir, which was constructed to raise the water level by 7.5 metres. Limerick city lies some ten kilometres distant where towers poke through tree cover. Our bird's-eye view, from left to right, takes in its built highlights: St John's Cathedral, Colbert Station, the Hunt Museum, St Mary's Cathedral, Roches Street Telecom Mast, the Riverpoint Complex, Clayton Hotel, the Railway Bridge, Thomond Park, the Gaelic Grounds and, in the far distance, the Mungret Cement factory. Territorial birds bicker in the trees and on power lines, jockeying for position. Skylarks shoot up and down, while swallows swoop in and out of hedges and buildings. Apart from the greenery, it looks like a 1930s' black-and-white film landscape. Hedges and walls form dark lines across the hillside. The wind rustles the tree cover, which resembles black coral. A buzzard hovers, looking for its lunch.

Alan points to the new developments in Limerick and speaks about the importance of the scheme when it opened. 'It was,' he said, 'a phenomenal undertaking, and the construction of the Shannon Scheme remains a source of inspiration for all of us at ESB as we face into the energy challenges of the coming decades.'

13

'A town of spires, gossip and lots of frustrated people'

HURTLING DOWN AT an unstoppable pace, the Curragower Falls bubbles in a mass of flying spume. Water gushes over the weir in what is one of the Shannon's most dramatic spectacles. Gulls swirl, screeching high-octane outrage in a squalling mêlée. Cormorants song-flight over it like black crosses in the sky. A playground for the brave, the Falls also excites a wobble of kayakers testing their skills on the white-water tides. Named after an ancient crossing point for goats on the Shannon, the Falls represents my late-morning introduction to Limerick coinciding with the best time to view the tidal surge.

Underneath Sarsfield Bridge, two long-haired men enjoy an alfresco aperitif from blue cans of Bavaria beer. From their seat on a girder, rusted to burnt umber, the pair throw their scrunched empties under the heavy machinery of the bridge's rack-and-pinion system on which it used to turn. This allowed ships to pass but no longer swivels since it has been closed to river traffic since 1928. Alexander Nimmo designed Sarsfield Bridge based on the plan of the Neuilly Bridge near Paris. It was completed in 1835. Each of the five river-arches is designed with a flat segmental curve on the facade, changing to an elliptical shape on the inside, and when it was built it was considered a masterpiece of function.

In the early years of the twenty-first century there was a vast amount of Limerick-directed abuse. It was a place in perpetual turmoil, verging on anarchy. This was caused by a vicious gang feud, revolving around the control of drugs, which was rampant in several estates for up to ten years. Because of this, the press nicknamed it 'stab city', a hard cliché to shake off. More recently, to a large extent, the city has turned around its fortunes, some even now calling it 'fab city' although this might be pushing it for old-timers. A couple of businesses have latched on to this: The Fab Lab and Chez le Fab café, and you can even buy a 'Fab City' Limerick lapel pin. It has reinvented itself, reconnected with its old buildings and re-orientated towards the river. Former corn stores and granaries, as well as derelict warehouses, have been repurposed and given life again. Like many towns and cities in Ireland, the waterfront has undergone a beautification project. A three-bridges health-giving walk takes in the impressive Shannon, Thomond and Sarsfield bridges. Fairy lights brighten up the surroundings, along with flags and hanging baskets of petunias. The 'warfare' has died down, although there are still exceptions, and while it has striven hard to overcome prejudices, parts of the city are riddled with social deprivation. Ironically, its motto – carved on its Treaty Stone – *Urbs Antiqua Fuit Studiisque Asperrima Belli*, translates as 'An ancient city well studied in the arts of war.'

The commercial centre is made up of a grid of five long streets running parallel with the river, intersected with eight cross streets. Vestiges of old Limerick remain. Walk along its historic lanes, funky alleyways or pedestrianized streets and you will soak up echoes of the past. The city feels remarkably free of the creeping homogenization that flattens the sense of serendipity in other places. Deep-rooted connections with the past are reflected in traditional shopfronts. The city is saturated with thirty-two cafés, leading to nose-tickling coffee aromas infusing many streets. A sign scrawled on a blackboard outside one of them states: 'Keep calm, we have Wi-fi.' I stroll around looking for the old in the midst of the new, for the twentieth century in the twenty-first, struggling to find it amongst the surveillance culture of CCTV cameras,

Sculpted geese are captured in a pose at the waterfront in Limerick.

Puffa-jacketed tourists, ATMs, pop-up shops, patisseries, gleaming gastropubs and glass and steel high-rise hotels. The multicultural food scene represents one of the biggest differences. Temples of gastronomy featuring Japanese, Thai, Indian, French and Texan food sit next to stalls in the urban garden selling Mexican fare, hot dogs, waffles and crêpes alongside a candy stall. The city has been awarded Purple Flag status and has committed itself to improving its environmental image, including green growth and sustainable jobs. In another development Limerick has just been chosen to take part in a futuristic European pilot project on reducing the carbon footprint of cities. The project will lead to a transformation of a cluster of buildings in the city centre with extraction of wave energy from the Shannon, which means it will become an energy generator rather than an energy consumer. A tidal turbine, developed by a local company, is being placed in the river, generating electricity for what is termed 'the positive energy zone' in the Georgian neighbourhood. This pioneering role means that Limerick will become a 'European lighthouse smart city' and ultimately, it is hoped, a model for other places to follow.

Parts of 'old' Limerick, around Rutland Street, where most buildings are derelict, still have an edgy decrepitude. Many of the corn stores and stone mill buildings, some of which lined the riverbank, were closed in the 1960s. I beam myself temporarily back to 1939 and it is not hard to imagine what Hayward would have seen. In fact, he had a passion for the eighteenth century and liked the Georgian houses at one end of O'Connell Street. But he also mentions the decorated houses of Athlunkard Street, which he felt showed a civic pride. The city reminded him of Athlone. He describes soaking up the atmosphere by the river from where he appreciated the architectural and historical value of the ancient buildings of King's Island but notes a noisy interruption to his enjoyment:

Many thoughts came into my mind as I stood here looking at this pleasant prospect with the history of age lying heavy upon it, and then suddenly my ears caught a faint whispering sound which must be common in Limerick, but which was new to me. The sound came from the pitter-patter of the crubeens of a great flock of pigs being driven from somewhere in the County Clare to be made into Limerick bacon. And I remembered the incident of the good lady in Limerick who fainted when a pig belonging to just such a flock was run down and killed by a motorcar, never thinking that within an hour it would have been dead anyway at the hands of the butcher.

Pigs no longer run around the roads although pony and traps are still to be seen, but no rag-and-bone men. The streets are threaded the same way as Hayward knew them although the character of the city in those days was changing rapidly. The 1930s was a period of social housing developments caused by a revolution in the building industry. Hayward described Limerick as having two sides, but if he was to return today he would divine a feisty city that has restyled itself in the form of brash hotels, bijou apartments and business quarters: the Medieval Quarter, based on

Sir Terry Wogan statue in Limerick, which has divided opinion.

King's Island, incorporating the castle and St Mary's Cathedral, has preserved its historic core; the Market Quarter houses the renovated Milk Market; elegant boutiques have collectively been rebranded as the Fashion Quarter, and the sedate area around Pery Square is known as the Georgian Quarter. Statues abound: at every turn the city remembers its singers, poets and actors. Hurlers and rugby players stand with memorials to dockers, seamen and other workers. Wild geese and a broken heart symbolize the Famine beside Shannon Bridge roundabout. Near the castle, Michael Hogan, the bard of Thomond, is reading his book *The Lays and Legends* in his outstretched palm.

In the summer of 2017, a bronze statue of one of the city's most famous sons, Sir Terry Wogan, who had been made a Freeman of Limerick, was unveiled at Harvey's Quay. The statue divided opinion, causing controversy. On an elevated circular stage, the amiable broadcaster sits life-size on a chair with a microphone in one hand and a book in the other. The statue, which cost almost €60,000, was created by the sculptor Rory Breslin and was unveiled by the Major of Limerick, Councillor Kieran O'Hanlon. But it has brought derision from some in the art world. One artist, John Shinnors, was quoted in the press as saying that council officials and politicians 'wouldn't know a Turner from a turnip'. Frolicking pigeons are now making a mess at Wogan's feet, pecking around his shoes. A woman throws bread at his feet, encouraging pigeons to jump on them. There is something forlorn-looking about the statue, especially his gaze up Bedford Row, giving him the appearance of a *Spitting Image* caricature.

'It's horrible,' a passer-by says. 'The artist should have asked people what they thought about spending all that money on it.' A cycling couple pull up to look around it. The man likes it, apart from the microphone in his hand, which he thinks is 'almost pornographic-looking'. He adds, 'Limerick people will always gripe and complain about everything, about what a kip it is and how awful a place it is to live. And this is no different. We came here from Dublin with no plans when I was eleven and we're still here fifty years later, so we must like something about it. Cycling along the new boardwalks and discussing the art along the way is one of the pleasures.' Another man says that Wogan's head is out of proportion and he does not like the cut of his sculpted chin. There has been a huge amount of commentary about the statue in the local and national press, as well as on social media, bearing out how Wogan once described Limerick: 'It is a town of spires, gossip and lots of frustrated people.'

Farther along, a search and rescue operation is underway and a small crowd has gathered to watch. Fire and rescue service crews and police have cordoned off the Shannon Bridge after a man walked into the river. Red-jacketed volunteers from Limerick Suicide Watch, formed in 2013, patrol the riverside and quays and walk the bridges to help if needed. No motive was known for the incident, but I was later told by one of the watchers that the man was rescued. 'The tide was very low and we calmly talked him out of it. Sometimes people will go in for a dip to cool off, but this wasn't the case with him.'

Keen to sample some of the exotic food the city offers, I opt for the Poppadom Indian restaurant near the Milk Market. Fortunately, the hot food comes with a large jug of water and is washed down, naturally enough, with a Kingfisher beer. Just when I am resigned to the sight of the bird being an eternal mystery, here it comes again, flying out from the label of the bottle with its motto 'The King of Good Times'.

Later that night good times continue in the company of Limerick's beautiful people, raising the roof at Jerry Flannery's bar. I am familiar with the Percy French song 'The Four Farrellys' but have never heard of 'The Five Flannerys' until I meet Michael Flannery. One of Limerick's longest-serving publicans, Michael's family name is inextricably linked as part of a drinking dynasty that has cornered a sizeable slice of the Limerick pub market. Michael's grandfather, William Flannery, opened the first bar in 1898 and the business has thrived. He explains the complicated breakdown of who runs what.

'My son, Seamus, runs a bar in Upper Denmark Street, while further along, in Lower Denmark Street, Philip Flannery, who is a brother of mine, owns a bar there and another in Shannon Street – each of those bars is managed by Philip's two sons, Philip and Paul. Patsy Flannery, who is my nephew, runs a bar in Wickham Street, and on Catherine Street, Jerry Flannery runs this bar with his son, also called Jerry, who was a hooker for Munster and Ireland. It's a well-known rugby bar for both players and garrulous alickadoos. Jerry retired from playing in 2012 through injury and now concentrates on bar duties.

'We like to keep it in the family and have five bars in the city and one in the county at Caherconlish out the Tipperary road ... I'd say we are unique in Ireland, or at least in Limerick. People often ask why we picked bars and I said that you have to remember there wasn't much in Ireland in the 1950s, which is why 400,000 people emigrated. We're lucky in what we bought, and despite recessions and setbacks, we were able to keep everything together.'

The youngest of fourteen, Michael's father was born in Co. Limerick and learnt the bar trade in Dublin, serving an apprenticeship with his uncle at the Palace Bar. This sparked off his interest in the business and in 1959 he leased his own bar in Wickham Street for two years.

'We bottled our own Jameson, which you could buy in casks for jars, and we sold it down through the years and now there's a big swing to whiskey and gin. In those days there wasn't much interest in the river; there were coal boats coming in and there could be thirty or forty men drawing coal to various parts of the city and barges with Guinness up to the early 1960s, until they started to bring it by road. There were pig and shoe factories and clothes and toffee makers such as Cleeve's. Farmers would bring pigs to the market with horse and carts with four of five pigs and there were two cattle marts in Limerick. It was a common sight to have seen somebody walking up the street with ten or fifteen pigs going to the bacon factories. The country people were good for business as a lot of small towns had a half day on Wednesday and would come in to shop and have a drink. Going back even twenty years ago there was a queue to open the door in the morning – at 10.30 am some would have soup or a few pints. They would sit around reading the paper or talk, so it was a bit of a sanctuary, but all that's gone now. Sure doesn't the time fly when you're enjoying yourself.'

On the walls, memories of the October 1978 'match of all matches' in which Munster beat the All Blacks are recalled in framed reports from the *Limerick Leader*. Munster supporters will never forget how they beat the mighty New Zealanders 12–0. The story is told in an exhibition at Thomond Park, the shrine of rugby for sports followers.

I come across a framed poster for an old film, *The Voice of Ireland*. It does not attract any interest but when I take photographs of it, it raises questions amongst the drinkers. The poster was produced to promote a black-and-white film about Ireland made in the early 1930s, I tell a gap-toothed drinker with a shock of white hair. Hayward appeared in the film along with Mick Gleeson, the Limerick singer about whom I am seeking information and whom Hayward had met in the Killaloe section of his book. The

Film poster from
The Voice of Ireland
hanging at Flannery's
Bar in Limerick.

drinker tells me he knows nothing about it but if I'm looking for some songs then the back room is the place to go. The theme of time is covered in some songs when a female vocalist breaks into Cyndi Lauper's 'Time after Time', followed by Roberta Flack's 'The First Time Ever I Saw Your Face' bringing the evening to a thought-provoking end.

BEEFY CUMULUS CLOUDS billow into cauliflower heads and long towers that soar over the river the next morning, a sure sign of an imminent downpour. Within ten minutes the first heavy drops of rain begin and the streets are deluged. Shoppers scarper for cover and I dive into a riverside café. There is something soothing about watching water falling into water, an elemental force mingling with itself. The waitress says the mercilessness of the rain sluicing the windows is a normal way to start the day in Limerick. 'It's best to get it out of the way early on but you can be sure it'll return later – that's why we call this place a Celtic rainforest.'

Aside from the weather, many people in the city are talking about the musical version of *Angela's Ashes*, which opened the previous week when it was given its world premiere. The musical grew out of Frank McCourt's misery memoir, which later became a film. It is the story of his impoverished childhood and the book for which he is best known. Although he died in 2009, his name is enshrined in the city and his classroom has been recreated from the 1930s with posters and photographs and a replica of the McCourt bedroom and kitchen. To give me a feel for what life was like then, Michael O'Donnell has offered me a personalized tour of this part of the city where both he and McCourt grew up. As the sun emerges, we meet beside a bronze bust of the author on a plinth and leave from the redbrick Tudor-style Leamy House (formerly Leamy School) in Hartstonge Street, which he attended, and which is now the Frank McCourt Museum. Our trail to where the McCourts lived starts through the well-ordered geometry of the streets of the Georgian district of Newtown Pery and includes stops at places drawn from his book. It is a step back into 1930s' Limerick, a place with which Hayward was familiar, now officially designated an Architectural Conservation Area. We turn a corner into the spacious Pery Square, an elegant terrace of four-storey brick townhouses dating from the 1830s where Limerick's wealthy families once lived. The houses, adorned with distinctive first-floor cast-iron balconies, show the patina of age. Doorcases are flanked by narrow window lights. Fine-boned elliptical fanlights are de rigueur over brightly painted front doors: blood red, gentian blue, canary yellow and bottle green. One building with a classical cut-stone portico has been converted into a boutique hotel and restaurant.

Across the road from this architectural grandeur, office workers are enjoying their sandwiches on grass and benches in the People's Park. It is somewhere, Michael says, that has always had an affectionate place in the hearts of Limerick people. Between the trees we make out the monument of Thomas Spring Rice, an

MP for the city from 1820 to 1832 who represented the political interests of the merchants of Newtown Pery. We walk down Barrington Street and a tight network of alleys and lanes, along the narrow Carroll's Row and on to St Joseph Street, which has not changed since McCourt's day.

'There are many examples of the old houses that are still standing and today some of them are rather desirable because people have added extensions, new roofs and extra rooms upstairs. In fact, my aunt and uncle lived there in the very last street that was called Vises Field. Now there are new houses for old people and they have tried to retain the ambience of what it was like.'

At the junction of Wolfe Tone and Bowman Streets we pause to look up Barrack Hill, which leads into Roden Street.

'The McCourts had a house in Roden Lane and they thought they were going to be comfortable there but they realized that when it rained, the water would flow down the lane, under the door and the whole place would be drenched. Eventually their father Malachy decided they would have to move upstairs. When they did, he said it was warm and they called it "Italy" because it reminded him of a warm country. Off Barrack Hill, in Roden Lane, there was a lady called Mrs Purcella and she was going blind. Frank sometimes would sit under the windowsill of the house, listening to Billie Holiday's jazz singing and other artistes on a radio that was given to her by the Blind Association of Ireland. And I can relate so much to that too. My grand-aunt was very ancient – probably only sixty-five but that was very old to us then – and she had a radio given to her by the Blind Association. She brought that with her and moved into our house and I would tell people I had a radio bought by my parents, which was not true of course, but in the 1940s we would have listened to John Count McCormack while Richard Hayward was on Radio Éireann with Delia Murphy.'

Michael leads through back alleys to Quinlan Street and on to The Crescent, which is a double crescent, an oval-shaped area whose two- and three-bay houses are occupied by solicitors, consultants and insurance brokers. Sections of Georgian Limerick – often touted as an essential and irreplaceable part of the city's heritage, especially along O'Connell Street – are crying out for much-needed stimulation. Standing on a traffic island, amidst the thrum of vehicles, a red-scarfed man takes a selfie in front of a bronze statue of Daniel O'Connell where metre-high water snorts from a fountain. The statue stands on a granite pedestal amongst flowerbeds overlooking O'Connell Street, which was named in his honour.

We pause outside the classical facade of St Joseph's Church before stepping inside. There is a Romanesque effect to the interior, caused in part by a series of single-light round-headed windows, as well as the arcades along the side walls of the transepts. Two women light candles and walk around the nave admiring the stained-glass window of St Patrick produced by the Harry Clarke studio. A young man approaches us, asking if he knows where he could find a priest because he is in urgent need of one. Michael suggests calling at the sacristy, then picks up the thread of his story.

'This is a place that McCourt knew well. At the time of his confirmation, he was feeling sick and the doctor was sent for. He was put into what was called the City Home Hospital because he had typhoid fever. He was in hospital for some days and was very upset because like any young lad he did not want to be there. Then one day from the ward next door he heard a girl's voice.

"Boy next door, what's your name?"

"Frank McCourt."

"And what's wrong with you?"

"I've got typhoid. And what's your name?"

"Patricia Carmody."

"And what's wrong with you?"

"I've got diphtheria."

The ward sister did not want typhoid talking to diphtheria, so she moves him upstairs to another ward, but he doesn't want to be there because he thinks the place is haunted. Eventually Patricia gets books sent up to him, including works by Shakespeare and he loves them because he has never read them before. He constantly repeats some of the sentences from one of the works: "I do declare induced by potent circumstances that thou art mine enemy." Frank gradually got better and one day the doctor came and sat beside his bed, leant across Frank to take his pulse and farted. And Frank smiled to himself and said he knew no doctor would fart in front of a dying child.

'When he returned to Leamy's National School and went back into fifth class all his friends had gone into sixth class. He asked the teacher if he could pass on and when he refused, Frank was very disappointed. He asked again and the teacher told him to go home and write a composition on Limerick and then he'd see what he could do. Frank came in the next day and read his composition:

"The name of my composition is 'Jesus and the Weather'. I don't think Jesus who is our Lord would have liked to have been born in Limerick. It's always raining, and the River Shannon keeps the whole city damp. My father blames the River Shannon for the death of my two brothers. Is it any wonder he chose Israel in which to be born – a lovely warm country?" He moved up to sixth class the next day.'

The general conditions of the time were also to blame for ill health.

'The Shannon played quite a part in the sicknesses that were prevalent in the late 1930s and into the 1940s. Work was scarce and there was no nourishment. Having come from that background, I know what McCourt means when he said about all the clouds in the Atlantic gathering together drifting up the Shannon, dumping their contents in Limerick causing all kinds of coughs, flus, fevers and consumption – and it certainly did. The consumption was tuberculosis, which was huge then … I had an uncle, Paddy, who got consumption and he was put into the City Home Hospital with typhoid fever. Very few people escaped.'

When we arrive back at Leamy House, Michael speaks about the new musical, which has reignited interest in McCourt's life and brought the Shannon to wider attention again.

'It's very well done, and I think Frank would be happy with it,' Michael says. He knew McCourt well. In 1998 he came up with the idea of a walking tour and asked Frank how long he thought it would run for. "'Michael," he replied, "you have a job for life" and sure enough I'm still at it twenty years on.'

Frank McCourt had a difficult relationship with the Catholic Church. When asked for his thoughts on his mortality, he once quipped to the *Limerick Leader*: 'I don't want funeral services or memorials. Let them scatter my ashes over the Shannon and pollute the river.' In his time there were numerous religious orders in Limerick, many of them now closed. As I walk around the streets, I am conscious of church buildings that have been deconsecrated or repurposed. The Franciscan Church in Henry Street has been turned into a museum dedicated to the memory of Jim Kemmy. In *City of Churches*, a gazetteer of Limerick's ecclesiastical buildings, Emma Gilleece quotes a history lecturer from Mary Immaculate College Chapel about students turning up for mass: 'In the 1980s and 1990s, the numbers attending mass in the church always increased dramatically before exams, with hundreds of students crowding in, praying for inspiration.' While the face of church-going in the city has been transformed in the last thirty years, its many surviving places of worship represent a variety of denominations. African culture and heritage is celebrated with a special week-long series of events. The levels of immigration from various African countries and eastern Europe has led to the term the 'new Irish'. The numbers of overseas workers have been especially swollen by the Polish community. Michael O'Donnell suggested I call at St Michael's Church in Denmark Street for a feel of this multicultural and ethnically diverse aspect of Limerick life today.

Since 2012 Fr Leo McDonnell, the parish priest of St Michael's, has worked alongside Fr Andrzej Sroka, the Polish chaplain in the church. Fr McDonnell was born and brought up in Limerick and trained in hotel management in Europe. He returned to Ireland in 1980 and entered the seminary in 1987.

'I grew up in Barrington Street, which is now the parish of St Joseph's, but back in those days St Michael's was the busiest parish in Munster,' he says. 'It incorporated the church here, and St Joseph's, and the parish got so big that it included another church,

Our Lady of Lourdes, which meant there were three churches in St Michael's parish with seven priests.

'Limerick, and elsewhere in Ireland, started off with the Celtic Tiger so it is a world of difference from the homogeneous society that it was. New workforces were needed from different countries in Europe, and they came from Poland with degrees and skills. If you walk down Henry Street, you'll hear a lot of east European languages, as well as Brazilian. They are very well spoken in English. Their children are now going to school and some of them are even learning Irish, which is extraordinary as they are becoming more Irish than Polish. They have assimilated well in all aspects of Irish life and business. Believe it or not, the next spoken language to English in Ireland now is Polish.'

Fr Sroka says the Polish people who came were from the northern part of the country and were first and foremost seeking jobs. Initially they were not interested in the place itself, its culture or history. In Limerick there are an estimated 10,000 Poles out of a population of 75,000 and five Polish masses take place in the church every week. The overall experience has been a positive one.

'We have six Polish supermarkets,' Fr Sroka says, 'and at least 500 people for mass at 12.30 pm, and in Newcastle West we have more than sixty people every Sunday. Many attend church in local parishes and St Joseph's, and wherever they are living they speak good English. When it's busy I call in help from Polish chaplains in Clare and Galway. I need two or three masses on special feast days at Christmas and Easter since so many people are coming here because of the Polish tradition, which is a little different from the Irish one. Our mass is longer since it lasts ninety minutes. But now they also like aspects of the cultural life and attend Culture Night, and there are many kids who enjoy taking part in Irish dancing. Sometimes the Polish families sing Irish ballads and they like going to pubs to hear live music. They also like singing in the church choir but they are not as talented as the local people.'

Some Poles have gone back because the economy in the country has improved but accommodation and costs are rising so a substantial number remain in Limerick. Polish energy and culture is contributing to parish life and the general business world of Limerick. Fr Sroka also leads pilgrimage groups from Limerick to Poland and talks about the language problems they encounter.

'I was in Poland with an Irish pilgrimage last week and we went to a shop in the Sanctuary of Divine Mercy shrine in Kraków. The woman in charge asked me how long it took me to learn and speak English because she could not understand their accents. She knew English well but could not pick up a single word of any of the Moyross accents. I told her it took me six months to realize what people were saying.'

Fr McDonnell reflects on the differences that have taken place in his time in the streets around the church. 'A number of years ago we had the closure of the Franciscans, then the closure of the Jesuits – although there is a group of priests in there now – then the Dominicans left. The Dominican nuns have taken their place and are very involved. The Augustinian Church is still going strong, but the priests are getting on there in years too. The Redemptorists have survived but owing to falling numbers they have now scrapped the last mass solely for men in Limerick. At one time more than 10,000 men attended the archconfraternity masses, amounting to thousands each night.'

Despite this decline and the fact that significantly fewer people live in the city centre, Fr McDonnell says the Catholic church is thriving in Limerick. 'People may not be going to mass to the same extent, but they are constantly praying, and we have the shrines here. The number of candles being lit in the church on a weekly basis is huge. We have a large number of confessions too, especially amongst the Polish community – and that's the way Ireland was of old, perhaps fifty years ago or more, but we don't have the queues that the Polish have. The Polish people used their skills as carpenters, electricians, and painters and built the whole interior again, which is now beautiful and is used for prayer groups and meetings, and the two communities generally work well together. It would be a much smaller parish if they weren't present.'

14

The 'clean dirt' of Mungret

FOR SEVERAL DAYS I have explored Limerick on foot but feel the need for a perspective on the city from the river. I'm given the name of Pat Lysaght, who helps navigate people on Shannon boat journeys as a water taximan.

I had arranged to meet Pat at 1 pm but with an hour to kill I decide on a haircut and find a barber called Pat Stapleton, who classifies himself as the Best Barber in the World. Framed newspaper clippings describe Pat as the 'Barber of Limerick', a man with banter, comedy and an 'amazing raconteur'. When I open the door into the salon a woman is cutting a man's hair while Pat is finishing off snipping someone else's. He wears a white jacket and a traditional handmade hat from Uzbekistan with a hammer-and-sickle cap badge. Without a word, he motions me to wait. He shows me to the chair and I explain that I just want a tidy up. He nods but says nothing. I wonder why, for such a garrulous man, he is not speaking. He points to a sign on the mirror in front of us: 'I can't speak well anymore so you will get a quiet haircut. Relax and enjoy it.'

Pat has lost his voice and I have lost my chance of talking to him about old Limerick. His wife Brigid, who acts as his mouthpiece, explains that ten years earlier he developed a problem with his voice box and no one has been able to diagnose what caused his loss of speech. She suggests, with a laugh, that it was due to talking to too many customers for more than fifty-three years of his working life. Many of them, she says, are reliable and one man has been coming from Tipperary to get his hair cut since 1952. I had not had a chance to find out about specific aspects of the city in the middle decades of the twentieth century but left with a smart Limerick-style short back and sides, and a line from one of Pat's best quotes ringing in my newly cold ears: 'Absence makes the hair grow longer.'

Before meeting Pat Lysaght for my boat trip, I have one other call to carry out. Hayward mentions in the Clare and Limerick section of his book about his friend Mick Gleeson whom he knew through their work in the early days of filmmaking in Ireland. On my street peregrinations I had come across a couple of Gleeson businesses, including a Spar supermarket. The man in charge of it is not aware of an actor or singer called Mick Gleeson.

'All my Gleesons came from Tipperary into Limerick around the time of the Famine and settled in tenements in Ellen Street. They were from around Borrisokane – who of course was a well-known Russian-Irishman of his time.'

My best bet, he says, is to call with Michael Gleeson, who runs shoe shops in William Street. While I wait to speak to the owner, I browse the first shop. Tables are crowded with a variety of soft-cushion shoes and multicoloured running shoes for normal feet, flat feet and high-arched feet. Racks hold polished shiny shoes, sweet smelling and made of high-quality deer leather. The aroma pervades the shop, a rich sensory experience.

'You're in the right place – you rang the right bell coming here,' Michael Gleeson says when I explain my interest in Mick Gleeson. 'I am his godchild, nephew and namesake.' A be-suited and affable man, he motions me to sit down beside a stand of shoe polish, laces and universal cleaner.

'My uncle used to sing and ran a pub in William Street in the late 1950s under the name P.J. Gleeson, which had originally opened in the 1880s. He appeared in a film called *The Voice of Ireland* in 1932 in which he sang 'The Stone Outside Dan Murphy's Door'. It was filmed in Mungret. Richard Hayward also appeared in that film and that is how he knew him. It was a travelogue promoting Ireland as a place to come to for a holiday. Mary Begley was in it too, as well as Frances O'Toole and Kathleen Conroy. I wouldn't know all the names of the singers and actors, but it was popular in its day.'

Several customers and a salesman are waiting to speak to Michael and a woman asks when she can see the in-store chiropodist. He breaks off our chat and returns a few minutes later.

'I've spent fifty-odd years successfully selling and fitting shoes. I like to say that I have been in shoe business while my uncle was in show business ... As regards your interest in uncle Mick, he was a reasonably good singer although he wasn't Pavarotti or Belafonte or anyone like that, but he had a strong voice. He spent time in Lisdoonvarna playing the fiddle where he entertained crowds in the Imperial Hotel each September. He was seventy-five when he died and although I knew him well, I had never really heard him singing. I don't know much more about him than that, but if you want to find out more, then the man you should contact is Nessan O'Donoghue out in Mungret.'

Mungret must wait until tomorrow. Time is running out and I hasten to meet my boat taxi at the appointed rendezvous. In the lunchtime sunlight, Pat Lysaght swings around in a small red boat into the marina at Custom House Quay behind the Hunt Museum and nods up at me from the water. He wears a racing green peaked cap and navy anorak. Although the sun is bright, it offers no warmth. I have already prepared for the near certainty of getting wet, but he hands me yellow leggings, a red anorak and a lifejacket, saying it will be cold later. When I ask about the length of time our journey might take, he replies, 'Don't worry about time, when you step on this boat you forget about time and move into another world – but we'll be back by dark o'clock.' His five-metre boat, *The Eye of the River*, is made of polyurethane plastic with an outboard motor.

'It's a real flier,' he says as we set off. 'It does a great job hopping off the old walls of Limerick. I know every rock in the place because I've hit every one of them at one time or another.'

Pat carries oars as a safety measure in case the engine packs up. Although retired, he works for a variety of contractors on river-based jobs, regularly assisting and advising rowers, canoeists and paddleboarders, as well as the owners of cruisers. He is familiar with the river's perilous tricks and blinds me with tides and half-tides, neaps and springs, high and low water.

'As it's tidal it's a difficult stretch of water and if you don't know the river it can be dodgy getting through the Limerick lock. I bring people with me in the dinghy firstly and show them what it's like. But I also bring out groups and a few old fogies like myself to places such as Plassey, or up the headrace or the tailrace where we're going this afternoon.'

Known as 'Mr Navigation', Pat is well versed in the Shannon and familiar with its tributary, the Abbey River, an uncelebrated, lesser-known waterway that flows around the eastern and southern shores of King's Island before re-joining the Shannon at Hellsgate. The Abbey may play second fiddle to its more glamorous neighbour, but its status as a river of importance was enhanced after dredging in 2000. Like the Shannon, it still rises up in anger after heavy rainfall to flood some areas. This afternoon Pat has brought his boat down the Abbey from Corbally near St Thomas' Island in the northern part of the city where he lives. He makes balanced judgements on the ebb and flow of the tide, and the water and air draft of the boat. It is now half tide, the best time to be out because it is low water, which will give us at least three hours.

'The tides are predictable and accurate, along with the tide book and charts that I study every day as it is my Bible,' he says.

As we leave the quay, parties of rooks and jackdaws clatter about London plane and lime trees. Sand martins make a commotion from their grass-and-feather nests in the walls of the former potato market. The calm and glassy water looks as brown as a bottle of Limerick Treaty City ale. Workmen shovel up leaves from the boardwalk, throwing them into the water. Orange sandbag levees are piled up to one-metre high along the front to help prevent flooding. We head downriver under Sarsfield Bridge with its candelabra-style lamps, unique to the city. Most people never see

A one-legged Limerick gull on display at the waterfront.

the bridge's elegant underside curvature with fluorescent lights, which were added some years ago but no longer work. We pause beside the steel-and-timber locks, which all boats are required to pass through on their way into Limerick.

'The lock-keeper is part-time and may open the gates only once a week,' Pat says. 'But if he isn't around and a cruiser wants to come up, I get them over the weir and then help with the other problem of getting them under the bridges. Because of their height, it means they may have to wait up to four hours for the tide to drop.'

We rub faces with the natural world, all animals keeping their own eyes on the water. A young river-watching heron hunches with a statue-still stance, giving the impression of enjoying meaningful solitude. The kingfisher continues to elude me, but I have decided by now that it has been more about the quest for it than the result. As we look back into town, a yellow crane swings around on the building site of the former Roche's Hanging Gardens that is being turned into a multi-storey block of offices and shops. In the early 1800s these vertical gardens, created by a banker called William Roche, were one of the marvels of Ireland. Exotic fruits were grown in hothouses and vegetables, flowers and fruit trees all flourished. In the clear air, the pin-sharp circumambient sights and sounds are more intensely defined.

The twin towers of the sixteen-storey Riverpoint building with blue-mirror glazing, flanked by apartment blocks, glint in the sun as our speed reaches nine knots. Nearby, the eye-catching Clarion Hotel is one of the most photographed architectural sites on the river. Little business goes on now at the port, apart from crushing scrap metal from factories and old cars, which is why it is known to some as the 'dock of the dead cars'. Grey crows scavenge from the top of sheds and mini mountains of scrap up to ten metres high, an eyesore for those arriving into Limerick by boat. Piles of disused tyres add to a picture of desolation. In the 1930s Limerick was a prosperous port with buoyant trade. The commissioners funded a dock extension in 1937 and by 1939 more than 365,000 tons of cargo was moving annually through the port. In those days, trading links with Britain and Europe were strong. The traffic port has migrated downstream with most business nowadays concentrated on Foynes along the estuary.

We pull over at a moss-covered quay wall with long strips of Greenheart timber, the stiffest wood in the world, used because of its durability and resistance to insect attacks. Pat points out the Bannatyne corn mill looking like an abandoned castle, and the tall, grey Rank grain silo, an austere and unadorned rib-like structure of reinforced concrete. The silo, now obsolete, was completed in 1935 for the government's wheat-growing scheme – a subject with which Hayward was familiar since he later made a documentary film, *Tomorrow's Bread*, in 1943 for the de Valera government. The building was used to dry wheat and is now a protected structure but its distinctive tilt led to the local name, the Leaning Tower of Limerick.

We have almost reached the point where the river will shortly surrender itself to the estuary. From here the river and sky are flung wide open. Pat swings around heading for Clancy's Quay, where plastic cartons and bottles surface. We drift past a discarded shopping trolley. Ahead of us he spots a strange piece of flotsam, which turns out to be the corpse of a seagull with its wing upended. It was caught in a fishing lure, a type of artificial fishing bait. Doing his bit to help keep the river clean, he hauls it in.

A small school of fish disappears quickly into their hidden subaqueous world. Pat explains that anglers are usually looking for salmon, eel, trout, common dace or flounder, which are strange flat fish whose eyes move across to the side of their heads. We progress upstream passing the Arts-and-Crafts-style Shannon Rowing Club dating from 1868 and make our way safely over the Curragower Falls, now becalmed compared to my first sight of them a few days ago. The tide kills the rapids, which is why early afternoon is the best time to approach it. We reach Thomond Bridge, where repair work on capstones and stabilizing the parapets is underway with one side closed and a stop-go system for traffic. The bridge dates from 1845 and its stone is crumbling badly, Pat says, and needs urgent attention.

Riverine Limerick is a place from where to appreciate the past and the present. Major public buildings seem naturally to find their place beside the river showing that it is still of paramount importance. History is deeply etched in the form of King John's Castle, an Anglo-Norman fortress whose walls are besieged by giant hogweed. Its towers and turrets represent a conspicuous and imposing five-sided fortification inaugurated by the king himself in 1210 which now comes with the addition of a new glass room. St Mary's Cathedral, dating from 1111 AD, as well as other buildings such as St Munchin's Church, founded in 1827 and named for the patron saint of the city, and the cut-stone and Gothic-designed Toll House beside the bridge, were all familiar to Hayward. The city hall and the extensively renovated courthouse encroach on the horizon but illustrate that the river is still *the* place to be located.

Sandbags line a stretch of the waterfront in preparation for winter flooding. Pat explains the devastation caused by the flood in February 2014. As a result, the authorities raised the height of the wall with the addition of a concrete triangular top, shaped like a well-known bar of Swiss chocolate, which has earned it the nickname of 'Toblerone wall'. We make our way up to Thomond Weir, obsolete for more than forty years but still straddling the river. This was a place, according to Pat, where thousands of salmon were caught. It is in a dilapidated condition, with a dozen gulls patrolling around it. He picks up speed as we move into deeper water and a wider stretch of the river, leaving behind the city centre and passing the island field at St Mary's. Ahead of us lies the low range of the heavily forested round hills of Clare. Near the Barrack Lane Boat Club, half a dozen drakes and ducks are huddling together in lovebird companionship at the water's edge. Several of Limerick's quintessential flat-bottom boats, known as 'gandelows', are moored here. Some of them were used by lightkeepers or as tenders to harbour workboats. The derivation of their name is uncertain but one school of thought suggests it came from gondoliers who serenade lovers as they punt along the Grand Canal and other Venetian waterways.

The river cuts a crystalline path through the countryside. At a fork Pat branches off under the Shannon Railway Bridge and the concrete bridge at Parteen, passing red and white navigation markers into Co. Clare. Soon we reach the tailrace that leads up to Ardnacrusha, a green and serene two-kilometre corridor of trees. There is an electric energy to the air. We are hemmed in on both sides in our own private arcadia by a procession of tall, deep woody foliage where dappled sunbeams filter through, sparkling the water with ripples. The forest includes ash and pine, alder, beech and sycamore. Poking through branches, the vigorous climbing plant, old man's beard, known as travellers' joy, is taking over.

It is curious to discover such a pastoral waterway beside Ardnacrusha, an industrial plant that can shed up to 400 metres of water per second. When it opened, it disrupted the lives of fishermen, altering the flow of the river and affecting the way fish behaved. We spiral around and head for Corbally, where Pat lives. The banksides are cloaked with deep green mosses and waxy ferns. Pat reads the river- and skyscape, all the time watching the banks and trees, spotting snatches of movement. Then, out of nowhere, low and fast, it comes arrowing along the river, a streak of electric, laser-bright blue. Through my binoculars, I catch a glimpse of his dagger bill and a bright stripe, a flying furnace of magical colour. As the bird flies past, dead straight, wingbeats whirring, he winks at me – perhaps a wink for luck, a reward for patience, and most definitely not a waste of time. He banks and disappears all within a few seconds. The kingfisher sighting is not a surprise to Pat who is used to seeing them. In fact, he says that he has often watched them washing and cleaning themselves along sections of this waterway. 'They're just birds, aren't they?'

They may just be birds to Pat but seeing a kingfisher is, for me, one of the most purely elemental spectacles of my Shannon journey. With its vivid plumage, in beauty and form, the 'king of fishers' is an exotic enigma. It was a brief wildlife relationship but in ornithological circles, it is regarded as a privilege to see these Shannon supermodels of the avian world. Literature has romanticized the bird; its biographer David Boag says 'only the righteous ever see the kingfisher'. Words of the Scottish nature writer Jim Crumley snap into focus: 'If there is anything more flamboyantly *haute couture* in all the fauna of the land, I have not seen it.'

On the way to Corbally we pass through an area Pat calls 'the bend in the river', a meeting of the waters at St Thomas' Island, beside the remnants of the abandoned Lax Weir, which was made of solid cut stone built by the Danes. In its heyday, the weir was 457 metres long and extended from the water mill at Corbally to Parteen. Little is left of it now. Sections are overgrown with vegetation and ivy covers the remains of a caretaker's house. Salmon cribs were once positioned at the weir and meant that the fish could not return once they passed through their narrow vertical openings. Hayward referred to Corbally, which, he wrote, came from the Irish *corbhaile*, meaning 'the odd town'. The Lax Weir was built by the Norsemen as a salmon trap; 'lax' is the old Norse word for a salmon. The fierce weather in the winter of 2015 wreaked havoc, flooding houses and submerging cars after the Park Canal burst its banks.

'The silt is building up and islands have cropped up where there never were any before. If a sally tree comes down and catches on a rock, then the river surge of leaves and branches creates a new island. St Thomas' has even grown in size since I was a kid. It was twenty-three acres and is now twenty-five. There was also a sandbar, which has been pushed back with the floods, so it has changed a huge amount.'

As well as a meeting of the waters, this is also an area where social history meets natural history and has been designated a wildlife sanctuary. Although I am still in an epiphanic trance from having seen *Alcedo atthis* burn into my retina, Pat tells me to keep an eye and ear out for other birdlife, including greylag geese. 'They usually come through here about ten minutes to four, which is about now.' On cue, a pair of thick-necked greylags with their distinctive bright orange bill perform a low-altitude flypast. Next to the weir on the island is a peculiarly shaped ivy-smothered building. Pat describes it as a 'garderobe', a historic term for a castle, which comes from the French for wardrobe and was used as a storeroom for valuables.

'We had baths up here in Corbally in the 1940s and '50s. It was a place of fun and recreation, especially for the Abbey fishermen. I supplied a boat and worked with them on the dredging and when the marina opened, I was part-time with the city council helping to keep the navigation clear and looking after lifeboats.'

The Shannon and Abbey rivers pulse through Pat's veins all year round as he keeps a steady hand at the tiller. They often cause sleepless nights as he ponders what the next day's river expedition might involve.

'I was awake last night wondering if the turbines are going to be on tomorrow for a job I'm doing for a company. I've been asked to put up booms and need to check if they have told the power station that the tide is at five o'clock in the morning and will have dropped after three hours. Reading a river is just the same as driving a car, and you lose touch if you don't do it often. Sometimes I might just look at the birds or a couple of fish might jump. But I don't want to be doing nothing and love to get out and to have an excuse to bring people like yourself out for a spin.'

A lover of rivers and the doyen of boatmen, Pat makes his way around without the need of maps, compass or GPS, which is why he is known to his friends as Pat Nav.

THROUGH A SERIES of telephone calls and emails, I eventually track down Nessan O'Donoghue, who is involved with the Mungret Heritage Society. He agrees to meet me at the Milk Thistle Kitchen Café, housed in the former Mungret Jesuit College. *You'll find me easy enough*, he says in his email, *I'll be standing, Richard Hayward-like outside the front door, puffing my pipe.*

Hayward was often photographed with a pipe or cigarette in his hand or mouth. But during his time in Limerick he had difficulty finding a camping site anywhere near the water. His perambulations took him to Mungret, south-west of the city, where he found a suitable spot. Apart from having read in Hayward's Shannon book that it was a place that boasted of having wise women, I know little about the area. Early Christian Ireland had a monastic school there, founded co-incidentally by St Nessan, who died in 551. Its fame as a seat of learning spread fast, with students arriving in large numbers. The monks of Lismore felt jealous of the growing fame of the monks of Mungret and sent them a challenge to meet them in a scholarly disputation. The men from Mungret were not happy at the thought of the encounter with the giants of Lismore but they devised a plan. Shortly before the visiting scholars arrived, they dressed up a number of their cleverest monks as old women washing clothes at a point in a stream which the visitors would have to cross as they approached Mungret. They spoke Greek and Latin with such fluency that it frightened off the Lismore monks.

Uncertain of how to reach the area by car or which bus to take, I decide to jump in a taxi from the city centre. My taxi driver is filled with swearword-infused anger, as well as love-hate bitter laughter about the city, exemplified in a fifteen-minute vitriolic tirade about life on the Shannon.

'There's no jobs here, no industry, the docks are long gone, the place is lifeless and all they do is put up statues to the dead,' he rants. 'They're good at commemorating long-gone people in this town but they don't do much for the living. Fab city me arse, dead statue city is more like it ... and don't get me started on kami-bloody-kaze cyclists and the mad zombies on smartphones – they'll all be dead before me. And people like you just want to go to the cement capital of Limerick – best of luck with that one.'

As good as his word, Nessan O'Donoghue – a calm counterpart to the taxi driver – is surrounded by a fug of Mick McQuaid tobacco smoke outside the café. Nessan taught economic history and business in the diocesan college in Limerick and when he retired pursued his first love, the history of Mungret, which he felt had been neglected.

'The Jesuits came here in 1882 and stayed until 1974,' he says. 'In the space of that time they sent more than a thousand priests all over the world to missions. St Patrick is said to have founded the schools and promoted St Nessan to take charge of them. The most famous of all former pupils is the Vatican's so-called 'Scarlet Pimpernel', Monsignor Hugh O'Flaherty, who defied the Nazi command in Rome. During the Second World War he hid thousands of Jews and Allied soldiers from the Germans in safe houses in and around the Holy City. He later got a knighthood from the Pope. It all started here, where he blossomed as a student at the college and was a senior apostolic.'

He explains how his interest in the work of Hayward came about. 'It was through *The Voice of Ireland* because I grew up listening to stories about this famous film made in Mungret. My father had an appearance in it too, shooting pigeons. A few years earlier, my mother had featured in a silent film by Victor Haddick called *Ireland's Rough-Hewn Destiny*. It featured a scene in Mungret where the locals were filmed dancing at the crossroads with music by a piper. In *The Voice of Ireland*, people were also dancing on a timber platform. This film was a photographic study of the four provinces and the first indigenous sound picture ever made in Ireland. When the filmmakers had finished, they left the platform to the locals who moved it up to the village and the dancing continued one night a week. I started doing research on it and wondered if I could get a copy of the film. It was then that I came across Hayward, who would have been known to the older men around Mungret. He took part in the film too and was known as the Ulster bard. The film was a talkie version of the earlier one and it was made to promote Ireland and its products for the Empire Marketing Board whose purpose was to encourage trade between Ireland and the colonies.'

The ninety-minute film, which was premiered simultaneously in Limerick and Philadelphia in November 1932, was shown twice-nightly for three weeks in Limerick, with a special showing for the people of Mungret. We talk about Hayward's time in Mungret gathering material for his book, which was seven years after the film was made. He found the area highly industrial because of the cement factory:

> While it is undoubtedly a great boon to the work-people and merchants of Limerick it is nothing but a menace and an eyesore to people who are only concerned with the beauty of the country. For over a wide area this factory has spread a mantle of limestone dust and is a considerable nuisance. Everything within sight of us, fields, trees, hedges, cottages, shrubs, and vegetation, was reduced to one monotonous prospect of dirty grey. Even the Shannon itself was saturated with the dust.

Hayward contemplated swimming in the river at Mungret but was reluctant because of the dirty water. He included a short conversation he had with the postman whose bicycle had been lying in bushes:

> 'A swim,' said the postman. 'Sure this is the grandest place in the world for that same, and it's meself should know, for I'm only just out of it.'
> 'But it's so dirty,' I protested.

'If it's dirty it's clean dirt that's in it,' said the postman, 'and the best thing in the world for you at that … You'll get the best swim you ever had, and when you come out of it you'll find no trace at all of the mud you're talking about.'

Hayward took the postman's word, stripped off his clothes and enjoyed a pleasant swim in the water, finding it buoyant.

Our conversation turns to the factory, which today still produces cement. There is a worry about a controversial €10m plan by the company to burn used tyres and solid recovered waste. The Limerick Against Pollution group has expressed concern about health implications. Recently Irish Cement held a family fun day to welcome the local community and show them round the site. The purpose of it was to mark the arrival of a new digger, known as a 'front-end loader', which is taller and wider than a double-decker bus.

Nessan says that although the chimneys were removed in the 1990s, cement is still being made from crushed limestone. His memories of it are vivid. 'When I was a kid in the 1940s the factory was in your face, everything was coated in white dust and it was a sensory experience. You could see it, you could hear it because it was very noisy, especially when the hooter went off and the crows would rise out of the quarry, you could feel it when the rumble of the big explosion went off when they were detonating the limestone, and you could taste it with the dust. It was the first major industrial activity that we were close to and was very impressive because it meant that the twentieth century had arrived. In Hayward's time they were using crushed limestone and mud from along the Shannon. They mixed these into a slurry and then it was put into a kiln and came with stuff called clinker, which was heated at 1500 degrees and ground into cement by gypsum.

'That mud along the Shannon had a great deal of uses before the cement factory came. It was used to make plaster cast if you broke your arm and for floors in cottages. They would spread out mud on the floor, let it dry and then you would invite in the kids to dance on the floor and play music, then add another layer of mud and another session of music. It was also used to make bricks. In Limerick, before the concrete blocks came along, there were brick factories along the river and in Mungret but Hayward is not wrong when he complained about the smoke. When the tide is out it is still muddy as the estuary stretches at least forty miles to the sea and Limerick is unusual as being tidal so there is a high tide content. The little creek where Hayward swam is still in use – although not to the same extent because it used to be where the local fishermen kept their boats, but around 2007 they finally stopped net fishing on the estuary.'

During his visit Hayward found the people friendly. He was given apples and accepted hospitality. 'He was probably regarded as quite an exotic character with his caravan and smoking his pipe and his love of people and his singing. People who smoke pipes are rarely threatening. In the 1930s it was common for people to walk from the city out along the riverbank to the quay in Mungret, then walk into the village and back into town. The bank is still there but the road has disappeared and been swallowed up by the quarry. We've always regarded Mungret as separate from the city.

'At the start of this century we were getting thousands of new houses, but we had no community centre, just more houses and a shopping centre. The green area in the college grounds presented an opportunity to maintain a community centre and it has been developed for walks to help people identify with the area. We have organized interpretative panels for visitors, which tell the story of the monastic site and of Mungret in different languages and we recorded a huge amount of detail on the history of the graves.

'I felt that a Mungret identity had been lost. When we were growing up, we were proud to be from this area because of the monastic connection or even, God forbid, the cement factory. I began to wonder what I could do to preserve it. The population of this parish in the 1950s was about a thousand – we wanted to let them know the history so they could identify with it. In the latest census the population has grown to almost 20,000. Most of these people come from elsewhere but their kids are going to the schools here as two new ones have opened. There's a fine GAA club too.

'There is a strong connection between the community here and the Shannon, which has existed since Mesolithic times as we are effectively on the Shannon's shore. That connection has unfortunately been lost because of the cement factory, which quarries the land between Mungret and the Shannon so people are now not conscious of feeling close to the river. I decided to bring a group every year to make them more aware of it and travel the river by boat on what we called pilgrim voyages. We went to Scattery Island, Lough Derg, Clonmacnoise, Lough Ree and Carrick-on-Shannon. In the sixth century there was a big spread of monastic activity along the Shannon, right down to Scattery. They would have known and visited each other and called into St Nessan in Mungret and St Senan in Scattery. There was also contact between the Shannon and the continent with a flow of activity and the river was the conduit as the rest of the country was largely forested. People are drifting away from the institutional church but still want a religious experience.'

15

'Source of its soulfulness'

FOR THE GRAND finale to my journey I begin by sitting on the dock of the bay, or more correctly, Beagh Castle, near the hamlet of Ballysteen, perched on a promontory of the Shannon estuary, about ten kilometres west of Limerick where it unspools into what might be termed a middle-aged spread. The estuary is an ambiguous place with a dual personality, which borders on the southern portion of Clare and the northern section of Limerick leading to Co. Kerry. With one of the deepest natural watercourses in Europe and stretching for over a hundred kilometres, it is the largest estuary in Ireland, and somewhat intimidating in terms of trying to work out an approach to it. Having cycled, driven and boated, I wanted to test my walking boots for part of the way on the Limerick side since I had already covered the Clare coast out to Loop Head in my book on the Wild Atlantic Way.

On my journey I had seen where the river had been forded and bridged, harnessed and dammed, diverted and pinched, so it is now time see what the estuary offers. Beyond the city the river divides into the North Channel and South Channel. Carved with a crooked knife, the Limerick shoreline has numerous secluded slips and jetties, turf piers, quays and small harbours, sequestered headlands, points and creeks, sandy shallows and lumps of rock. The poetry of the waterway is apparent through its alluring names:

The Whelps, Rincawinaun, Ilaunavoley, Gammarel, Knockfinglas, Sturamus Island, Mount Trenchard Point and scores of others reflecting heritage, history and lore. They all sit alongside forts, castles, churches, holy wells and standing stones.

The ancient ruin at Beagh (Hayward translated its meaning as 'a place of birch trees') is a strikingly tall abandoned square tower house with window slits, but it is a long way from being a fairy-tale castle. In May 1827 twenty-five people boarded a boat from the castle to collect seaweed for manure on the islands. After the weather changed quickly, twelve of them decided to remain on the island while the other thirteen – eleven men and two women – set sail in heavy seas. The boat overturned and all thirteen drowned, their bodies being washed ashore in just a few minutes. The castle, which dates to the early thirteenth century, was built as a defensive outpost by the FitzGeralds of Desmond on the grounds of a former Viking settlement where a chapel had been erected around the 820s. During its chequered history, the building came into the possession of the Knights of Glin and remained in the Glin lineage for three centuries. In 1569 Thomas Fitzgerald, the fifteenth Knight of Glin, was beheaded in Limerick. One story claims that his mother, who was present at the execution, seized his head, drank his blood and put the dismembered body parts into a linen sheet. When she set out for home with his body she was followed by a large funeral cortege and keening women. After a battle thought to have been near Beagh Castle, his body was buried in Lislaughtin Abbey, west of Tarbert.

In Cromwellian times, the castle was occupied by Sir Hardress Waller. As a major general in Cromwell's army, he captured Carlow Castle in 1650, playing a key role in the Siege of Limerick in 1651, and eight years later led the officers who seized Dublin Castle in 1659. The following year he was jailed in Athlone, sent to England as a prisoner and later sentenced to death, but his life was spared through the intervention of his friends. During the Napoleonic Wars, Beagh Castle was used as a defensive outpost. Its spectacular position led to it being painted and explored by artists, architects,

The historic Beagh Castle, which overlooks the Shannon estuary, is a tall, abandoned square tower house.

archaeologists, writers and sailors. It was painted by the landscape artist Samuel Brocas in the 1840s and is mentioned in several books of sailing directions for the estuary. From the 1830s the castle served as a coastguard station with the staff living in the cottages. By the late nineteenth century, the pier was a stopping point for the popular Shannon steamers, which ran from Limerick city to Kilrush and called at Beagh. A new quay and slipway were built in the early 1900s. In 1969 an Italian Count and his American wife bought the castle. They passed it on to their daughter, who was given planning permission for the conversion of five adjoining dilapidated former coastguard cottages to holiday rentals, but the development did not proceed.

However, a new lease of life could be underway since a *For Sale* board by Scanlon Auctioneers is in place beside the cottages, comprising 17.5 acres of grazing land. The cottages, dating from the mid-nineteenth century, are a roofless and windowless shell, exposed to the elements and in need of much TLC – a snip, along with the castle, and a slice of history for a mere €260,000. It is being sold with a view to restoration as a 'once-in-a-lifetime purchase of a famous Shannon landmark steeped in beauty and history'. It is fascinating to reflect on what went on in this castle and in the area surrounding it, but also curious to think of who would wish to turn it into a holiday home. Stone steps lead up to a door along a path filled with clover and bird's foot trefoil, while wild woodbine, and tall stands of rosebay willowherb grow profusely. Elder, ash and sycamore trees surround the castle along with a tangle of bramble and blackberries. Its side door flaps half-heartedly in the breeze and inside is a jumble of stones and rubble, a place inhabited nowadays by owls.

The tide is out. Thick Limerick mudflats throw up a large amount of detritus, some of it worked by crows. It is a chaotic jumble of rock, scree, stones and boulders. A single discarded red shoe waits for Cinderella. There is a dizzying variety of packets of anti-static spectacle wipes, computer and sterile wipes, everything for cleaning industrial machinery to applying insect repellent. This appears to be one of the fastest-growing non-biodegradable categories being casually thrown away. Despite the chaotic and unsightly debris, the river is placid but generates a silky grey texture, a liminal landscape of waste, dereliction and memory.

An overwhelming sense of emptiness prevails, although the area is imbued with a romance of remoteness. Few boats are on the water until the appearance of a long red and white vessel, *Priscilla*, moving slowly in the mid-stream on its way into Limerick. My gaze is ineluctably drawn to the large oil tanks, the flashing beacon light and runways of Shannon International Airport. Under impossibly large skies, I walk as close as possible to the edge, working out somewhere halfway along where I might take the pulse of the estuary and gain a feel for its marshes and birdlife. There are so many villages to discover here: Kildimo, Kilcornan and Pallaskenry; Patrickswell, Crecora and Cappagh; Caherconlish, Ballyneety and Ballybricken-Bohermore. Although sparsely populated, the communities have their own identity and appear to be thriving since they support a national school, church and resource centre. Sometimes just a crossroads marks a townland. A dog-walker pauses to talk to me about the castle. 'If you wanted to buy it, you'd need a bit of money behind you and be prepared to spend a few million to bring it up to standard. It wouldn't suit everybody.'

Twisting threads of narrow roads lead me through Ballysteen where signs promote it as a community text alert area. Gated houses and mansions, some secreted behind trees, are neatly manicured with high privet hedges alongside honeysuckle, the bright yellow of coreopsis and Mexican orange blossom. The tarmac is splattered with dung, providing a fast-food festival for insects. Since it is milking time, Friesians have primacy, walking slowly over the cattle-crossing tracks leading into lanes with grids.

I make my way past Bushy Island and Bushy Point, circumventing Washpool Creek and via a narrow back road regain the estuary, tracing a pathway along a bank to Ringmoylan Quay where the weather throws up a stiff breeze. A sign at a crossroads advertises a gandelow boat race at the pier, but the heavy swells have led to a delay. However, the rowers are determined to press ahead with their annual event, which is now in its third year. Several participants warm up by shovelling buckets of water from the inside of the simple light blue wooden boats with fixed seats. The race has been delayed for thirty minutes in the hope that the weather improves. The darkening clouds lie low, obscuring the hills of Clare on the other side. Several people speak about the area and what it means to them. One man used to come to the pier as a child and remembers an open-air swimming pool to the west of Ringmoylan quay. He talks about the fishing boats, which are typical of Limerick and were operated by three men.

'They were specially built for the mudflats and designed to slide along the mud,' he recalls. 'The boats were unique to this part of the Shannon and went down as far as the Fergus estuary. They were light and at the same time strong and had a shallow draught, which made them manoeuvrable, allowing the crew to row them easily over long distances. Their versatile shape enables them to cope with the short steep seas generated by a fast-running ebb tide against strong prevailing westerlies.'

On the water, the crew of the Bunratty Search and Rescue lifeboat bobs contentedly up and down. A jet-skier powers his way through waves like a bucking bronco rider, creating lines of white disturbance in his wake. The number of spectators has swollen to almost a hundred, gathered along the pier while the swell on the water is decreasing. Another man, who has built the boats, talks about people who used them.

'Limerick was a major port for timber and because of that there were good clean spruce boards and that's why the boat became popular. You had fishermen, farmers and lightkeepers who all had gandelows and it was their only means of contact with people on the mainland. But the gandelow was also used for cutting thatching reed from the beds along both shores of the river so it had a practical nature. In certain areas it had a different shape and in some places, it came with a narrow, tapering transom.'

Dog-walkers are out in force to cheer on the rowers. Eleanor Purcell, a businesswoman in Limerick city who lives nearby, has come to support the race. She has also brought her two animals, Fonsie, a retriever Labrador cross, and a three-legged mongrel called Puppy, both of whom enjoy a swim. Eleanor speaks about her love of the estuary, which she looks out at every day from her house.

'For the people from the city and especially the fishermen all the way out to Askeaton, the gandelows would have been the boats that were used in the early twentieth century. They like really low water and I have one still tied below on the mooring. Now it's just a sport, but they're the same design of boats that would have been used to bring turf and milk over from Clare and handle all the commerce that took place on the Shannon. Ringmoylan was one of the strongest piers nearest the city. As children we were always brought here if it was too short a day or too bad a day to go to Ballybunion, the seaside resort of choice for my father. Part of a day out to Ringmoylan would have been to walk back the shore. Fifteen years ago, when I found myself

Gandelow Boat Race underway at Ringmoylan on the Shannon estuary.

homeless and somebody said there was land for sale down here, after some trials and tribulations, that's where I bought my present house, right beside the beach here.'

We watch the casual transit of birds. Six duck take flight heading west. A slender herring gull slices through the air with uninterpretable cries while four others enjoy a gabfest on the pier. A herd of curlew sweeps down to one side of us. Eleanor says there are often oystercatchers, shelduck and mallard but no plover anymore. She is trying to put together a bird sanctuary and a total of seven snipe, whose numbers have been reduced along the Shannon, now live beside her. The energy of the tidal flow shapes the water, curls the waves, swirls and snaps it, giving it a brown, syrupy look.

'There are two tides every twenty-four hours and as the tide comes in, it creates a kind of great solidity and then it goes out and everything changes again. I find a sense of peace, which is to do with the tide. In an average year you have a change in tide of about five metres maximum running up to seven metres. You have a massive volume of water displaced in itself twice a day. And that affects the sky. Now, I don't know how, but as the tide is coming in the clouds can go electric. Most people experience it only when they're on their holidays. I often have discussions with friends of mine, that when you live in a beautiful place, it gives you an obligation to be happy all the time. That doesn't always work out.

'There's no sunset in Ireland, not even below in Dingle, to compare with the sunset here. The refracted light from the water is absolutely wonderful on the estuary, and from my house I have one of the best views in Ireland. My house is nearly a mile and a half off the road and prior to the Famine, nineteen families lived on my road. Now there's just me, I'm the only person living on this road, and I'm living here for the past fourteen years. And although I love the hot weather, I rather like Ringmoylan in the wintertime.'

Four teams of men and women of all ages line up with the boats. The flagman in charge assembles the teams and they are finally under starter's orders as the 'Sporting Limerick' flag is dropped. To get down to the business of rowing, several participants remove their T-shirts. Furiously, they battle against the breeze towards the buoy cheered on by the crowd. Every stroke is a strong effort as they pull in unison. The races are over quickly but confusion reigns as to which boat is the overall winner. After a lengthy discussion, no one is clear who is victorious, but the organizers finally decide that the Bill Fitzgerald Memorial Race – known as the Masters' Race – should be awarded to the team from Newtown-Clarina.

By 9 pm the estuary is modulated by the atmospheric light of evening, the colours of the day have been desaturated and a quietude is restored once more to the water. The light is darkening with a widescreen starriness as I absorb myself in the soundscape where minor shushing has replaced the battle of the boats. I mull over what Eleanor Purcell had said about the estuary.

'Even when I saw it as a child as the storm broke through the clouds, the spears of light came down. My mother called it the light of heaven and here we have such wonderful light over the river because if the sun is in the sky these shafts of light come down to earth and it's something I always look at. I find the constant changing of the river, and the light on a river, is good for your soul – well it's good for my soul anyway, and it's the source of soulfulness.'

In the community-run tourist office in Askeaton, a former butcher, Anthony Sheehy, is busy explaining the highlights of west Limerick to a Mexican couple using a map of the estuary, outlining a place in which he is well versed. He ends with a cordial greeting, *Go raibh maith agat*, which confuses the woman. 'It means thanks and good luck in Irish,' he explains as she tries to repeat the phrase. Anthony says business is quiet and he readily agrees to lock up the small tourist office shop and show me around town. Anthony was born and bred in Askeaton, and his butcher's shop is a local hub on the quay.

'My father owned a butcher's shop here in 1939 and sold beef, mutton, fish and ammunition for fellows who were wildfowling as there was no lamb in those days. We had a mini supermarket and I trained under him and took over when he retired. I had a good name for the home-made Irish black pudding and supplied the big locations such as Dunraven Arms, Adare Manor, The Mustard Seed and Aghadoe Heights in Killarney.'

Hayward described Askeaton as a 'rambling' village and wrote about the River Deel, which is tidal and widens into a navigable creek on its two-mile journey down to the Shannon. The Deel makes its way up through Askeaton, which Anthony says is the second oldest town in Co. Limerick.

'It's quite a big river and was fantastic for fishing salmon and trout. There are still some trout in it upriver but for my part I just fish to get tourists into the town. You can see the Franciscan friary, a historic building, which has featured on six television programmes and I've been on them all. Beside us is Desmond Castle, built on an island on a rocky outcrop, where they're carrying out work at the moment. There are a lot of mudflats and the gandelow would slip down on to the water easily enough.'

The Askeaton of the twenty-first century is a straggling place with a population of 1200 which, like many villages near the Shannon, needs to be urgently re-energized. Many dilapidated properties are boarded up and there is feeling of desolation.

'It's sad to see what has happened,' Anthony says. 'The town needs an injection of money to improve the properties and we need a hotel or a good restaurant. We have banks and the credit union and a small coffee shop, we have a marina and a creamery and the Aughinish Alumina factory and every Friday morning we have the farmers' market, which attracts visitors, but the town has been neglected and so too has the estuary. Some people have discovered Askeaton and there is a big interest in what we have.'

Anthony feels if everybody pulled together, they would be doing more to promote small towns and villages along the river. He has taken on many different jobs to help in the development of Askeaton and multitasks in his varied roles.

'I'm a member of the community council, tidy towns, swimming club, civic trust and a volunteer tour guide. A sister of mine died back in 1964 and she is buried in the Franciscan friary. And I would meet people like yourself asking questions about the ruins. It was divine inspiration that got me interested in it and I said to myself we have something here in our own town. North Americans were great and were the first to have the money to come to Ireland, and they were amazed at our historical ruins as we took them for granted. I brought people around the friary and it developed from there. Then I had to meet the OPW to satisfy them that I knew what I was talking about. A professor from Limerick University came out some years ago and went through the tour guiding that I was doing. He said I knew more than he knew, so I'm obviously the only fool in Ireland.'

We walk through the garden of remembrance around St Mary's Church and I note down a heart-warming quotation: 'How very softly you tiptoed into my world / Almost silently for only a moment you stayed / But what an imprint your tiny footprints have left on my heart.'

Never mind touring the suite of historic buildings, which includes the church, the friary, Desmond Hall, or the abbey mill and corn store – the place Anthony wishes me to see in all its glory is the Askeaton pool and leisure centre at the Green. It is a place where he spends a considerable amount of time, since Askeaton has been a renowned swimming location for decades.

'The first gala was held in August 1959 when the club was formed and I began swimming in the masters' competitions in Dublin, continuing in that for many years. I'm in the pool five mornings a week and used to do distance swimming. In fact, the longest swim I ever did was across the estuary from the jetty at Shannon Airport on the Clare side right over to Beagh Castle.'

In the past year two men separately swam the length of the Shannon but I had never heard of anyone crossing it. 'You swam the whole estuary?' I ask incredulously.

He grips my forearm. 'As sure as my name is Anthony Sheehy, I swam the whole way across. It was the fifteenth of August 1993 on the Feast of the Assumption as it's called, although I'm not a holy roller. Me and another guy did the whole thing in one hour, twenty minutes and fourteen seconds. That was two-and-a-half miles in a straight line. We were confident of being able to swim it and now we count ourselves as true swimmers. It was a hot day and the river was like a billiard table but there were three pockets of water that I went into and they were freezing and I never have forgotten it. These were cold springs that were shooting up. I had always wanted to swim across the Shannon and it was the crawl that I was doing so there was a great sense of achievement. For some people the estuary is muddy and inhospitable, but to me it has a sense of mystery about it. And don't forget this is the estuary that carries the river's secrets out to the sea.'

A NARROW ROAD takes me to one of my final ports of call, at Aughinish, where I have come to wander the fields of this little-known island where two worlds collide.

'I'm only the boy doing the tour,' Liam Dundon laughs when I greet him at the Aughinish Alumina factory. 'But I'm groundsman, steward, ranger and wildlife warden so I wear different hats – not bad for an eighty-year-old.'

Liam meets me at the visitor information centre on Aughinish Island, right on the estuary front. It is home to a startling juxtaposition that intrigues me: a large chemical plant belching out smoke and high-pressured clouds of steam, alongside a nature reserve teeming with rare wildflowers, a butterfly and dragonfly sanctuary and a haven for birds, all set in a rural farming hinterland. Liam, who was a mechanical fitter, explains what happens in the factory, which has a workforce of 450.

'It's a bauxite refinery, which includes a deep-water jetty through which the refinery imports bauxite from Guinea and Brazil and exports alumina to be refined into aluminium metal. Bauxite is a sedimentary rock, reddish-brown with a high aluminium content, and the world's main source of aluminium. Alumina is a fine white granular powder exported to aluminium smelters for processing into aluminium metal. The factory featured in the news recently because of a crisis looming over the possibility of U S sanctions imposed on the company's owner, Rusal. It's majority-owned by a company controlled by the Russian billionaire Oleg Deripaska, who was targeted because of his purported close ties to the Kremlin. If you'd worked in Auginish in recent times some of the local banks refused to open an account for you because of the Russian money.'

Liam was born in Swindon, where his father had gone to look for a job at the start of World War II, and has a connection to the year of Hayward's journey. 'I was born in December 1939. My father moved over there to work on the railways as Swindon was the centre of the whole operation. Hitler bombed the area and as soon as that was over, they took out sections of steel track and tried to get the trains running as quickly as they could. My father was originally from Aughinish so I came back here as a boy to live on the island. In those days it had no industry but plenty of animals and I got to love cocker spaniels. It was a rugged place in its natural state – it was like part of the Burren and full of deep limestone. There were a few old roads with bicycles and horse and carts the only means of transport as no one had cars. It was known as the rough causeway.'

Aughinish Alumina Factory on Aughinish Island is part of an important nature reserve.

After the war Liam's father came back to the estuarine island. 'My father worked in the docks in Foynes as a thatcher and stonemason and repaired mowing machines that cut the hay, which were then drawn by horses. The ring of the machine was just magic. When it was cut, the place was full of corncrakes, and you could hear them all over the place and would often see the mother with the chicks, but they don't come any longer and we are all the poorer for their loss.'

Liam is employed by Aughinish two days a week to deal with wildlife queries. He likes raising awareness of the diversity of birds, plants and insects found around the refinery. We study the map and he points out that the island resembles the shape of a horse's head. He hands me safety glasses and we jump into his white Nissan van, driving slowly past disused oil tanks and then the pumping station where steam rises from hot tanks.

This part of the estuary is largely unknown and unvisited, apart from the workers and those interested in wildlife. With its constantly changing light it is wild and inhospitable. We look across to the Fergus estuary and to the islands at its mouth, including Canon, Inishmacowney, Inishcorker and Inishtubrid, which can be reached only by boat.

'Some people think the estuary is dismal and boring,' says Liam, 'but everything changes on it through the seasons when you watch it closely. The dolphins come up here regularly and magnificent flocks of waders in the winter arrive from Iceland and Greenland, so birdwatching is a big growth activity. I often have botanists and ornithologists in my company. The mudflats are nationally important, especially in January when you see a colourful array of dunlin, golden plover, lapwing and shelduck.'

Liam now spends his time looking after the plants, photographing the flowers and birds and trying to identify anything that he has not already noticed. 'In the old days everybody had a boat and it was our way of getting around. When the banks broke and the tide came in my father would repair them, drawing stones, sand and cement to the area, which was a lifesaver. We had nothing, only a horse and cart, and the boats brought it up and down. One of the things that local people love about it is the sea breeze. You come here on a hot day and you will have a cooler air and it's a healthy salty smell.'

We pass small lakes and mud ponds, then stop and walk around rough ground filled with flora. Liam knows the names better than the members of his family: buddleia, beloved by the hummingbird hawkmoth, milkwort and carline thistle, St John's Wort, greater knapweed, primrose, cranesbill, sea buckthorn and bindweed. Along a narrow, red dust-covered road we pause at a deep jetty where the boats bring in caustic, acid or red bauxite. In the fields, quaking grass is common alongside yellowwort, ragwort, ox-tongue ferns, plantain, and the little brown stems of bird's foot trefoil, or *Lotus corniculatus*, which he knows more expressively as 'old granny's toenails'. In 2014 Aughinish was awarded the best semi-natural grasslands in Ireland because of its diversity of habitats.

Liam speaks about the fauna and overwintering estuarine birdlife. 'You could get duck, pheasant, rabbit, woodcock and curlew all in here. It's now a sanctuary visited by BirdWatch

Ireland and wildlife service rangers, and scores of species have been counted here.'

He feels it is important to state that regular inspections are carried out by the Environmental Protection Agency to verify the running of the factory and there have never been any problems. 'The company is conscious of its responsibilities and there are stringent requirements placed on it. We have a network of air quality monitors in place around the hinterland. There is no pollution, because how would the flora survive? Animals such as newts, which particularly love clean water, are a barometer of purity. Every modern environmental safeguard is employed, from multi-stage electrostatic precipitators to the specially engineered mud storage area.'

The grounds are well maintained and the whole area has been landscaped with nature trails. Chaffinches and goldfinches chatter past us feeding prominently on knapweed and teasel. Liam drives his van carefully up a small stony incline with a hidden dip, stopping suddenly at the top of it. We get out and stand on the edge, drinking in the scale of it. In front of us lies a vast, red, flat ochre pond. It consists of a spacious panorama of hardened earthy mud cracked with lines in places that fills my eye and floods my senses. Every few metres, tall water sprinklers are in operation, otherwise it is empty. Reminiscent of the turloughs found in the limestone pavement of the Burren, it is made up of waste from the red bauxite and stretches for more than a square kilometre, ranging from blood red to pink – a completely unexpected, jaw-dropping sight. It reminds me of something in Arizona or the Grand Canyon, rather than west Limerick. Liam explains that the purpose of the sprinkler system is to moisten the dust to prevent it from rising and is an essential part of its working. We turn around and follow the course of the wide Roberstown River at Aughinish West beside a railway line and close to a row of Sitka spruce and eucalyptus trees.

'Many parts of the island have gone back to nature, so as well as scrubland, hay meadows and salt marsh, we have extensive woodland. The company has planted tens of thousands of trees all around the island. Alder, ash and birch are common, and you can find varieties of horse chestnut, beech, sycamore and holly. In fact, they all seem to know each other because they are on nodding terms!'

Of all the wild plants and trees there is one special flower that Liam holds close to his heart. He drives me over to a bumpy meadow where we park, pull on our boots and walk across to another field, part of which has been cordoned off. Here we find, growing in abundance, the great burnet, a rare plant that is deep purple claret. It is a native perennial herb growing up to 1.5 metres with crimson flower heads and showy, healthy-looking, bright green leaves.

'The flowerhead turns deep purple and becomes corky on ageing. The ecologists moved all the protected plants such as Irish meadow barley and the great burnet and when they saw the grassland around the red mud, they could not believe the high quality of it. The botanists wanted to put Aughinish's name into the surveys for grassland — one man said he had never seen so many types of grass.'

The original land has been allowed to grow wild and there is a restrained untidiness about it. Liam is constantly coming across flowers such as foxglove, sea lavender and juniper shrub, whose crushed leaves have a strong scent. At other times, Aughinish has a theatrical side to it and the fauna of the estuary is a pageant. There are days when he marvels at stoats and otters, while seal pups bark alongside crabs, frogs, gulls and coots. It is also an orchid lover's island and on the right day, the common spotted, pyramidal and bee orchid can all be seen. The complexion of the river changes here — its pace is slow, and it is a transformation of appearance and temperament. It had been an absorbing walk spent in Liam's company, enlivened by his knowledge, enthusiasm and awareness.

A POWERFUL VULCAN bursts into the airspace over the estuary on Saturday afternoon with a screaming roar reverberating through the small town of Foynes. Such is the intensity of the noise children dive under picnic tables and cover their ears. It marks the start of the fifth year of the air show, animating the skies. The Vulcan is followed by two Mustang flying high in close formation. The planes take off from Shannon Airport, out of sight across the estuary, and make their way over to Foynes Island and the airspace beyond. Emerging through the elephantine clouds with a splutter, flying low over the tops of nearby trees, and leaving a thick trail of black smoke comes a home-built plane, a Van RV-7, piloted by Gerry Humphreys. Painted in the colours of a Friesian cow, it is fitted with strobe lights and a unique smoke system to help it stand out – the first of its type to be flown in Ireland. Gerry indulges in a series of rolls and spins, thrilling the crowd with his aerobatics. Next are two blue military aircraft, playing follow-the-leader at a cruising speed of 180 knots. The planes are from Baldonnell Aerodrome, south-west of Dublin, and are making their debut at Foynes. Part of the Air Corps, they are used for patrolling the Irish sea space.

Young children, quickly bored by the activity in the skies, are brought to the Shannon Ices van for 99s. The streets are engulfed in amusements with circus acts, stilt walkers and aerialists, while the screams of teenagers from the Sky Fall fill the air alongside the legendary Red Baron struggling to walk with his wooden plane. Yachts with names such as *Star Fisher*, *Leigh Mary*, *Marengo* and *Kilteery* sit bumper-to-bumper, their halyards creating their own calming noise at the marina. Spectators cram into the grounds and the pier where metre-long camera lenses, balanced on tripods, are trained overhead.

A biplane in Union Jack livery swirls uphill, flicks, suspends itself in mid-air, cartwheels in daredevil fashion, turns this way and that, showing off for all its worth, making the airspace a playground, and leaving a long smoky trail in its wake. A restored Douglas DC-3, painted in Aer Lingus colours, performs a steep turn, and is followed by a gleaming pair of BAC Strikemaster jet fighters from north Wales, with their powerful Rolls-Royce Viper engines, flying in unison so close that they are practically touching. The planes, in a grey and desert colour, were originally in the Sultan of Oman's air force. They perform a spectacular formation before disappearing in a carefully choreographed flypast.

Crowds enjoy a flypast at the Foynes Air Show over the Shannon estuary.

The highlight comes at the end of the afternoon when a Catalina flying boat pays a visit. It flies low over the water and makes a distinctive turn, but it is not possible for it to land on the estuary. Smooth and steady in flight, it is a perfectly preserved aircraft and a piece of aviation history. The original name of this model was *Miss Pick Up* and it has been faithfully recreated by an aviation artist who has reproduced a digital version printed onto vinyl stickers and applied to the hull. This is a similar type of plane to that which Hayward saw in 1939. It made an unforgettable appearance at the end of the documentary that accompanied his book, and because it arrived twenty-five minutes ahead of schedule it took them by surprise:

A deep-throated roar came from the heavens, and, like a beautiful silver bird high about the Cross of Foynes, we saw the American Clipper gracefully sweeping across the deep blue of a perfect summer sky. It was one of the most exciting moments of my life, and, indeed quite too exciting, for so intent were we in watching the great ship that we almost forgot to get our cameras out to photograph what I had planned would be the last thing you would see in my travel picture … The camera turned, and the Clipper came on, high above our heads, gigantic as any fabled monster, yet graceful in flight as a wild swan.

RIGHT TO THE end of his journey, Hayward remained outspoken about the small Shannon towns. He called Ballybunion 'a rather untidy, rather vulgarised little town' and it was there that he and his fellow adventurers ended their trip. Looking back on his 'darling journey' from the start at the Shannon Pot, he concluded that the river is not sufficiently known to those in search of a holiday that is different: 'Those who read this book, or see my Shannon picture in some cinema, will surely realise the wonderland of river and lake and history and good company that is lying waiting for them, waiting to be enjoyed. That, indeed, is the fondest hope of my heart.'

It has been a privilege to look over Richard Hayward's shoulder eighty years later and see the changing face of Ireland. Were he alive today, he would be gladdened by the fact that the tourist board launched a plan to promote 'the Shannon corridor' as well as the wider 'Hidden Heartlands' – although the cynic in him would probably question why it took so long. He ends his book by describing the sight of a Clipper winging its westerly way to the next parish, which was in America, and of how peace and a great contentment descended upon him.

BIBLIOGRAPHY

Barry, M., *Across Deep Waters*: *Bridges of Ireland* (Frankfort Press, 1985).

Bellamy, D., *The Wild Boglands*: *Bellamy's Ireland* (Christopher Helm, 1986).

Bielenberg, A. (ed.), *The Shannon Scheme and the Electrification of the Irish Free State* (The Lilliput Press, 2002).

Boland, D., *The Mid-Shannon Waterway: A pictorial book of designated and tranquil moorings* (James & Mary, 2016).

Broderick, J., *The Waking of Willie Ryan* (The Lilliput Press, 2004).

Byford, G., *Reedbound: A year on Ireland's waterways* (Matador, 2015).

Cahill, S., O'Brien, G., & Casey, J., *Lough Ree & its Islands* (Three Counties Press, 2006).

Casey, J., *Lanesborough-Ballyleague: A living history 1939–1955* (Rathcline Heritage Society, 2003).

Cassells, B., *IWAI and the Waterways of Ireland* (Cottage Publications, 2014).

Claffey, T., *Tapestry of Light: Ireland's bogs and wetlands as never seen before* (Artisan House, 2017).

Clements, P., *Romancing Ireland: Richard Hayward 1892–1964* (The Lilliput Press, 2014).

Colwell, M., *Curlew Moon* (William Collins, 2018).

Conwell, J.J., *Portumna: A Galway Parish by the Shannon* (2017)
———— *A Galway Landlord During the Great Famine: Ulick John de Burgh, First Marquis of Clanricarde* (Four Courts Press, 2003).

Cooper, A., *The River Shannon, A journey down Ireland's longest river* (The Collins Press, 2011).

Cunningham, B., & Murtagh H. (eds), *Lough Ree, Historic Lakeland Settlement* (Four Courts Press, 2015).

Delany, R., *The Grand Canal of Ireland* (The Lilliput Press, 1995)
———— *By Shannon Shores*: *An Exploration of the River* (Gill & Macmillan, 1987)
———— *The Shannon Navigation* (The Lilliput Press, 2008)

————— (ed.) *Shell Guide to the River Shannon* (Irish Shell, 1993).

Dunne, L., & Feehan, J. (eds), *Ireland's Mushroom Stones: Relics of a vanished lakeland* (University College Dublin, 2003).

Fallon, M.R., Murray, P., & Ní Mhuirí, S. (eds), *Clonown: A County Roscommon Shannonside Community* (Clonown Heritage, 2006).

Feehan, J., *A Long-Lived Wilderness: The Future of the North Midlands Peatland Network* (Department of Environmental Resource Management, 2004)
————— *Croghan, County Offaly* (Offaly County Council, 2011)
————— *The Landscape of Clonmacnoise* (Offaly County Council, 2014).

Feehan, J. M., *The Secret Places of the Shannon* (Royal Carberry Books, 1980).

Fogarty, P., *Whittled Away: Ireland's Vanishing Nature* (The Collins Press, 2017).

Foy, P., *A Lifetime on Lough Ree* (PubliBook Ireland, 2013).

Gardner, R., *Land of Time Enough: A Journey thorough the waterways of Ireland* (Hodder & Stoughton, 1977).

Geissel, H., *A Road on the Long Ridge: In search of the ancient highway on the Esker Riada* (CRS Publications, 2006).

Gibson, P.J., *Heritage Landscapes of the Irish Midlands* (Geography Publications, 2007).

Gilleece, E., *City of Churches: A Skyline of Spires* (Limerick Archives, 2014).

Groarke, V., *Selected Poems* (Gallery Press, 2016).

Harbison, P., *Irish High Crosses* (The Boyne Valley Honey Co., 2001).

Hayward, R., *Where the River Shannon Flows* (Dundalgan Press & G. Harrap, 1940).

Henry, M., *The River Shannon* (The Conna Press, 1996).

Heery, S., *The Shannon Floodlands: A natural history* (Tír Eolas, 1993).
————— (ed.) *Birds in Central Ireland: Sixth mid-Shannon Bird Report* 2012–2016 (BirdWatch Ireland, 2018).

Higgins, M.W., & Aherne, S. (eds), *Introducing John Moriarty: In his own words* (The Lilliput Press, 2019).

Holmwood, J., *Under the One Roof: A creative memory document of the Bush Hotel* (Leitrim County Council, 2013).

Kavanagh, P.J., *Voices in Ireland, A Traveller's Literary Companion* (John Murray, 1994).

Kay, M., *The Limerick Flood of 2014: Climate Change and a Case of Unpreparedness* (Original Writing, 2014).

Kenny, J., *The Hills Speak: History and Mystery* (Dbee Press, 2016).

Kiely, B., *The Waves Behind Us: Further Memoirs* (Methuen, 1999).

Kingston, M. (ed.), *Stimulus of Sin: Selected Writings of John Broderick* (The Lilliput Press, 2007).

Ledbetter, G.T., *The Great Irish Tenor John McCormack* (Town House, 2006).

Lee, T., *Offaly: Through time & its townlands* (Ottait Publishing, 2009).

Long, M. (ed.), *The Collected Letters of Flann O'Brien* (Dalkey Archive Press, 2018).

Mac Cárthaigh, C. (ed.), *Traditional Boats of Ireland: History, Folklore and Construction* (The Collins Press, 2008).

Madden, G., *For God or King: The History of Mountshannon, Co. Clare, 1742– 1992* (East Clare Heritage, 1993).
——— *Holy Island: Inis Cealtra, Island of the Churches* (Holy Island Tours, 2008).

Madden G., & Creamer, S., *Lough Derg and its Islands*: A *voyage of discovery by road and water* (Holy Island Tours, 2016).

Manning, C., *Clonmacnoise, Co. Offaly* (Office of Public Works, 2016).

Meehan, R., & Parkes, M., *Karst, Turloughs and Eskers: The geological heritage of County Roscommon* (Roscommon County Council, 2014).

Moore, A., *Water Spirits of the World* (Python Press, 2008).

McInerney, T., *The Gandelow: A Shannon Estuary Fishing Boat* (A.K. Ilen Co. Ltd, 2005).

Murtagh, H., *Lough Ree: A short historical tour* (The Old Athlone Society, 2016).

Nowlan, N., *The Shannon: River of Loughs and Legends* (Frederick Muller, 1966).

O'Brien, F., *At Swim-Two-Birds* (Hart-Davis, MacGibbon, 1976).

O'Brien, G., *Athlone in Old Photographs* (Gill & MacMillan, 2002)
——— *Athlone in Old Picture Postcards* (European Library, 1996)
——— *Athlone on the Shannon* (Cottage Publications, 2008)
——— *Athlone Miscellany* (The History Press Ireland, 2011).

O'Brien, S., *Powering the Nation: Images of the Shannon Scheme and the electrification of Ireland* (Irish Academic Press, 2017).

O'Carroll, B., & Felton B., *The Story of Clonmacnoise and Saint Ciarán* (Ely House, 2013).

O'Connor, J., *On Shannon's Shore: A History of Mungret Parish* (Pubblebrien Historical Society, 2003).

O'Conor, K., & Shanahan, B., *Rindoon Castle and Deserted Medieval Town: A Visitor's Guide* (Roscommon County Council, 2018).

O'Farrell, P., *Shannon Through Her Literature* (Mercier Press, 1983).

Oram, H., *Bygone Limerick: The city and county in days gone by* (Mercier Press, 2010).

Pedlow, A., *Did you know? 100 quirky facts about County Offaly* (Offaly County Council, 2013).

Prendergast, F., & Seoighe, M., *Limerick's Glory: From Viking settlement to the new millennium* (Cottage Publications, 2002).

Rice, H.J., *Thanks for the Memory: Being personal reminiscences, traditions, history and navigational details about the River Shannon* (1st edn 1952; Inland Waterways Association of Ireland, 1974).

Rolt., L.T.C., *Green and Silver* (1st edn 1949; Inland Waterways Association of Ireland, 1993).

Sherlock, R., *Athlone Castle* (Westmeath County Council, 2016).

Somers, D., *Endurance: Heroic Journeys in Ireland* (O'Brien Press, 2005).

Somerville-Large, P., *From Bantry Bay to Leitrim: A journey in search of O'Sullivan Beare* (Gollancz, 1974).

Spellissy, S., *Limerick: The Rich Land* (Spellissy-O'Brien Publishers, 1989).

Tierney, A., *Central Leinster: Kildare, Laois and Offaly* (Yale University Press, 2019).

Trodd, V., *Banagher on the Shannon: A Historical Guide to the Town* (1985).

Tubridy, M. (ed.), *The Heritage of Clonmacnoise* (Trinity College Dublin & Co. Offaly Vocational Educational Committee, 1987).

Walker, S., *Hide and Seek: The Irish priest in the Vatican who defied the Nazi command* (Collins, 2011).

Warner, D., *Shannon-Erne Waterway Users Guide* (ERA-Maptec, 2000).

Warner, D., & Fallon N., *Waterways: By steam launch through Ireland* (Boxtree, 1995).

Wibberley, L., *The Shannon Sailors: A voyage to the heart of Ireland* (William Morrow, 1972).

ACKNOWLEDGMENTS

THE MAIN PLEASURE of writing this book has been meeting and conversing with people far more knowledgeable than me. I owe a debt of gratitude to them for their unstinting generosity, time, knowledge and hospitality along the route of the River Shannon, its lakes and islands. The following people stimulated, inspired and helped navigate my journey, whether at kitchen tables, over caffeine-infused chats, or in boats, barges or barrooms:

Alan Bane, Flan Barnwell, Anthony Barry, Colin Becker, Donal Boland, Kate and John Brennan, Gerry Burke, Brian Caffrey, Emma Caffrey, Michael and Kevin Casey, Nick Condon, John Joe Conwell, Nicola Daly, Joe Dolan, Steve Dolan, John Donohoe, Timmy Donovan, Liam Dundon, John Feehan, Michael Fewer, Maura Flannery, Michael Flannery, Michael Gleeson, Eileen Gibbons, Edwina Guckian, Paddy Hanley, Patsy Hanly, Conor Harrington, Stephen Heery, Mick Hough, Kealin Ireland, Nick Kaszuk, Dan Kavanagh, Barry Keenan, Mickey Kelly, Derry Killeen, Gráinne Kirwan, Susan Leen, Pat Lysaght, Ger Madden, Basil Mannion, Alanna Moore, Tom Moore, Dermot Moran, Diarmuid Mulvihill, Harman Murtagh, Oliver McGrail, Fr Leo McDonnell, Mike McDonnell, Stephen McGarry, Terry McGovern, Gearoid O'Brien, Michael O'Donnell, Nessan O'Donoghue, Beth O'Loughlin, Eleanor Purcell, Dick Ridge, Seadna Ryan, Anthony Sheehy, Gerard Shortt, Fr Andrzej Sroka, Canon Trevor Sullivan, Bee Smith, Brigid and Pat Stapleton, Sean Ward and Sean Wynne.

Particular thanks are due to Norma Herron and Nuala Reilly at Waterways Ireland for their interest and assistance, and to Mary Cosgrave at Fáilte Ireland. John Morton of Carrickcraft was extremely helpful in sourcing old maps and kindly supplied the historic charts of Lough Ree (1837) and Lough Derg (1839) for the endpapers. I am grateful to Trevor Ferris for his skilful photographic work in putting together a slide show of my Shannon travels.

I would like to thank Antony Farrell at The Lilliput Press for embracing the motive behind this journey, and to Ruth Hallinan, publishing manager, for her resourceful work in overseeing the production lifecycle of the book from conception to completion. Djinn von Noorden is a sensitive editor who lavished attention on the manuscript, suggesting cuts and comments with panache, and I am grateful to her. Sincere thanks are also due to the graphic designer Niall McCormack, Amy O'Sullivan in publicity, and Bridget Farrell for their enthusiastic and meticulous work.

I am indebted to Richard (also known as Ricky) Hayward, son of the writer Richard Hayward, author of *Where the River Shannon Flows*, who was encouraging from the outset about a book following in his father's footsteps.

Mid and East Antrim Borough Council have supported several Richard Hayward projects, including an exhibition held in 2019, and I would like to record heartfelt appreciation to Marian Kelso of Larne Museum & Arts Centre for her assistance. Several heritage officers from county councils in the midlands agreed to support the production costs of this book and thanks are due to Ann-Marie Ward (Cavan), Nollaig Feeney (Roscommon), Máiréad Ní Chonghaile (Longford), Melanie McQuade (Westmeath), Amanda Pedlow (Offaly) and Majella O'Brien (Limerick).

I owe special thanks to my agent, Jonathan Williams, for reading the proofs, and for his wisdom, valuable insight and suggestions, which are immensely appreciated.

After the journey, the process of writing a book is a lonely business of self-isolation, and I have been fortunate to receive loving support at home from my wife Felicity and son Daniel. Any sins of error and omission are, of course, my own.

Finally, a proportion of the royalties from the sale of this book will be donated to assisting the research of the Brainwaves charity.

INDEX